Recruiting People of Color For Teacher Education

Judith R. James, Editor

Hot Topics Series
Center for Evaluation, Development, and Research
Phi Delta Kappa

The Center for Evaluation, Development, and Research (CEDR) dedicates the Hot Topics series to administrators and board members who must make responsible, data-based decisions, to teachers and paraprofessionals who must interpret a constantly changing curriculum, and to students and parents who must deal with the current problems and issues in education.

The Hot Topics series presents readers with a selection of the best research and practice available. Topics are based on information gathered from a poll of leading educational organizations. Each volume contains articles carefully selected by the CEDR staff from a number of sources to help readers avoid the repetition and irrelevance that characterize the literature gathered from searches of larger databases. Each topic reflects a holistic approach by introducing many sides of an issue, and each year the variety of topics will reflect the spectrum of education concerns.

One of CEDR's most important missions is to help educators identify ways to solve problems by seeing the successful solutions of others. We sincerely hope that this volume will fulfill that purpose.

The Hot Topics series is prepared
under the direction of
Larry W. Barber, CEDR Director
January 1993

WANTED

One million caring, culturally sensitive, ethnically diverse men and women with the patience of Job, wisdom of Solomon, and the ability to prepare the next ethnically diverse generation for productive citizenship, usually under adverse conditions. Applicants must be willing to fill gaps left by absent or working parents, satisfy demands of state politicians and local bureaucrats, impart moral values, and – oh, yes – teach the three Rs 50-60 hours a week.

Pay: Fair (getting better)

Reward: Mostly intangible

INTRODUCTION

The research literature is replete with statistics to document the precipitous decline of minorities who are willing to accept the challenge described above. The interest of college freshmen in teaching peaked in 1968, dropped sharply by 1976, and continued to decline throughout the 1980s. The most commonly mentioned reasons for the decline in minority teachers include broader career opportunities, teacher testing, fewer minorities enrolled in higher education, poor working conditions, lack of respect from the communities in which they teach, and low salaries.

Three tightly intertwined developments have begun to generate unprecedented change: 1) a new corps of teachers who will be the products of radically revised teacher preparation programs, 2) an increased demand from the public to educate the present generation of Americans better and more effectively than any previous generation, and 3) shifting demographics that foretell of a more culturally diverse student population. These three forces are beginning to converge in dynamic interaction to produce change within schools, classrooms, and communities – affecting the recruitment of minorities by colleges and universities across the nation.

Demographics define the challenge. According to the latest projections, by the year 2020 minorities will constitute 35% of the students in our public schools. Our nation's Hispanic population on the mainland will expand from 11% to 14%; the Asian population will expand from 1.5% to 5%; and the Native American population will double to 1%. If the present educational system is failing to teach minority students to write well, speak articulately, and appreciate the importance of mathematics, science, social science, and the humanities, then change must occur in the system. The difficult task is aggravated by the shortage of minority teachers in the system, a trend that threatens to deny minority students the positive role models they need to succeed in school.

This volume is intended to provide a comprehensive treatment of the central issues related to the recruitment and retention of minorities in teacher education. Specifically, the volume covers: 1) the scope of the problem, 2) the reasons for the shortage, 3) the pipeline issues, 4) the impact of testing, as well as the validity issues in testing minority candidates, 5) a review of the recommendations for recruiting minority teachers contained in most of the major national reports and by most well-known authorities, and 6) implications for establishing demonstration recruitment and retention models.

Chapter one will describe the problem surrounding the declining number of minority teachers and discuss the need for a diversified teaching staff. Chapter two will focus on barriers in the educational pipeline – e.g., tracking, testing, and admissions criteria. Chapter three will discuss the factors that influence one's decision to enter the teaching profession. Chapter four will feature "success stories" and recommend strategies and models for increasing minority student enrollment in teacher preparation programs. Chapter five will present information on retention strategies for prospective and currently employed minority teachers.

We hope that this Hot Topics volume will be helpful to school, college of education, and university personnel seeking information pertaining to the recruitment and retention of minorities in teacher education.

The editor wishes to acknowledge David Carter, Ben Chavis, Jesus Garcia, Howard Hill, William Husk, Lloyd Hackley, Daniel Levine, Sheryl Santos, G. Pritchy Smith, Raymond Wong, and Elaine Witty who participated so faithfully on the national panel of experts for this volume.

Judith R. James, Editor

TABLE OF CONTENTS

NOTES

NOTES

NOTES

NOTES

NOTES

NOTES

The Need for a Diversified Teaching Staff

OVERVIEW

This chapter analyzes the minority teacher shortage. Although much of the research has focused on the shortage of African-American teachers, it is clear from the articles in this chapter that the minority teacher shortage includes Asian-Americans, Native Americans, and Hispanics.

The first article describes the significant historical, political, and economic factors impinging on the number of minorities working or seeking careers in education. Given the educational system's failure to work effectively with learners with variant ability levels and racial, linguistic, and socioeconomic differences, there is an increasingly justifiable expectation that minority students would benefit more directly from a teacher role model when the teacher is a member of the students' own minority group.

The second article describes the problems related to the past and current shortage of Native American teachers and teachers who are sensitive to the "Indian condition." As a result, the quantity and quality of educational services and opportunities for Native American children are limited.

Recruiting Teachers of Color: Problems, Programs and Possibilities

A Paper Prepared for the
Fall Conference of the Far West Holmes Group
Reno, Nevada
4-6 October 1989

Michele Foster
Assistant Professor
Graduate School of Education
University of Pennsylvania *

* on leave 1989-1991 at the University of North Carolina at Chapel Hill

The Problem

The precipitous decline in the number of teachers of color has prompted some to note that they are an endangered species (Cole, 1986). Though the statistics are well-documented, well publicized and undoubtedly familiar to most in the field of education, it is important to restate the severity of the problem. Between 1971 and 1986, the percentage of Black teachers declined 1.2% from 8.1 to 6.9%, while the percentage of other minorities dropped from 3.6 to 3.4%. During the same period, the percentage of white teachers grew from 88.3 to 89.6, an increase of 1.3% (NEA, 1987). In 1987, although African-Americans constituted 16.2% of the children in public schools, they comprised only 6.9% of the teachers. Latinos represented 9.1% of the children in public schools, but only 1.9% of the teachers. Asian/Pacific Islanders comprised 2.5% of the children in public school, but only 0.9% of the teachers. Native Americans and Alaskan Natives represented 0.9% of the children in public schools, but only 0.6% of the teachers (NEA, 1987; OERI 1987). At the present rate, some estimates are that by the year 1995 teachers of color--Asian-Americans, Native Americans, Latinos and African-Americans--will be less than 5% of the entire teaching force (Stewart, Meier & England, 1989).

The situation is even more critical when one considers that this decline is occurring at the very same time that the number of pupils of color is growing rapidly. It is estimated that, by the year 2000, children of color--"minorities"--will comprise the majority in 53 of the nation's largest cities (Goertz & Pitcher, 1985). In order to keep pace with the growing percentage of pupils of color, at least one third of the 500,000 new teachers needed by the mid 1990s will have to be minorities (Stewart, Meier & England, 1989). Yet a recent survey has revealed that at all levels of satisfaction, teachers of color are more likely than "white" teachers to report they plan to leave the profession (Metropolitan Life, 1988).

The purpose of this paper is to analyze the reasons for this shortage, describe some promising practices and programs for recruiting and retaining teachers of color and suggest additional possibilities for reversing the situation.

The Past

Wider career opportunities and teacher testing are the most commonly mentioned reasons for the decline in the numbers of teachers of color. Without a doubt, these trends have taken their toll on the number of minorities who choose or qualify to enter the teaching profession. In 1950, half of the Black professionals in the United States were teachers (Cole, 1986). Twenty-seven years later, of the 58,515 bachelors degrees earned by African-Americans, 22% (12,922) were in education. By 1983, only 9% or 5,456 of the bachelors degrees earned by African-Americans were education degrees (Stern, 1988).

Even historically Black colleges, located in the southern and border states, which over the years have prepared the majority of African-American teachers, have experienced a marked decrease in the number of students studying education. Nationwide in 1974, historically Black institutions graduated 9,051 teachers, compared to only 4,027 seven years later (Cole & Horton, 1984). Although specific data are not available for all historically Black colleges, some examples demonstrate the severity of the decline. In 1963, Florida A&M graduated 300 education majors; however, by 1985 it enrolled fewer than 100. Two historically Black institutions in Louisiana awarded 33% and 41% of their degrees in education in 1976 in 1977, whereas in 1982 and 1983, only 11 and 14% of the degrees awarded were in education (Irvine, 1988). Norfolk State University graduated 69 Special Education teachers, 42 Early Childhood Education teachers, and 18 English Education majors in 1975; by 1983, Norfolk awarded only 22, 18 and 2 degrees respectively in each of these fields (Witty, 1984).

Teacher testing, at both entry and exit stages, has also sharply reduced the number of candidates who become certified. In 1980, the first year in which the Florida Teacher Exam was given, 85% of all candidates who took the test passed. For

African-American candidates, however, the pass rate was only 35 - 40% (Dupre, 1986). The failure rate for Blacks in North Carolina was 87% compared to a rate of only 17% for whites, prompting one researcher to predict that, should the rate remain constant, North Carolina would be left with a teaching force that is 96% white (Hilliard, 1980).

Not only are teacher candidates being required to pass qualifying tests in order to be certified, but many states are now requiring those seeking admission into teacher training programs to qualify by passing an entrance exam. A required score of 835 on the SAT reduced Florida's entire candidate pool by 25%; this cut-off score reduced by 90% the number of Black candidates who were eligible to matriculate into teaching training programs (Bray, 1984). The statistics in California are not much better. There, of 6,644 minority candidates who sat for exams given to prospective teacher candidates in 1983, 3854--58%--failed. African-Americans had the highest failure rate with only 530, or 25% of 2,040 candidates passing. Other candidates of color also failed at substantially higher rates than whites. Only 39%--834 of 2,133--of all Mexican-Americans, and half of all Asian-Americans--637 of 1,259--taking the test qualified for entry into teacher education programs. Anglos passed at a rate of 76%, with 18,856 of 24,540 candidates qualifying for admission into teacher education programs (Gifford, 1986). Comparable statistics are available for a number of other states, including

Alabama, Texas, Pennsylvania, Georgia, Oklahoma and Louisiana (Collins, 1989; Irving, 1988; Gifford, 1986; Bray, 1984).

Though less widely discussed, at least two other factors, one historical the other more contemporaneous, have impinged directly on the number of candidates of color working or seeking careers in education. Historically, because of dual school systems, the underrepresentation of African-American teachers was less severe in southern than in northern states. An immediate consequence of desegregation, however, was that between the 1954 Brown vs. the Board of Education Decision and the early 1970s, approximately 31,584 African-American teachers lost their jobs in 17 southern and border states (Ethridge, 1979). African-American teachers in Kentucky declined by 41% between 1955-65, even though an additional 401 would have been needed merely to keep pace with the increasing numbers of pupils. Moreover, a study of Kentucky school districts revealed that 127 of 467 had dismissed 462 African-American teachers. By 1970, the African-American teacher student ratio in the south was over twice that of the white student teacher ratio (Stewart, Meier & England, 1989). Negative evaluations resulted in dismissal for many. In some cases African-American teachers and administrators were demoted or stripped of their responsibilities. In other situations, the most competent Black teachers were reassigned to white schools. The permanence of after-effect is not surprising, for rarely have

African-American teachers been in demand in unitary school systems (Tyack, 1984).

The second factor directly influencing the number of prospective teachers results from the decreasing number of students of color enrolling in and completing college. For instance, only 7% of Hispanics graduate from college (Carnegie Forum, 1986). Moreover, although African-Americans comprise 13% of all 18-24 year olds, they represent only 9.6% of those enrolled in college. Half of all Black high school graduates enrolled in college in 1977, but by 1982 that figure had fallen to 36%. Of Blacks who do go to college, 42% attend two year colleges; of these, only 25% graduate (Irvine, 1988). It would be counterproductive, given the complex and interactive nature of causes for this drop-off, to try to account for the extent to which each is individually responsible for the declining numbers of minority teachers. Only by attacking all of them simultaneously can the situation be reversed. While there must be efforts to increase the number of well-prepared candidates of color who enter teacher education programs, this strategy alone will not solve the problem. Schools of education will always be in competition with engineering, medicine, law, business and arts and sciences for the most academically talented and well-prepared students. Rather than pilfering students from other professions, schools of education must work to enlarge the pool of students of color who are interested in and eligible to enter teacher education. Making sure that more students are prepared to enter and complete college is the only way to accomplish this goal. This will require forming partnerships with educational institutions below the baccalaureate level, since it is at lower levels of the educational ladder--community college, high school and junior high school--that attendance and completion of college are made possible.

Policies

In a 1987 policy statement titled "Minority Teacher Recruitment and Retention: A Call to Action," the American Association of Colleges for Teacher Education designed a set of initiatives to reverse the declining number of teachers of color. While not specifying programmatic details, the AACTE did broadly sketch several approaches to ameliorating the problem. Included among the recommendations were the development of national as well as state scholarship programs, high school and college work-study programs; two year/four year college articulation programs; assistantship and grant programs; early incentive programs; support programs for reentry and career change; teacher induction programs and assessment demonstrations grants programs (AACTE, 1987).

Programs

Within the past two to three years, some programs have shown promise of staying and perhaps eventually revising the declining numbers of teachers of color. Because the programs are relatively new, few data are available by which to evaluate these programs. In presenting these programs, it is not my purpose to suggest they be adopted wholly without regard to local situations and specific contexts. Indeed, it is adaptability to local needs and contexts that make such programs possible. The interventions undertaken by individual programs vary, but they share two common elements. Each has at least one person who is directly responsible for implementing and overseeing the program; and each program hinges on inter- or intra-institutional efforts.

Pre-baccalaureate Programs

Programs can be divided into two types--pre-baccalaureate and baccalaureate--depending on the educational level of the population they serve. Pre-baccalaureate programs can be further divided into two types, those that serve students at the secondary level and those that prepare postsecondary students to matriculate into teacher education programs, usually through articulated agreements between member community colleges and universities.[1]

Many of the secondary programs are resurrections of Future Teachers' Clubs of 30 to 50 years ago. These clubs meet regularly for activities, which include guest speakers, college visits, presentations on college attendance and requirements, and study skills workshops. Some of the programs pair students in mentor/protoge' relationships with student teachers or practicing classroom teachers and arrange a day when club members can shadow teachers. Programs can be open to members of all ethnic and racial groups, or they can be targeted to specifically underrepresented groups. An example of the former, the YES program, is a collaborative between the Milwaukee Public Schools and the University of Wisconsin at Milwaukee School of Education, which sponsors Future Teachers' Clubs in 15 high schools. Project: I Teach, a collaborative of the University of Texas in San Antonio, the Educational Testing Service and the San Antonio and Edgewood School Districts, has been started to increase the number of Hispanic students who pursue careers in education. Through a combination of academic year and summer programs,

---

[1] Except where otherwise indicated in the text, the information in this section comes from a report by the Appalachian Educational Laboratory and the Tennessee Association of Colleges of Teacher Education, titled "Programs of promise: A summary of current programs focusing on the recruitment of minority candidates to careers in professional education," ERIC Document Reproduction Service No. ED 301 556.

Project: I Teach provides academic support, test taking and study skills, career planning, and financial aid to high school students in an effort to ease their transition from high school to college (Zapata, 1988). In other programs, the University of Arkansas at Pine Bluff, and Keane State University in New Jersey, two examples, target high school students of color, enrolling them in a type of Upward Bound with a specific focus on the field of education.

Courses of teaching, as well as opportunities for tutoring and teaching, are elements of many secondary programs. Sometimes these approaches are combined, as they are at California State University at Dominguez Hills. Dominguez Hills, an institution with an excellent reputation for recruiting as well as retaining minority students, has designed a program to expand the pool of recruitable teachers. Program participants take an introductory teaching course, and students interested in pursuing careers in education can take a second course that combines theory and practice. Under the auspices of the course, enrollees conduct a Saturday enrichment program for students at a local elementary school. Working in teams of three for ten weeks, and each week changing roles--teacher, support person who assists the teacher, observer who provides feedback--participants prepare and teach lessons to groups of six elementary students. New groups are formed after ten weeks, and the cycle is repeated.

Community College/University Transfer Programs

Significant numbers of minority students, many of whom are first generation college students, begin their college careers in two year schools. Since teachers have customarily come from the ranks of first generation college students, well-designed two year/four year college transfer programs have the potential to enlarge the pool of teachers of color considerably. Faculty at Virginia Commonwealth University, a historically Black institution in Richmond, visit local community colleges and develop mentor/protege' relationships with students at these schools; these relationships continue until the students graduate from the university (Reed, 1986).

Milwaukee Area Technical College (MATC) is beginning the second year of its Urban Teacher College Program. MATC has developed articulation agreements with four of Wisconsin's State Universities--Madison, Milwaukee, Whitewater and Oshkosh. The universities guarantee admission to MATC students who pass the PPST, have a 2.5 GPA and meet all of the other program requirements. Fifty students enrolled in the first year, and 27 students began the program this September. The retention rate for the first cohort is 90%. A brochure was printed to aid in recruiting; however, students most often hear about the program by word of mouth.

Paid for out of the college's regular budget, the program receives no special funding. The college does provide the personnel who staff the program. Included among the program staff are a full-time coordinator/director, a tenured member of the Developmental Studies/English Department, who spends most of her time coordinating the academic program and support systems and hammering out the articulation agreements with the receiving schools, and three other regular full-time faculty assigned to the program on a part-time basis, who spend between 25 and 40% of their time arranging field placements, campus trips and events, doing administrative tasks, record keeping and academic advising.

Although the program used the existing curriculum for the first year, two new one-semester courses, titled Issues in Urban Education Modules I and II, totalling three credits and taught by the director, were developed. Field experiences are built into the modules; in the first, students observe an urban teacher; in the second, they do 15 hours of field placement, which is applied to the seventy hour field placement required at the university. All field experiences take place in effective schools with large populations of minority students and in effective schools with large populations of minority students and in the classrooms of successful teachers of color. In an effort to insure cross-pollination of ideas and more contact between diverse groups of teacher education students, the coordinator co-teaches an introductory teaching course at the university in Milwaukee, attended by students from the community college as well as the university. Required for admission into the teacher education program, this course will be offered at both sites beginning this year.

During the academic year, students in the Urban Teachers Program visit the cooperating universities and the attend local professional development activities, such as teacher workshops and conferences. For eight weeks during the summers, students attend classes and workshops designed to help them prepare for and pass the Pre-Professional Skills Test (PPST). With money acquired from the state and a basic literacy grant, students are paid $8.00 an hour to work up to 15 hours a week as teacher interns in community literacy centers or in public schools. As part of their internship, students attend mini-workshops on how to teach someone to read, or on other related topics.

Through a recently funded Title VII grant, the Urban Teachers Program has begun a bilingual teachers component. This year six Hispanic and two Hmong-Lao students entered the MATC program. The grant provides money for tuition, books and a living stipend for students, who sign an agreement that they will remain for as bilingual teachers for a specific period (personal communication, 1989).

Loan Forgiveness Programs

A second set of programs offers financial incentives to high school students who indicate a desire to pursue careers in education. Most of these programs are designed to attract outstanding students who might opt for a career other than teaching. South Carolina has begun a Teacher Cadet Program that offers forgivable loans to candidates of outstanding ability who agree to teach in critical subject or geographic areas. Loans are reduced by 20% for each year the graduate teaches in a critical need subject or geographic area. The first cohort of the South Carolina Teacher Cadet Program included 32% minorities. Through the Public Forum of North Carolina, fellowships are offered to outstanding students never before enrolled in two or four year colleges. These forgivable loans are reduced by 25% for each year the candidate teaches in a North Carolina School District. These fellowships are offered at 13 colleges and universities throughout the state and, while not specifically for minority students, the first cohort of students to receive them included 65 minority applicants and yielded 51 minority participants, out of 400; the second cohort included 112 minority candidates out of 400. At the University of North Carolina at Chapel Hill, 16 of the 80 students enrolled in the 1989-90 Teaching Fellows Program are Black. North Carolina student fellows also participate in summer programs that provide teaching-related enrichment activities.

Georgia Southern University (GSU) has entered into a cooperative agreement with several school districts. Both GSU and the school districts offer matching funds for forgivable loans to students of color. In return, the students agree to return to and teach for a specified time in the school district, which agrees to hire them. As with most loan forgiveness programs, should students decide not to teach in the state or school district after finishing their education, they are required to repay the loan.

Magnet and Theme Schools

Magnet schools whose themes emphasize careers in education form a third set of pre-baccalaureate programs. Magnet school programs currently exist at Austin High School in Houston, Texas, and Crenshaw Teacher Training Academy in Los Angeles. Students enrolled at Austin take college preparatory courses and educationally-related electives such as foundations of education and methods courses. Also included in the Austin curriculum are field observations and classroom practica. As a capstone experience, students complete a one semester practice teaching internship.

One hundred-forty of the 1,000 students at Crenshaw High School are enrolled in the Teacher Training Academy. Ninety percent of the students enrolled in the high school and all of the students in the Teacher Training Academy are Black. In 1988, the third year of the Crenshaw Magnet Program, there were 54 seniors, with equal numbers of males and females. A component on pedagogy and method is attached to each subject in the curriculum, and students participate in several multicultural teaching experiences over the three year program. Enrichment activities include visits to universities, attendance at conferences and participation in Future Teachers' Club activities. A similar magnet program has begun its first year in San Jose.

A review of the existing programs seems to indicate the following:

- Pre-baccalaureate programs require resources and cost money. Preparing students of color who have poor educational backgrounds is labor-intensive and costly.

- Recruiting students of color is influenced by many factors. Although no one model will guarantee success, outreach into minority communities through contact with churches, schools, organizations and media is essential.

- Institutional and state efforts must be well-coordinated with public schools.

- Pre-college programs that begin at the high school may be too late. Other pre-college programs--math, engineering, and science--have found that in order to be successful, interventions must begin in junior high school.

College Level Programs

For minority candidates, many barriers block the road to certification; however, the biggest barriers are the standardized tests. While the literature indicates that there are a number of college programs whose emphasis is on helping minority candidates successfully complete teacher education programs and pass standardized tests, detailed written information about them is sparse. The University of Florida in Gainesville is one such program. During the past two years, 200 candidates, including 50 minority students, have participated in Florida's program. The overall pass rate on the Florida Teacher Education (FTE) test of candidates enrolled in this program was an impressive 91%; for minority candidates it was 86%.

Grambling State University in Louisiana, on the other hand, has implemented a program that has been well-documented. In 1980, Grambling, in danger of losing its accreditation because of its students' poor showing on the National Teachers Examination (NTE), undertook a comprehensive plan to insure that its students could pass the certification requirements. Five years later, Grambling received the Showcase of Excellence award presented by the American Association of State Colleges and Universities to institutions that had significantly improved the quality of their undergraduate teacher education programs. During this five year period, Grambling raised its students' NTE pass rate from 5 to 85%. It accomplished this by adopting a three-pronged approach to helping students prepare for standardized tests. Grambling's program sought to: improve students' basic skills; equip students with test taking skills and strategies; and assist faculty in aligning their courses more closely with the professional competencies required by the NTE.

Diagnosing and remediating students' basic skills were made priorities. Students who wanted to major in education were tested and required to achieve a grade equivalent of 11.0 before admission into the College of Education. The program enables students to work on their communication skills in a Reading/Writing Development Center housed in The College of Education until they meet this requirement. Passing required standardized tests is emphasized throughout the teacher education program. Before entering formal preparation for teaching, sophomores must take the Communication Skills and General Knowledge sections of the National Teachers Examination and students must pass the Professional Knowledge Sections of the NTE before they can begin student teaching. Finally, in order to graduate from the program, students must pass the College of Education Senior Comprehensive Exam and a Specialty Area of the NTE in addition to completing an approved program. Using content related materials developed according to test specifications along with instruction on test taking skills, students receive 10-12 hours of preparation for these tests. By requiring students to meet state requirements before graduating, Grambling insures that its teacher education graduates will be eligible for state certification. One result of Grambling's new program is the increased numbers of students seeking admission to the College of Education. After averaging 1,200 students between 1972 and 1975, enrollment in the College of Education dropped to 200. By the spring of 1986, enrollment had reached 850, and was reported to be growing faster than any other program in the university (Spencer, 1986). This suggests that students will enroll in teacher education programs when they can be reasonably sure they will be able to meet the certification requirements upon graduation.

In response to low test scores that threatened the accreditation of their teacher education programs, at least two other historically Black institutions have designed and implemented plans for improving their students' test scores. The University of Arkansas at Pine Bluff and Norfolk State University have successfully raised the percentages of students passing the NTE--Pine Bluff from 42 to 67% between 1983 and 1985, and Norfolk

State from 28 to 71% between 1982 and 1985 (Whitehurst, Witty & Wiggins, 1986; Antonelli, 1985).

Critics may argue that programs like Grambling, Pine Bluff and Norfolk concentrate too much on helping students prepare for tests, shortchanging more important aspects in teacher preparation. Such concerns are legitimate. The validity of tests and appropriate weight to be accorded tests over other characteristics are widely addressed and debated in the literature. Almost everyone agrees that the tests currently in use do not tap the energy, adaptability, perseverance, sense of humor or other qualities that are indispensable to teaching. Reasonable people do disagree, however, about what should be done. The flaws that exist in standardized tests notwithstanding, most teacher educators, those mentioned earlier as well as others, have turned their attention to what they believe is the more critical task of helping students pass the tests.

We can ill afford to lose two or more generations of teachers of color while we wait for better tests. Nor should we be overly optimistic about the new certification tests for teachers. The evidence to date suggests the newer tests may end up replacing a set of correct answers with a set of preferred teaching styles, styles unrelated to academic growth in students least well served by the schools. Despite promises that this new generation of tests will be more faithful to what teachers actually do in the classroom, there is little reason to believe that minority candidates will fare better on them than they do on the National Teachers Examination or on state tests.

Pressing for minor changes in the testing conditions--eliminating the rule that limits the number of times a candidate may retake a test, allowing students longer than 30 minutes to complete the essay on the PPST, a test condition that discriminates against Black dialect users or English as a second language speakers--is an intermediate goal worth pursing, one that may enable more students to successfully negotiate the tests. In the meantime, however, making sure that students of color are adequately prepared pass the tests must become a priority. There is ample evidence that, with coaching and remediation, students of color can pass standardized tests.

When it comes to testing, teacher educators must be pragmatic at the same time they remain idealistic. Lobbying for major reforms in teacher testing is a worthwhile long range goal, although recent Supreme Court decisions upholding the use of the NTE in North and South Carolina indicate that this may be a long and difficult struggle.

Possibilities

The most commonly advanced argument for recruiting minority teachers is that their presence in the classroom makes them available as role models to students of color. Speaking to this point, the Carnegie Task Force on Teaching comments: "The race and background of their teachers tells them [students] something about authority and power in contemporary America. These messages influence children's attitudes toward school, their academic accomplishments and their views of their own and others' intrinsic worth" (Carnegie Forum, 1986). While shared cultural background does not guarantee that teachers will be successful with students, there is an unspoken belief that teachers from similar backgrounds may be able to relate better to students' experiences, understand their motivations and forge productive alliances with their parents. Recently research has been undertaken that seeks to understand the influence of cultural background on pedagogy and practice (Joint Center for Political Studies, 1989). Though sparse, evidence is slowly accumulating that shows that teachers of color do relate to minority students and their parents in ways that are culturally congruent and pedagogically responsive. And, despite institutional constraints, they act as surrogate parents and counselors. Finally, many believe that one role of teachers of color is to prepare students for individual and collective responsibility as well as for leadership (McCollum, 1989; Foster, 1988; King, 1987; Erickson & Mohatt 1986; Barnhardt, 1982).

Unfortunately, institutions--schools, colleges and universities, including teacher preparation programs--ignore the unique strengths and experiences that students of color bring to institutions of higher education, usually subtracting rather than adding to their knowledge, and eventually discouraging them from teaching in areas with large concentrations of minority students. For almost a year, I have been corresponding with African-American teacher education students from a midwestern university in Milwaukee in their final year of college and throughout their first year of teaching. The dilemma facing students of color who have strong cultural ties to their families and communities and who want to return to teach in communities similar to those in which they grew up, is best illustrated by presenting excerpts from the letters of one young woman, whom I'll call Josephine.

2 November 1988

> I love teaching and have an intrinsic need to teach. I want to change the injustices imposed by the education system on innocent Black children. I thought going to a well reputed university and majoring in education would be a stepping stone in my career. But something has been missing in my

> professional preparation--in the university education system.
>
> My education at ______________ has not been negative, but I cannot quite explain or describe my feeling of unfulfillment. When I read your work, I felt the closest I have ever felt to being able to express to my professors what I and many other minority education students have been missing in our professional training here. There are important, vital understandings and sensibilities about what teachers of Black children need to know to teach them in a way that capitalizes on the strengths of their background instead of punishing them for it.

Josephine goes on to describe briefly the family, neighborhood and community with which she identifies and wants to remain connected. Seven month later, she had completed her degree, had been hired by the urban public school system where she lived and was waiting for her assignment. On 29 June, 1988, she writes:

> I was hired by the ______________ Public School System. I will not be assigned to a specific school or grade until the third week of August. I

> am truly EXCITED. I have been reading children's books and doing literary expansions for a variety of ages.
>
> Unfortunately, some teachers are discouraging me from working in neighborhood school areas where 90% of the students are minorities. Many teachers have stated, "They are terrible and disrespectful!!!" The general attitude of teachers toward teaching especially in urban areas is often times negative. ... I will take each comment with a grain of salt and continue to prepare myself. I feel confident that where I lack the Lord, love, determination, and hard work will make sufficient.

I am pleased to report that Josephine has begun teaching and all reports indicate that she shows promise of becoming an excellent teacher. Still, I wonder how many other Josephines have become disillusioned, discouraged and turned away from teaching or, worse, how many have adopted the negative attitudes of their more experienced colleagues who long ago gave up trying to teach pupils from minority backgrounds.

Colleges and universities ought to help teachers, school psychologists and counselors acquire the cognitive and affective competencies necessary to teach students of color successfully. Unfortunately, many schools of education have trained teachers as if teaching were a set of technical skills to be mastered. These same schools are also guilty of advancing paradigms, theories and doctrines that have served to educationally disenfranchise subordinated groups. Twenty-five years ago, schools of education promoted ideas of cultural deficit and cultural disadvantage on a large scale. Now, it is "common wisdom" among teachers that minority group children have been so neglected by their parents and communities before coming to school, that there is little or nothing that schools can do to overcome these deficiencies. In the past few years, these same ideas have been promoted under the new in vogue "at risk" label. The result is that explanations cloaked in science will continue to be used as excuses for the massive educational failure of large groups of children. Teaching students of color successfully will not come from merely mastering a set of technical skills. Nor will it come from blaming families and children for the underachievement.

Earlier I mentioned a survey that indicated that minority teachers at all levels of satisfaction were more likely to report that they were likely to leave teaching. Forty percent of minority teachers, compared to 25% of non-minority teachers, said that they were possibly or very likely to leave the profession. Minority teachers will fewer years' experience were most likely to indicate that they planned to leave teaching, with 55% of those with less than 5 years' experience and 43% of those with 5 to 9 years' experience stating that they were very or possibly likely to leave teaching. The corresponding figures for non-minority teachers were 31% for those with less than 5 years' experience and 27% for those with 5 to 9 years' experience. One explanation for this disparity is differences in work conditions; the minority teachers surveyed were three times more likely than the non-minorities to work in the inner-city, where difficult teaching conditions are the norm (Metropolitan Life, 1988).

Another explanation, however, is that minorities feel alienated from the institutions where they work and believe that they have little or no voice in the educational establishment. Changes in our educational institutions, partly the result of desegregation, have sharply curtailed the influence that adults of color have over the education of their children. Ongoing discussions about what curricula pedagogy and teaching styles are appropriate for children from their communities have excluded the voices of minority researchers, teacher educators, teachers and parents (Joint Center for Political Studies, 1989; Delpit, 1988, 1986; Grant & Gilette, 1987; Bell, 1980). It should not surprise us that individuals are reluctant to enter or stay in a profession where their views are neither heard nor respected.

Increasing the number of teachers of color provides schools of education with the perfect opportunity to improve the instruction that students of color--those least well served by the schools--currently receive. How might we design a program that would serve the twin goals of providing more equitable access to schools of education for students of color while at the same time effecting a change in the quality of instruction that children of color receive in the nation's public schools? What would such a program look like? These are some of the questions that teacher education programs must answer in order to make the kinds of changes necessary to make these two goals a reality.

Any teacher education program that seeks to increase the number of students of color must be comprehensive. It will have to include coursework, tutoring, academic advising, and field placements. In order to be successful, it will require fundings, resources, and commitment from top level administrators as well as from the faculty. The teacher education programs for students of color will have to be scrutinized carefully. Do courses include issues of equity and diversity? Are issues of language and culture, child-rearing and socialization in non-mainstream families, testing and tracking, power in the classroom (discipline) included in the curriculum? Do political science courses address court cases--Brown vs the Board of Education, Ann Arbor, Larry P.--that affect schools and schooling? Do the psychology courses include a cross-cultural perspective?

Are minority perspectives and the works of minority scholars included in the readings? Do students have a chance to study under African, Native, Asian-American and Latino professors? Are students encouraged to compare their personal, family and community experiences with the findings in the research literature? Is the curricular emphasis only psychological or does it also include an anthropological focus?

Do students of color get enough chance to observe, have field placements and student teach under the direction of an exemplary role model? Are there opportunities for these students to attend workshops, conferences and professional meetings? Are there opportunities for students to work as paid interns in day care centers, elementary schools, and literacy centers? Are students encouraged to compile a portfolio of experiences, workshops, or other activities relevant to their professional education?

Are students of color given instruction especially tailored to helping them pass the SAT, PPST, NTE or other teacher certification tests? Are students encouraged to form and maintain connections with each other? Are they encouraged to study together? Are they encouraged to depend on each other for mutual support?

It should be obvious, whether attempts to increase the number of teachers of color are developed through collaboratives with middle or high schools, transfer programs with community colleges, or through partnerships with predominantly minority institutions, that schools of education need a major restructuring and refocusing of their teacher education programs. Actually, this will be true in order to prepare all teachers, but especially applies to our topic--recruiting teachers of color. These are the teachers for the pupils of the 21st century, whom they will face in little more than a decade. We know the problems. We must hasten to apply the programs, in order that we may realize the fullness of the possibilities.

References

American Association of Colleges for Teacher Education. (1987). Minority teacher recruitment and retention: A call to action. Washington, D.C.: Author.

Antonelli, G. (1985). Reconceptualization of teacher education in Arkansas. Pine Bluff, AR: University of Arkansas at Pine Bluff Forum.

Appalachian Educational Laboratory, Charleston WV and Tennessee Association of Colleges of Teacher Education. (1988). Programs of promise: A summary of current programs focusing on the recruitment of minority candidates to careers in professional education. Washington, D.C.: ERIC Clearinghouse on Higher Education. (ERIC Document Reproduction Service No. ED 301 556)

Barnhardt, C. (1982). Tuning-in to Athabaskan teachers and Athabaskan students. In R. Barnhardt (Ed.), Cross-cultural issues in Alaskan education. Fairbanks: Center for Cross-Cultural Studies.

Bell, D. (1983). Time for the teachers: Putting educators back into the Brown remedy. Journal of Negro Education, 52(3), 290-301.

Bray, C. (1984). _The Black public school teacher: Alabama's endangered species_. (University of California). Washington, D.C.: ERIC Clearinghouse on Higher Education. (ERIC Document Reproduction Service No. ED 255 476)

Carnegie Forum on Education and the Economy. (1986). _A nation prepared: Teachers for the 21st century_. (Report on teaching as a profession). NY: Author.

Cole, B. (1986). The Black educator: An endangered species. _Journal of Negro Education_, _55_(3), 326-334.

Cole, E., & Horton, F. (1984). _Trends in recruitment, retention and placement of prospective Black teachers_. (Paper presented at the Fifth National Invitational Conference on Teacher Preparation and Survival, Norfolk, VA). Washington, D.C.: ERIC Clearinghouse on Higher Education. (ERIC Document Reproduction Service No. ED 263 046)

Collins, H. (1989, May 17). Most pass teaching exam, but Blacks don't fare as well. _Philadelphia Inquirer_.

Delpit, L. (1986). Skills and other dilemmas of a progressive Black educator. _Harvard Educational Review_, _56_(4), 55-66.

Delpit, L. (1988). The silenced dialogue: Power and pedagogy in educating other people's children. Harvard Educational Review, 58(3), 280-298.

Dupre, B. (1986). Problems regarding the survival of future Black teachers. Journal of Negro Education, 55(2), 55-66.

Erickson, F., & Mohatt, G. (1988). Cultural organizations of participant structures in two classrooms of Indian students. In George Spindler (Ed.), Doing the Ethnography of Schooling, pp. 132-174. Prospect Heights, IL: Waveland.

Ethridge, S. (1979). Impact of the 1954 Brown v. Topeka Board of Education decision on Black educators. Negro Educational Review, 30(3-4), 217-232.

Foster, M. (1989). It's cookin' now: A performance analysis of speech events of a Black teacher in an urban community college. Language in Society, 18(1), 1-29.

Foster, M. (1988). Who we really are: Black women speak about their lives as teachers. Paper presented at the American Anthropological Association Conference, November 1988.

Gifford, B. (1986). Excellence and equity in teacher competency testing: A policy perspective. Journal of Negro Education, 55(3), 251-271.

Goertz, M. & Pitcher, B. (1985). The impact of NTE by states on the teacher selection process. Princeton, NJ: Educational Testing Service.

Grant, C. & Gillette, M. (1987, November/December). The Holmes report and minorities in education. Social Education, 517-521.

Hilliard, A. (1980). The changing Black teacher and diminishing opportunities for Black teachers. (Paper presented at the national invitational conference on problems, issues, plans and strategies related to the preparation and survival of Black teachers.) Washington, D.C.: ERIC Clearinghouse on Higher Education. (ERIC Document Reproduction Service No. ED 212 565)

Irvine, J. (1988). An analysis of the problem of the disappearing Black educator. The Elementary School Journal, 88(5), 503-513.

Joint Center for Political Studies. (1989). Visions of a better way: A Black appraisal of public schooling. Washington, D.C.: Author.

King, J. (1987). Black student alienation and Black teachers' emancipatory pedagogy. The Journal of Black Reading and Language Education, 3(1), 3-13.

McCollum, P. (1989). Turn-allocation in lessons with North American and Puerto Rican students: A comparative study. Anthropology in Education Quarterly, 20(2), 133-156.

Metropolitan Life Insurance Company. (1988). The American teacher 1988: Strengthening the relationship between teachers and students. NY: Author.

National Education Association. (1987). Status of the American public school teacher 1985-86. Washington, D.C.: U.S. Government Printing Office.

U.S. Department of Education, Office of Educational Research and Improvement. (1987). Digest of educational statistics, 1987. Washington, D.C.: U.S. Government Printing Office.

Reed, D. (1986). Wanted: More Black teacher education students. Action in Teacher Education, 8(1), 31-36.

Spencer, T. (1986). Teacher education at Grambling State University: A move toward excellence. Journal of Negro Education, 55(3), 293-303.

Stern, J. (1988). The condition of education in postsecondary education. Washington, D.C.: U.S. Department of Education Office of Educational Research and Improvement.

Stewart, J., Meier, K., & England, R. (1989). In quest of role models: Change in Black teacher representation in urban school districts 1968-86. Journal of Negro Education, 58(2), 140-152.

Tyack, D. (1984). The one best system: A history of American urban education. Cambridge, MA: Harvard University Press.

Whitehurst, W., Witty, E., & Wiggins, S. (1986). Racial equity: Teaching excellence. Action in Teacher Education, 3(1), 51-59.

Witty, E. (1984). National invitational conference on problems, issues, plans and strategies related to the preparation and survival of Black public school teachers. (Proceedings of the Fifth Annual Conference.) Washington, D.C.: ERIC Clearinghouse on Higher Education. (ERIC Document Reproduction Service No. ED 263 046)

Zapata, J. (1988). Early identification and recruitment of Hispanic teacher candidates. Journal of Teacher Education, 39(1), 19-23.

PREPARING TEACHERS OF AMERICAN INDIAN HANDICAPPED CHILDREN

Bruce A. Ramirez & John W. Tippeconnic III

INTRODUCTION

> Properly equipped personnel is the most urgent immediate need in the Indian education service. At the present time the government is attempting to do a highly technical job with untrained . . . people. It is not necessary to attempt to place blame for this situation, but it is essential to recognize it and change it. (Institute for Government Research, 1928, p. 359)

More than 50 years have elapsed since this statement appeared in the Meriam Report, an extensive survey of the American Indian social and economic situation; yet the education of Indians, including Alaskan Native handicapped children, is today confronted with a similar challenge. Statistics within a recent report to the Congress indicated that for the 1978-1979 school year, federal Indian schools throughout the country would require approximately 386 additional special education teachers and 455 related school personnel, as well as extensive in-service training of existing staff (U.S. Department of Health, Education and Welfare, 1979). Note that these shortages and training needs pertain only to the Bureau of Indian Affairs school system, which annually enrolls slightly less than 25% of all Indian children residing on and near Indian reservations. And there is increasing evidence that public and tribal or Indian community controlled schools have similar needs.

While it is important to be aware of the present personnel shortages in special education, it is equally important to recognize that very often educators working with Indian children and youth have not had the benefit of training in Indian education. This can be traced to the widely held belief that Indian children are no different than other children. As a result, the curriculum and instructional strategies practiced in most schools serving Indian children have historically not differed substantially from those of middle-class suburban schools. More recently, preservice and in-service teacher preparation programs have begun to offer training opportunities in the education of culturally diverse children.

Over the past decade, several major studies have called attention to the general failure of public and federal schools to adequately educate Indian children (Fuchs & Havighurst, 1973; U.S. Congress, 1969). A major reason cited for this failure has been inadequately trained and sometimes insensitive school personnel. Unfortunately, many of the difficulties identified by these earlier studies continue to plague school systems serving Indian communities today. Some of the more frequent problems, particularly with regard to reservation and rural settings, include:

- Recruitment of teachers who have little knowledge of teaching in culturally diverse reservation settings and who have ideas about upgrading the "Indian condition."

These individuals all too often become impatient and disillusioned and opt for more familiar settings.

- Low expections from educators that lead to poor student performance, drop-outs, and negative attitudes toward Indian students.
- High teacher turnover rates due to the isolation of the reservation schools and communities, inadequate or minimal housing facilities, and feelings of not being a part of the community.
- Inadequate numbers of Indian and Alaskan Native teachers, administrators, and other specialized school staff.

Public Law 94-142, The Education for All Handicapped Children Act of 1975, requires that handicapped children receive the special education and related services necessary for each child to reach his or her full potential. A fundamental step in providing these services to Indian handicapped children is the preparation of necessary special education teachers and related school staff with training in Indian education. In view of the recurring personnel difficulties associated with Indian education, and the various kinds of staff required to fully carry out the requirements of federal education laws for the handicapped, it has become increasingly evident that these problems, if left unattended, will further delay the provision of a free and appropriate public education to Indian handicapped children.

FEDERAL RESPONSIBLITY IN INDIAN EDUCATION

The unique relationship between Indian tribes and the national government, reflected in treaties, legislation, executive orders, and court decrees, has required the United States to assume obligations and responsibilities to fulfill the rights of Indian people to health, education, welfare, and economic advancement (American Indian Policy Review Commission, 1976). Based on this special relationship, the federal government provides educational opportunities and services to Indian children, youth, and adults. The 1975 Indian Self-Determination and Educational Assistance Act (P.L. 93-638) reaffirmed this responsibility and committed the Congress to assuring maximum Indian participation in the direction and provision of educational services to Indian communities. In a futher declaration of policy, the Congress stated that:

> . . . a major national goal of the United States is to provide the quantity and quality of educational services and opportunities which will permit Indian children to compete and excell in the life areas of their choice, and to achieve the measure of self-determination essential to their social and economic well-being. (Sec. 3 (c))

In this respect, the principles of Indian self-determination and Indian preference are directly related to the need for substantive federal involvement in the preparation of Indian educational personnel to educate Indian children — including the handicapped.

INDIAN PREFERENCE IN EMPLOYMENT

Beginning as early as 1834 and continuing through the late 1800s, several laws were enacted by the United States Congress directing that Indians be employed in the federal Indian Service as herders, teamsters, laborers (25 U.S.C. 44) as well as matrons and industrial teachers (25 U.S.C. 274). Preference to Indians was also extended to qualified individuals of Indian descent "in all cases of the appointment of interpreters or other persons employed for the benefit of the Indians" (25 U.S.C. 45). In 1934, qualified Indians were accorded preference in appointments to vacant Bureau of Indian Affairs positions (25 U.S.C. 472). Forty years after the 1934 Indian preference law, the United States Supreme Court reaffirmed the legality of this tenet as it applies to the Bureau of Indian Affairs. In stressing that the intent of these laws was the promotion of Indian self-government rather than racial discrimination, the court observed:

> . . . it (preference) is an employment criterion reasonably designed to further the cause of Indian self-government and to make the BIA more responsive to the needs of its constituent groups. It is directed to participation by the governed in the governing agency. (*Morton* v. *Mancari*, 1974)

INDIAN PREFERENCE IN TRAINING

In addition to the employment preference within the Bureau of Indian Affairs, Congress has seen fit to extend Indian preference to the training of individuals serving Indian students. The Indian Education Act of 1972, P.L. 92-318, allows for special programs to train educational personnel to serve Indian students. Under this discretionary grant program, institutions of higher education, state and local education agencies, Indian tribes, organizations, and institutions are to apply Indian preference in the selection of program participants.

INDIAN SELF-DETERMINATION

In order to make federal services to Indian people more responsive, P.L. 93-638 encourages Indian tribes to contract through the Bureau of Indian Affairs to plan, conduct, and administer their own educational programs and services. Prior to this, however, the federal government through Indian preference had sought to involve qualified Indians in the direction and provision of its services to Indians. As indicated in Table 1, these preference policies have not resulted in substantial numbers of Indian personnel within the federal Indian school system. In an apparent effort to correct this situation, Section 1135 of the Education Amendments of 1978 (P.L. 95-561) directs the Secretary of the Interior to institute a policy for the recruitment of qualified Indian educators, including a detailed plan to promote such employees from within the Bureau of Indian Affairs.

SPECIAL EDUCATION PERSONNEL PREPARATION

During the past several years, the Office of Indian Education and the Bureau of Indian Affairs have afforded only limited attention to the pre-service and in-service training of educators of Indian handicapped children. At the same time, the Bureau of Education for the Handicapped has provided sporadic support to projects to prepare Indian special educators.

OFFICE OF INDIAN EDUCATION

As previously mentioned, under the Indian Education Act of 1972 the Commissioner of the U.S. Office of Education is authorized to make grants to institutions of higher education and state and local education agencies to prepare individuals to serve Indian children as teachers, aides, social workers, and ancillary education personnel. In-service training to improve the qualifications of these personnel is also permitted. The Education Amendments of 1974 (P.L. 93-380) expanded this training authority to permit Indian tribes, organizations, and institutions to undertake special training programs and in-service training for teachers and administrators of programs serving Indian children.

The history of these personnel development programs within the Office of Indian Education shows that the training projects have focused on

Table 1

Bureau of Indian Affairs employees in the professional educator series (GS-1710) as of March 29, 1978

Type of personnel	Non-Indian	Indian	Total
Elementary teachers	722 (60.7)	468 (39.3)	1190
Subject matter teachers[1]	505 (77.5)	174 (22.5)	679
Special education teachers[2]	122 (79.2)	32 (20.8)	154
Guidance counselors[3]	182 (74.0)	64 (26.0)	246
Supervisory school positions[4]	228 (64.8)	124 (35.2)	352
Education specialist[5]	210 (67.3)	102 (32.7)	312
Education program administrators	31 (49.2)	32 (50.8)	63
TOTAL	2000 (67.4)	996 (32.6)	2996

Data provided by the Office of Indian Education Programs, Bureau of Indian Affairs, U.S. Department of the Interior, May 15, 1979.
1 Primarily secondary teachers specializing in a particular subject area, i.e., history, language arts, etc.
2 Includes remedial reading teachers and teachers of the handicapped.
3 Includes school as well as dormitory counselors.
4 Includes principals, assistant principals, principal/teachers and supervisor/teachers.
5 Educators at the area and agency administrative levels specializing in curriculum, language arts, guidance, special education, etc.

the preparation of elementary teachers, school administrators, and counselors. While there have not been specific projects aimed at preparing teachers of Indian handicapped children, a few existing projects contain special education components. In addition, the Education Amendments of 1978 (P.L. 95-561) increased the number of fields for which fellowships may be made available, making it possible for Indian students to pursue graduate degrees in specific areas of education for the 1979-80 school year.

BUREAU OF EDUCATION FOR THE HANDICAPPED

Part D of the Education of the Handicapped Act (P.L. 91-230 as amended) has authorized the Bureau of Education for the Handicapped to conduct an extensive preservice and in-service training program to prepare teachers and other specialists to educate handicapped children. Discretionary grants are available to institutions of higher education, state education agencies, and other nonprofit institutions or agencies in the areas of program assistance, special projects, and training grants to state education agencies. With the passage of P.L. 94-142, the thrust of this program has concentrated on preparing sufficient special numbers of education and school support personnel to assure the full implementation of this far-reaching federal law.

Through the special projects program, the Division of Personnel Preparation has supported several projects to train teachers to educate Indian handicapped children. These projects have included a special education teacher-training program for Navajos conducted by the Navajo Tribe Division of Education, a paraprofessional training program administered by one of the Indian community colleges, and a university graduate training program to prepare Indian special education teachers in South Dakota. In addition, a staff member has been identified and assigned to the area of Indian training programs.

BUREAU OF INDIAN AFFAIRS

There is no legislation authorizing the Bureau of Indian Affairs or the Department of the Interior to undertake training programs in Indian education. Rather, the 1921 Synder Act allows the Bureau of Indian Affairs to supervise and expend funds appropriated by Congress to educate Indians. This broad authority has been interpreted to permit postsecondary scholarships as well as specialized training projects. In the past the Bureau has supported training projects in areas such as law, social work, and educational administration. Bureau of Indian Affairs officials have indicated that in the future BIA will concentrate on making individual scholarships available rather than specialized training programs or projects.

Public Law 94-142 allows for the participation of the Secretary of the Interior on behalf of the Bureau of Indian Affairs school system. As a means of insuring that trained instructional and support personnel are available to serve handicapped children, P.L. 94-142 requires the development and implementation of a comprehensive system of personnel development. Besides the additional special education personnel needs mentioned earlier, the FY 79 Annual Program Plan identifies individualized education programs, procedural safeguards, confidentiality, evaluation procedures, surrogate parents, placement procedures, and physical education for handicapped students as priority in-service areas.

FUTURE NEEDS

The remainder of this article discusses issues and makes recommendations regarding actions that need to be undertaken to insure that appropriately trained special education personnel are available to serve Indian handicapped children.

FEDERAL LEADERSHIP AND COORDINATION

The preparation of teachers of Indian handicapped children will require the involvement of institutions of higher education as well as various federal, state, and tribal agencies. In this regard, coordination is especially critical, given the role each agency plays in the preparation of teaching personnel, e.g., the federal government provides financial support to train teachers, the university furnishes the academic program, the state certifies teachers, and Indian tribes can provide the necessary cultural activities as well as training programs in conjunction with colleges and universities. All too often, however, there is little coordination between these agencies, leading to confusion, conflict, and wasteful use of limited resources.

It is unrealistic to expect a vast increase in the

number of appropriately trained special education personnel to work with Indian handicapped children without leadership at the federal level. If priority is not given to this need, the Office of Indian Education will continue to address the basic need of training elementary and secondary school staff and the Bureau of Education for the Handicapped will continue to give priority to specific types of special education personnel. In either case, it is extremely unlikely that these separate practices will produce the number of special educators needed in Indian education.

This past year, the Secretary of the Department of Health, Education and Welfare established an Indian Initiative that has the potential to serve as the vehicle to improve the coordination of teacher-training programs in special education and Indian education at the federal level. Within the U.S. Office of Education, each program is to determine the type and level of services currently provided to Indian people. The Initiative further requires specific measurable objectives to be developed by these programs to increase the level of Indian participation in each program. In this regard, the Initiative provides an opportunity to focus federal resources for the benefit of Indian students, including the handicapped. Once the Indian Initiative has been developed and operationalized within the Department of Health, Education and Welfare, the special education training component needs to be coordinated with similar efforts in the Bureau of Indian Affairs.

TRAINING PROGRAMS TO PREPARE INDIAN SPECIAL EDUCATORS

Much has been written about the benefits of employing educators of the same cultural and language background to teach and administer educational programs for culturally diverse children. In light of the low achievement, high drop-out rates, and other difficulties experienced by Indian children in meeting school expectations, this has also become a primary consideration in the improvement of educational opportunities for Indian children. As previously indicated, ⅔ of the total number of professional educators employed in the Bureau of Indian Affairs school system are non-Indian. Similarily, a survey by the Arizona Department of Education (1975) of reservation public school districts throughout the state found that 85 to 90% of the teachers were Anglo, 5% other minority groups, and 10% Indians.

There is an urgent need to develop specialized Indian training personnel.

In view of the overall lack of Indian educators and the principles of Indian self-determination, there is an urgent need to develop specialized training personnel. Programs leading to a degree need to be developed by universities and colleges, or Indian tribes in conjunction with teacher-training institutions, to provide leadership and direction in the provision of services to Indian handicapped children. The major advantage of these programs is that they are able to concentrate on training a substantial number of participants at one time, using a curriculum that is based on their particular needs. Thus, a large number of individuals can be prepared in a relatively short period of time. For example, in the early 1970s specialized programs in educational administration were established at major universities throughout the country. By 1979, the graduates of these programs had a significant impact in administering education programs at the national, state, tribal, and local levels.

These programs also have the advantage of built-in awareness of Indian education. The sheer numbers and group cohesiveness of the program participants provide a force to modify program curriculum and focus on the needs of teaching Indian handicapped students. An important component of such a specialized program is a field-based internship, which allows participants to gain experience in working with Indian handicapped children or in agencies that have direct responsibility in special education or Indian education or both.

PRESERVICE TRAINING

Not only is there a need for more education personnel to teach Indian handicapped children but there is also a need to improve the manner in which these teachers are prepared. The typical teacher-training program in special education has not allowed for coursework in Indian education. Conversely, existing Indian education programs have not included experiences in special education. In teaching Indian handicapped children, a special education teacher should have some level of training in Indian education. This training should include instruction in areas such as the history and philosophy of Indian education, learning characteristics of Indian students, Indian cultures and languages, tribal diversity, Indian self-determination, and relevant curricula for Indian students. To facilitate the integration of special education and Indian education instruction, Indian education should be a component of a teacher preparation program and not added as an additional requirement.

An integrated approach will provide an opportunity to gain an understanding of Indian people, thus breaking down the barriers of stereotypes and misconceptions about Indians. Awareness and respect of cultural and language differences are critical and will improve the attitudes of teachers in working with Indian handicapped children. Ideally, university and college faculty members who teach about Indians should be Indian or have first-hand knowledge and experience in working with Indian people.

IN-SERVICE TRAINING

While much can be done through preservice training to increase the number and type of special education personnel educating Indian handicapped children, extensive in-service training will be required to develop the attitudes and skills necessary to serve handicapped children, as required by P.L. 94-142. As with preservice training, special education and related school personnel working with Indian handicapped children will require in-service training in special education and Indian education. With regard to Indian education instruction, in-service training can focus on the same areas as preservice training, with the exception that training can be more tribally specific.

In teaching Indian handicapped children, a special education teacher should have some training in Indian education.

CONCLUSION

The need for special education teachers and related school staff to educate Indian handicapped children is obvious. The academic preparation of these personnel should not only include the necessary coursework in special education, but also include experiences in Indian education. Public Law 94-142 and the basic federal policies of Indian self-determination and Indian preference in employment and training provide the impetus for the federal government to exert leadership. The government can give priority to specialized programs and projects to train teachers of Indian handicapped children. Without this emphasis, the mandate to provide an appropriate education to Indian handicapped children will not be met.

REFERENCES

American Indian Policy Review Commission, Task Force One: Trust Responsibilities and the Federal-Indian Relationship (Hank Adams, Chairman). *Report on trust responsibilities and the federal-Indian relationship; including treaty review.* Washington, D.C.: U.S. Government Printing Office, 1976.

Arizona Department of Education. *A study of selected public schools on and off Indian reservations in Arizona.* Phoenix: Author, 1975.

Fuchs, E., & Havighurst, R.J. *To live on this earth: American Indian education.* New York: Anchor Press, 1973.

Institute for Government Research. *The problem of Indian administration.* Baltimore: Johns Hopkins Press, 1928.

Morton, Secretary of the Interior v. *Mancari* 414 U.S. 1142 (1974)

U.S. Congress, Senate, Committee on Labor and Public Welfare, Special Subcommittee on Indian Education, *Indian education: A national tragedy, a national challenge.* S. Report No. 91-501, 91st Congress. 1st. Session, 1969.

U.S. Department of Health, Education and Welfare, U.S. Office of Education. *Progress toward a free appropriate public education—A report to Congress on the implementation of Public Law 94-142: The Education for All Handicapped Children Act.* Washington, D.C.: HEW Publication No. (OE) 79-05003, 1979.

U.S. Department of the Interior, Bureau of Indian Affairs. *Fiscal year 1978 annual program plan amendment revised for Part B of the Education of the Handicapped Act as amended by P.L. 94-142.* Washington, D.C.: Author, March 6, 1977.

Bruce A. Ramirez, The Council for Exceptional Children, Reston, Virginia.
John W. Tippeconnic III, Associate Deputy Commissioner for Indian Education, U.S. Office of Education, Washington, D.C.

Understanding and Overcoming Barriers in the Educational Pipeline

OVERVIEW

The minority teacher shortage must be viewed within the context of a larger educational pipeline issue. Given society's failure to provide successful school experiences for the increasing population of culturally diverse students, few minority students are successfully matriculating through the educational pipeline.

The first article in this chapter describes the historical, political, and economic context of differentiated schooling and the impact of inferior school programs on children from low income and diverse ethnic or racial backgrounds. The educational system has tended to sift and sort out the unmotivated and poorly performing students and favored those students who demonstrate promise of academic excellence. Consequently, many students from minority cultures are overrepresented in programs for underachievers and underrepresented in college preparatory and gifted programs.

Reginald Wilson and Manuel Justiz, in the second article, assert that the specific barriers in the pipeline leading to poor minority participation and graduation rates in higher education are related to academic underpreparation, a culturally insensitive curriculum, a hostile campus environment, and limited financial aid. The third article indicates that the traditional criteria – e.g., tests and admissions policies – used to predict a minority student's potential academic or career success have tended to discriminate against students from culturally diverse backgrounds. Both Garcia and Mercer recommend that alternative admissions standards and other multiple criteria be used in evaluating nontraditional and minority students for entry into teacher education.

From *Journal of Education*, vol. 168, no. 1, 1986, pp. 60-80. © by Boston University. Reprinted by permission.

TRACKING, INEQUALITY, AND THE RHETORIC OF REFORM: WHY SCHOOLS DON'T CHANGE

Jeannie Oakes
The Rand Corporation, Santa Monica, California

This paper looks critically at the historical, political, and economic context of differentiated schooling. The argument is made that this context explains the failure to address inequality in the current agenda for educational reform. The present inattention reflects the politics of economic scarcity and social conservatism, but, more importantly, it reflects persistent and deeply rooted assumptions about human abilities and the role of schools in providing equal opportunity. Neither the mood of generosity toward poor and minority children in the 1960s nor the current stinginess has altered the enduring differentiated structure of school.

In these times of perceived scarcity, the question that most threatens American ideology surfaces at every turn: If there isn't enough to go around, who gets it? The current supply-side, trickle-down answer is clear: Those who have, shall get. In education the question has been forced by diminishing resources and the withdrawal of public support. The answer is confirmed in the recent reform reports and in policymakers' enthusiastic response to them. There is a cynical common thread that both the detractors and supporters of these reports share, and the metaphor of the swinging pendulum serves to illustrate it. Sometimes we're more conservative, sometimes more liberal; sometimes there's money and confidence, sometimes we feel poor and hopeless. Back and forth. Everyone senses that the change is illusory.

The intent of this paper is to respond to that pendulum phenomenon, for until it is understood clearly, a powerful force—as little "seen" as gravity—will continue to shape our schools. That force, present at the turn of the century, almost unchanged in the generous '60s, and with us today, is the differentiation of schooling experiences according to the belief that some children can more easily or more deservedly achieve excellence.

This paper is an extension of the analysis included in *Keeping Track: How Schools Structure Inequality* (Yale University Press, 1985). While the views expressed herein represent only those of the author, thanks are given to Martin Lipton and Gary Fenstermacher for helpful comments on this work.

Current school reform proposals represent, for the most part, a stripping away of some of the contemporary guises of traditional schooling content and forms. This is differentiated schooling characterized by Anglo-conformity and meritocracy. Deemed "excellent" in the reform rhetoric, this mode of schooling has historically restricted both access to education and achievement of ethnic minority and poor children. Well-intentioned, progressive reformers have, at times, succeeded in mitigating the injustice inherent in these forms; even so, the current politics of social conservatism, far from inventing new inequities, appear to be largely capitalizing on endemic ones.

Prevailing Conceptions of Equality and Schooling

Traditional schooling forms, so clearly symbolized by the practice of tracking, are deeply rooted in assumptions about student differences and the meritocratic nature of schooling. Political and economic trends generate changes in rhetoric without addressing these assumptions or affecting the essential nature of schools as social institutions. Straightforward intents to eliminate inequality have given way to various rationales for inequality. Both are charged with a tangle of myth, unexamined assumptions, good intentions, and accurate and inaccurate beliefs.

Rarely do either those who press for equality or those who see equality as a costly luxury articulate the relationship between equality and schooling that permeates American schools. The following is an attempt to make explicit the prevailing conceptions of equality and schooling.

1. Educational opportunity, not educational results, must be equal in school.

2. Equal educational opportunity means equal opportunity to develop quite fixed individual potential (intelligence and abilities) to its limit through individual effort in school, regardless of such irrelevant background characteristics as race, class, and gender.

3. Providing equal opportunities to develop individual potential has instrumental value to both individuals and society. For individuals, it provides fair access to the world of work by providing fair access to the technical knowledge, the skills, and the attitudes that make possible the production of goods and services. Work is the way to attain the material and nonmaterial resources of society (wealth, prestige, power). For society, equal educational opportunity means that individuals' talents are developed for the benefit of all. These are contributions that could be thwarted under patronage- or inheritance-based systems.

4. Equal educational opportunity does not guarantee equal social and economic benefits to all individuals, because the rewards for various occupations are not equal. Rather, it provides a fair competition for

occupations and their accompanying unequal social and economic rewards. Thus, equal educational opportunity is the means for assuring equal economic and social opportunity.

5. Education provides students with the skills, attitudes, and technical knowledge required for participation in the workforce, but of course the requirements of different occupations vary greatly. They call for quite different levels of ability.

6. Equal educational opportunity does not require the same educational experiences for all individuals, but rather an equal opportunity to develop oneself for an appropriate future in the worklife of the community. This may, and usually does, necessitate quite different educational experiences for individuals of varying abilities and future roles. Equal educational opportunity, then, requires the provision of different educational experiences and the proper match of these educations to individual ability and suitability for future work. In that way all are served equally well.

7. Publicly supported schooling is a neutral, fair, and meritocratic place to determine who is best suited for various kinds of technical knowledge and skill, to provide appropriate educational experiences toward those ends, and to certify individuals for work roles. Further, school provides immigrant and minority groups opportunities to learn mainstream attitudes, values, and behaviors that are required for successful participation in American social, political, and economic institutions. School, with the provision of equal educational opportunity, fairly stages the competition for adult positions in the social and economic hierarchy.

The Content of Educational Opportunity

Equal educational opportunity, as expressed above, has shaped the structure of the contemporary school. This view has also led to the central struggle of contemporary schooling practice—the development of curriculum and instruction suited to the wide range of abilities and future needs of American children. Differentiated schooling is the structure for equalizing opportunity. But increasing evidence points to fundamental inequalities that result.

As a part of A Study of Schooling, data was collected about the curricular content, instructional processes, and classroom climates in nearly 300 secondary school English and mathematics classes. Over 200 of these classes were segregated by student ability or achievement levels.[1] Students had been assigned to these classes on the basis of teacher recommendations, test scores, or the advice of their counselors. Most of the students in upper-level classes were designated as academic-track students; most of the students in average or lower-track classes were in general or vocational programs. And, consistent with other studies of tracking, students in the upper tracks were disproportionately white; those in lower tracks were disproportionately minority. The data about these classes provided an unprecedented opportunity to look carefully at the principles of equal educational opportunity as they are played out in the everyday practice of schooling (Oakes, 1985).

There were considerable differences in the kinds of knowledge students in various tracks had access to. These differences did not represent equally valued alternative curricula. They were differences that could have important implications for the futures of the students involved. Students in high-track classes were exposed to "high status" content—literature, expository and thematic writing, library research, and mathematical ideas. Students in low-track classes were not expected to learn these topics and skills. They rarely, if ever, encountered them. They worked in workbooks and kits and practiced language mechanics and computation. The schools made decisions about the appropriateness of various topics and skills and, in doing so, limited sharply what some students would learn. The lower the track, the greater the limits.

Added to the unmistakable differences in the knowledge students had available to them were differences in their classroom learning opportunities. Both in the amount of time students were provided for learning and in the quality of instruction they received, there were significant differences among track levels. High-track students had more time to learn and more exposure to what seemed to be effective teaching than did other groups. These critical features of classrooms were not equally available to all students. Those students who were judged to learn most slowly and with greatest difficulty were provided the least time and the lowest quality of instruction.

Differences in the social milieus of the tracked classes were also found. In the high-track classes, teachers were perceived as more concerned and supportive; peers were often seen as nonthreatening allies. Students in low-track classes more often characterized their teachers as punitive and fellow students as unfriendly; their classes were more often seen as permeated with alienation, distance, and hostility.

What these students experienced in their classrooms shed considerable light on how equality of opportunity is manifested in classrooms. Despite meritocratic justifications and democratic intent, these data show an unequal distribution of learning opportunities in a direction that favors the already privileged. In the name of equal opportunity, track levels in schools, reflective of social and economic groupings in society, are provided with differential access to school opportunities that is likely to maintain or increase, rather than erase, the inequities in the larger social structure.

The Context of Educational Opportunity

To understand how schools arrived at this particular refinement of "separate-but-equal" one needs to look at the historical, political, and social context of differentiated students within schools. Shortly after the turn of the 20th century, as universal public secondary schooling was becoming a reality, the notions of equal opportunity and differentiated schooling converged in both the rhetoric and the organization of the urban high school. In 1908, the Boston school superintendent asserted, "Until very recently they [the schools] have offered equal opportunity for all to receive *one* kind of education, but what will make them democratic is to provide opportunity for all to receive such education as will fit them *equally well* for their particular life work" (Lazerson, 1974). Testing, tracking, and vocational education were the practices instituted to provide these equal opportunities. Both the rhetoric and the practices have changed little in this century.

Several related changes shaped the character of turn-of-the-century America: a switch from craftsman-based to industrial production, a population shift toward urban centers, a huge influx of poor, unskilled, and non-English-speaking immigrants, and the expansion of secondary schooling. Together they constituted a transformation of the economic, social, and political realities. All played a part in redefining the American conception of a democratic society. A central focus of this redefinition was establishing the prevailing 20th-century version of the relationship between equality and schooling. What resulted were the principles of equal educational opportunity outlined above.

The ideas undergirding these principles did not materialize from thin air. The air was thick with theories about the relationship of schooling to economic production and work, the value of a meritocracy, human evolution and the superiority of Anglo-Saxon cultures, and the unlimited potential of science and industry. A brief review of these ideas provides insight into the context of both turn-of-the-century and current definitions of educational equality.

School and Work. For the first time, students who would not become scholars, professionals, or gentlemen were attending secondary schools. The traditional academic curriculum seemed a mismatch, especially for immigrants who were difficult to keep in school. Yet it seemed important and humane to postpone these children's entry into the grind of factory life. At the same time industrial employers needed immigrants socialized with the work habits and attitudes required to "fit in" as factory workers (proper deportment, punctuality, willingness to be supervised and managed) and, perhaps less important, technical skills. Native-born youth needed a changed conception of work as well. The autonomy and complexity of a craftsman-based workforce were of the past. Work in the factory required respect for the industrial, in part to make the monotony of factory work tolerable. These requirements of industry coincided with the curricular vacuum in schools. Preparation for work became a central mission of secondary schools (Edson, 1982).

Social Darwinism and Differentiated Education. The misapplication of the theories of Charles Darwin to human society—social Darwinism—provided a *scientific* basis for viewing immigrant and minority groups as of lesser social and moral development than others. Their lives of squalor could be accounted for biologically, just as the disproportionate economic and social power held by men of Anglo stock could be justified by their "fitness." This misapplied social Darwinism, too, explained the disproportionate school failure and "retardation" rates of immigrant children. They failed because they were incapable, biologically unfit for an academic curriculum. The provision of different school content for these children—namely, industrial training—seemed not only democratic, but humane. Tracking into vocational or academic programs clearly provided equal opportunities for students with such inherently different capabilities (Hall, 1905).

Americanization and Anglo-Conformity. Not surprisingly, given social Darwinism, the languages and habits of the southern and eastern European immigrants were threatening to native-born Americans. They were numerous, strikingly different, and poor. There emerged a great concern about preserving the dominant WASP culture, eliminating the immigrants' "depraved" life style, and making the cities safe. It seemed absolutely necessary to bring the foreign-born into the American cultural mainstream by teaching them the Protestant American values of hard work, frugality, modesty, cleanliness, truthfulness, and purity of thought and action. The program to do so, closely aligned with preparation for work, was termed Americanization and located in the public schools. The rhetoric was one of an American melting pot, but in reality only certain people were to be melted. Americanization was driven both by a belief in the goodness of Anglo ways and by fear of the immigrants. Along with industrialism, Americanization provided much of the content of educational opportunities that were provided the children of the poor (Cremin, 1964).

Scientific Management. The concept of industrial efficiency shaped the *form* schooling would take to provide different but equal educations. The country had fallen in love with the idea of the factory busily engaged in a neatly standardized and controlled process of mass production. In went raw materials and, through the application of scientifically determined "best" methods and tools, out came ready-made goods and machinery—all designed to improve the quality of American life. The essence of the factory was efficiency. Human energies were controlled, coordinated, and channeled into machine-like parts, with little waste of material or duplication of effort. The "Taylor System" of scientific management made possible a system of production based on top-down decision making, a rigid division of labor, elaborate rules and regulations, and an attitude of impersonality toward the individual (Nelson, 1980). Schoolmen welcomed and often spearheaded the incorporation of "scientific management" into schools. Compared with the factory, schools seemed to be inefficient and unsuccessful. In an era of specifiable and measurable outcomes, what better way to manage the diversity of children's abilities and provide different educational opportunities than through the infusion of division of labor, standardization, specialization, and a division of labor into the schools?

Meritocracy. Fundamental to American conceptions of democracy is the principle that, while material rewards need not be distributed equally among citizens, the contest for these rewards must be fair. The American view of a "fair" contest is that it be won by effort and ability rather than by inherited status and privilege. Because of the central role of schools in preparing for work, educational opportunities determined by merit were seen as the fair and neutral means of providing access to economic rewards. The development of intelligence testing lent a "scientific objectivity" to the assignment of students to different curricula. Predictions about the appropriate futures of students could be made on the basis of their scores and then the requisite training could be provided.[2] It was clear from the beginning that the different educational opportunities were not equally valued. After all, they led to quite different social and economic outcomes. That poor and immigrant children consistently demonstrated the least merit and were consistently placed in the least-valued programs was not troublesome given belief in the link between race, inherited social and economic status, and ability.

The Struggle for Equality

Even with meritocratic selection, the consistent and obvious disproportionate placement of poor and minority students in inferior school programs required justification consistent with liberal and democratic intents. By mid-century biological explanations of group differences in capability gave way to environmental ones. Cultural deficits explained the gaps in achievement between minority and white student achievement. Poor and minority family life was disorganized, noncompetitive, and anti-intellectual; it provided little motivation for learning. The admission of environmental causes of inequities led, by the '60s, to efforts to use the regulatory power of government to "equalize" the competition by ameliorating these race and class barriers. Importantly, however, neither the neutrality of schools nor the concept of equal opportunity was questioned in these "compensatory" education efforts. School failure resided in the characteristics of the students, and it was these characteristics that must be altered. The influence of Darwinism had largely disappeared, but blaming the victim remained intact (Ryan, 1976). If disadvantaged children could begin school with a "head start," or be permitted to "catch up," equal results for children of various backgrounds would surely follow.

When equal results did not follow, political and social pressure led to the provision of more and more educational resources to poor and minority education. Generous funding was given to those programs that did not upset (a) the control of education, (b) the content or organization of schooling, (c) the pattern of distribution of educational resources, or (d) eventual social and economic payoff for differing educational credentials.

Some reform did question the *principles* of equality of opportunity. This questioning led to demands for educational interventions into previously protected areas. Affirmative action threatened "equal" competition for access; multicultural and bilingual education threatened the Anglo-conformity content and process of schooling (Banks, 1981; Cheng, Brizendine, & Oakes, 1979; Grant, 1977); and minority community control of schools, as in Ocean Hill-Brownsville, threatened elite power over education. Distributing educational resources on the basis of distributive justice threatened the concept of meritocracy (Bell, 1973). The push for reforms to enhance collective good, rather than individual gain (Cagan, 1978), threatened the very heart of society, i.e., individual competition for unequal economic benefits. And in fact those programs that called for significant restructuring to benefit poor and minority children were generally ignored, aborted, or only superficially implemented. What implementation did take place was accompanied by very little enthusiasm, great suspicion, and the closest of scrutiny (looking primarily for failures). For most people in decision-making positions, the only acceptable means of "equalizing" educational opportunities was to allocate additional resources to overcome deficits—to change individual students rather than to change the conduct of schooling or to examine its underlying assumptions.

What deserves our attention is not the evidence of a mid-century move toward greater equality. Far more striking is the evidence of the resilience of the ideology of opportunity and the intransigence of the essential structural properties of schooling. Even in a period of abundant educational spending and generosity toward poor and minority children, differentiated schooling remained essentially unchanged; its justification with notions of individual and cultural differences and democratic opportunity remained virtually unchallenged.

The Spectre of Scarcity

Seeing the mid-century push for better schooling for poor and minorities not as an *equalization* of education, but as an *extension* of educational opportunity permitted by a period of affluence and global supremacy, permits a clearer understanding of the retrenchment that quickly followed it. The 25 years following World War II were marked by unprecedented economic growth and material abundance. While this growth did not eliminate poverty, there was widespread optimism about prosperity trickling down to the poor. While inequalities and relative deprivation might still exist, in a period of abundance absolute deprivation could be alleviated.

The education enterprise experienced parallel surges in the amount of education and in the number of children served by the system of public schools. Demands for increased education were voiced by poor and ethnic minorities since schooling was seen as the means for commanding a greater share of the expanding wealth. The special needs and demands of poor and minority children in public schools were met by providing these children with additional educational resources, nearly always in the form of extra programs designed to ameliorate their background deficiencies and the difficulties they experienced in regular school programs. The add-on approach to enhancing educational opportunities and providing "equality" in schools was perfectly compatible with an expanding economy and abundant resources. In these times of seeming unlimited prosperity, society could provide Head Start, lunches, job training, and the like. Society could afford to be generous, even charitable, with the underprivileged. While these educational opportunities did begin to narrow the gap in educational attainment between the rich and the poor, they did not lead to any significant redistribution of economic, political, social, or educational power.

The 1970s, however, brought a set of social, political, and economic events that called this approach into serious question. For the first time, the prospects for unlimited economic growth and material abundance were called into question. The American economy reeled, first from the inflationary legacy of the Vietnam war and then from a dramatic rise in energy prices as Third World oil producers flexed their collective muscles. The second half of the decade of the '70s was plagued with inflation, recession, and unemployment.

Two quite different responses to the ecological and economic crises were voiced by scientists, politicians, and economists. One stressed the acceptance of the reality of shrinking world resources and encouraged the development of a cooperative human society in harmony with nature toward a no-growth end (see, e.g., Boulding, 1973; Commoner, 1977; Heilbroner, 1974; Schumacher, 1973). The second denied the doomsday prediction and condemned the limited vision of its spokespersons (see, e.g., Kahn, Brown, & Martel, 1976; Lipset, 1979; Macrae, 1972).

With the defeat of Jimmy Carter and the election of Ronald Reagan, the American public turned over political power to the champions of this second response. Government tinkering with the free play of the marketplace and excessive spending on social programs were blamed for inhibiting expansion, suppressing productivity, providing an easy life on the public dole, and leading to the current economic woes. "Social tinkering" had had a destructive effect on the healing and generating forces of economic growth, i.e. personal incentive, thrift, and hard work.[3] Economic recovery required a return to the values and approaches—hard work, free enterprise, and American ingenuity—that had earlier accompanied growth and prosperity. Government action must be limited to two goals: (a) eliminating controls and restrictions on the marketplace and (b) providing incentives to those with the talent, skills, and resources to spearhead the new technological advances. Gains to all would result from the "trickling down" of economic benefits. Needless to say, this approach has had ramifications for the schools.

Trickle-Down Excellence

Schools, as Seymour Sarason has so insightfully commented, serve as both scapegoats and sources of salvation (Sarason, 1983). That, of course, is the most salient message of current reforms. Although there have been hundreds of reports and state reform initiatives during the past two years, the tenor of reform is still best articulated in the 1983 round of commission reports. Their tone and substance have become recurrent themes in the educational pronouncements of politicians. Most states have followed their recommendations quite consistently in their efforts to upgrade their schools.

As the reports make plain, the current reform movement both blames schools for our current post-industrial economic woes and places on them the hope for recovery. We are all by now quite familiar with the warning in *A Nation at Risk* that "the educational foundations of our society are presently being eroded by a rising tide of mediocrity that threatens our very future as a Nation and as a people" (NCEE, 1983, p. 5). The reassertion of American dominance of a world of diminishing resources, voiced in terms of keeping and improving the "slim competitive edge we still retain in world markets," (p. 5) will result from re-establishing educational excellence in schools. "Knowledge, learning, information, and skilled intelligence are the new raw materials of international commerce and are today spreading throughout the world as vigorously as miracle drugs, synthetic fertilizers, and blue jeans did earlier" (p. 7). Given this conception of education itself as the medium of economic exchange it is not surprising that the report *Action for Excellence* claims, "Our future success as a nation—our national defense, our social stability and well-being and our national prosperity—will depend on our ability to improve education and training" (TFEEG, 1983, p. 14).

Equality issues are central to both the diagnoses of current educational troubles and the prescriptions for educational reform. The theme consistent in the diagnoses and prescriptions is that we have made a grave error in trying to be all things to all people. We have "squandered the gains in student achievement made in the wake of the Sputnik challenge" (NCEE, 1983, p. 5). After noting that efforts during the '60s and '70s to improve educational opportunities resulted in increased achievement for black students, *Action for Excellence* continues with an indictment of that era: "The fact remains, however, that overall performance in higher-order skills. . .declined in the seventies. . . .This suggests that we may be regressing from the standard of literacy which was considered adequate 15 years ago" (TFEEG, 1983, p. 24). The clear implication is that the price of extending educational opportunities was a decline in educational quality. Furthermore, providing resources to improve achievement exacted a social and economic price greater than the benefits received. *Making the Grade* is blatant in this regard: "Its [the federal government's] emphasis on promoting equality of opportunity in the public schools has meant a slighting of its commitment to educational quality" (TCF, 1983, p. 6).

The thrust of educational reform, then, is toward economic recovery through increased productivity and technological growth. Schools are to provide salvation from the crises of the '70s. The road to this salvation is clearly reflective of these crises and the lingering spectre of scarcity—even in the face of optimistic presidential promises for the future. It is clear that the central problem viewed by the makers of the reform reports is not an educational one. Educational issues have meaning only as they bear upon the issues of "real life": jobs, security, stability, defense, prosperity, and so on. And equality is given even less concern; it is tolerable as a goal only to the degree it is not perceived to stand in the way of these more important issues. And since the "real life" issues are so inextricably tied to perceptions of scarcity and abundance, education itself has meaning largely in the context of its contributions to the "good (economic) life"—Sarason's "salvation." Conversely, to the degree that prosperity, economic well-being, and so on are found wanting, all of education is suspect—Sarason's "scapegoat." If education is primarily a means to the goal of material well-being, it is not surprising that equality in education would receive little attention—no one has proven how to make equality pay. Still further, if equality is perceived as operating *against* life's real purposes (abundance) then it is all the easier to lay equality to rest with the claims that (a) we can't afford it, (b) it's bad for excellence, or (c) we solved the problem in the '60s.

It is in this context that current school reforms must be understood. Energy and resources for education are viewed as scarce. They must be expended judiciously and selectively with an eye toward maximizing economic returns. *Action for Excellence* seeks "more money *selectively invested* in efforts that promote quality" (TFEEG, 1983, p. 36). *Making the Grade* calls for public "report cards" assessing the effectiveness of funded programs (TCF, 1983, p. 18). Selective investment translates into extraordinary attention to preparing students for careers in scientific and technological fields and inattention to the worsening economic plight of the poor. This selectivity results in a reduced willingness to devote educational resources to poor and ethnic minority children. It is on those at the top that economic hopes, and therefore educational resources, are pinned.

It is in this regard that the College Board's report *Academic Preparation for College* (College Board, 1983) is of interest. The report focuses exclusively on the educational needs of the college-bound and is grounded in the view that improving college preparation is the first step toward educational reform. It is striking that a report so focused (and generated by an organization whose self-interest rests in the sale of SAT examinations) has assumed the status of a national report.[4] It symbolizes the current nearly exclusive attention on education for those students who can fulfill the hope for economic supremacy. In the current prevailing view, the provision of special opportunities or extra resources to those perceived as providing limited social and economic returns is a luxury permitted only in times of abundance. For these less promising students, financial stringency prohibits spending anything beyond what is required for preventing social disorganization (dropping out) and providing the minimum levels of competency required for low-level employment.

Still, those at the bottom are seen as benefiting educationally from this current emphasis. A more rigorously academic program at the top will create better programs for all students, it is claimed. Expanded course requirements and numbers of days and hours in school will benefit all—regardless of the differences that may exist inside their schools and classrooms. In this concentration of attention and resources on the best students there is clearly an expression of a "trickle-down" approach to educational excellence that parallels the prevailing mode of providing economic benefits. Emphasis on quality for those at the top will result in an enhanced quality of education for students throughout the system. This mood is made explicit by The College Board:

> Better preparation for the college-bound will spill over and improve the schooling of those who are not college-bound.... Just as the Advanced Placement Program has "rubbed off" on other teaching and learning in the schools, so better college preparation will strengthen the education of those who go directly from high school into the world of work or into the military. (Bailey, 1983, p. 25)

In all of this, little has really changed. The reform proposals are clearly shaped by the public response to scarcity. But the neglect of equality cannot be entirely explained as a response to the current economic crises. It must be viewed also in light of a neo-conservative reassertion of the turn-of-the-century values and beliefs considered earlier, beliefs that emerge virtually unaltered in the proposals for reform. The current crises have led to the stripping away of added-on programs that for a few years masked, but did not change, the fundamentally unequal structure of schooling.

Like the early 20th-century educational advocates, none of the current reformers state that equality should be sacrificed in the quest for excellence in schools. They even purport to uphold equality. But the view of equality presented—mostly by omission—is one firmly lodged in (a) a presumption of the neutrality of schools, (b) an Anglo-conformist perspective on educational excellence, and (c) faith in objective, quantifiable specifications of educational standards. From these proceeds a narrowly meritocratic allocation of educational opportunities and rewards. All of the above are simply variations on earlier themes—themes laid bare in times of crisis.

The Neutrality of Schools (Social Darwinism Revisited). In their general indictment of schools, the authors of the reform reports do not attach particular importance to the fact that schools fail to serve all students equally well. Consequently, they do not consider as targets for reform the school content and processes that limit school achievement for poor and minority students. Schools are seen as essentially neutral, and the reforms are presented as color-blind and affluence-blind. The failure of disadvantaged children (especially if they have had the additional benefits of remediation, free lunches, or other "compensatory" help) becomes a matter of their own deficiencies—social, economic, educational, or linguistic—and not of the schools' inadequate response to them. Social and economic inequalities are not seen as affecting students' access to high educational expectations or excellent treatment in school. All children are seen as entrants in an equal, fair, and neutral competition.

Current reform efforts do not address the unequal quality of school facilities, programs, materials, counseling, expectations, and instruction. No interest is shown, for example, in the unequal distribution of competent teachers. Neither do they address school organizational changes likely to equalize access to high-quality educational contexts— desegregation, the elimination of tracking, and reconceptualizing vocational education programs, for example. Even as an issue is made emphatically of increasing the skills and knowledge of teachers, the assumption is that teachers simply need to get better at what they've always done. There is little or no mention of the need for teachers to be more knowledgeable about how poverty, racism, and limited expectations affect the educational treatment of poor and minority children. The omission of these concerns makes clear the prevailing conviction that schools, *as they are now*, are neutral places. While many faults are found with schools, unfairness is not one.

Special resources are seen as necessary to provide separate and different schooling for those children with deficits that prevent them from succeeding in the neutral process of schooling. The assumption that poor and minority children are *unable* to learn lurks close to the surface of these recommendations. It certainly lies behind the assertion in *A Nation at Risk* that disadvantaged children (along with other "special needs" children—gifted and learning disabled) constitute a "thin-Market area" in education. They are a group of students for whom *regular* instructional approaches are not suited. That these regular approaches themselves might be a source of disadvantage is unthinkable, given the assumption of school neutrality. And given this inattention to the race and class bias of schooling, *A Nation at Risk*'s final admonition to students becomes a sad and painful message to the poor and nonwhite:

> In the end it is *your* work that determines how much and how well you learn. When you work to your full capacity, you can hope to attain the knowledge and skills that will enable you to create your future and control your destiny. If you do not, you will have your future thrust upon you by others. Take hold of your life, apply your gifts and talents, work with dedication and self-discipline. Have high expectations for yourself and convert every challenge into an opportunity. (NCEE, 1983, pp. 35–36)

A Single Standard of Excellence (Return to Anglo-Conformity). The elements proposed as the content and processes of excellent schooling are clearly reflective of Anglo-conformist values. Definitions of quality and standards are those that have historically served to discriminate against youngsters who are poor or members of ethnic minorities. There is nothing pluralistic or democratic about the educational content and processes that currently define "excellence." Perhaps *Making the Grade* is most straightforward in this regard. In a major section entitled "The Primacy of English," the report recommends that bilingual programs be replaced with programs "to teach non-English-speaking children how to speak, read, and write English" and calls the failure of bilingual programs to assert the primacy of English "a grave error" (TCF, 1983, p. 12). There is no recognition of the unique contributions of different cultures or of the special problems that arise from a history of discrimination and racism. There is not even a recognition that cultural differences are legitimate and can contribute to a broad general education for all American students.

Provisions of compensatory education are not to be interpreted as provisions for pluralism or, in the words of *Making the Grade*, "abandoning a single standard of excellence. There cannot be a white standard or black standard or a Hispanic standard when measuring educational performance"

(TCF, 1983, p. 22). This statement ignores the fact that there is a single standard posed in the reports, and that standard is undeniably white and middle-class.

Listen also to Secretary of Education William Bennett's response to a Latino teacher who had pleaded for a multicultural, multi-ethnic perspective in California schools. Bennett asserted, "I don't think it's the job of the public schools to introduce you to your grandparents" ("Bennett Says," 1985). Set next to Bennett's call for a reemphasis on the history and thought of Western Civilization in undergraduate collegiate education, the point becomes clear. Being introduced to your grandparents is an irrelevant educational matter—unless your grandparents represent the dominant cultural tradition. The current move in the Department of Education to dismantle bilingual education is a logical outgrowth of this perspective. Pluralism is seen as an intolerable shift from current dominance of Anglo values and interests.

At the same time, it is clear that what is valued for students with little academic promise is a quite different version of Anglo-conformity than that for the best students. The current system of differentiated curricula through tracking and ability grouping is clearly meant to be continued. The same subjects, the same "five new basics" of *A Nation at Risk*, are to be learned by everyone. But whereas the favored students will be helped to develop an *understanding* of science, mathematics, technology, and foreign language, a very different and "minimum-competency" education is envisioned for the rest who will be needed to fill low-status service jobs in a post-industrial economy. The emphasis for disadvantaged students is much as it has been, an emphasis on low-level basic literacy and computation skills (Oakes, 1985). There is no presumption that high-status knowledge is equally appropriate for all.

The Commodification of Educational Opportunity (Scientific Management Intensified). In the current push for productivity, education is increasingly treated as a commodity, measurable by objective tests. Like the scientific managers early in the century, current reformers appear to consider notions such as learning, knowledge, and experience to be soft and airy words unless they can be translated into numbers. Quantification, as expressed in the reports, is used as a quality-control check against the educational "factory workers" who might otherwise certify as "safe" high-risk minorities and poor. This emphasis on quantitative measures, in fact, signals a lack of trust in the responsibility of educators and their professional judgement (see Sirotnik & Goodlad, 1985). A disturbing result is that quantitative determinations of quality have a disproportionately negative effect on poor and minority children (Gould, 1981; Wigdu, 1982). Witness the disproportionate placement of black males in classes for the educable mentally retarded based on standardized ability tests (Heller, Holtzman, & Messick, 1983).

A Narrowed Meritocracy ("Opportunity. . . as will fit them equally well for their particular life work"). As a marketable commodity, education is increasingly subject to the same individualistic, competitive, acquisitive norms as are material goods (Slaughter, 1985). These norms are all grounded in the presumption of inequality. And in a period of perceived scarcity, there is likely to be a shift in how the poor are provided for. In fact, the meager level of concern in the reports for those on the bottom of the schooling hierarchy clearly indicates "stinginess" in the distribution of educational goods. It is painfully clear that the least promising students are expected to do least well. Staying in school, passing an eighth-grade proficiency test, getting a job, not being a criminal, and staying off welfare become "success" indicators. No report advocates substantive reforms to keep larger numbers of poor and minority students in schools or improve the quality of what they experience there. The expectations for poor and minority students, in other words, are far lower than in the reform proposals of a more abundant time.

The conception of school as a meritocracy is clearly reflective of the belief that some students can learn and others cannot or will not. In current reforms, promotion, assignment to various programs, graduation, and the kind of diploma received are all to be governed by merit in terms of objective measures of student learning. The fact that retention and low-track placement do not lead to increased student learning is irrelevant (see Larabee, 1984). As part of a meritocratic system, retention and low-track placement serve primarily to deny advancement in the educational system of those *not worthy.* "Student progress should be measured through periodic tests of general achievement and specific skills; promotion from grade to grade should be based on mastery, not age" (TFEE, p. 11).

Separate educations based on meritocratic selection within schools (tracking) or at different schools are recommended in several of the reports for students who do well or poorly on tests. *A Nation at Risk* suggests "placement and grouping. . . should be guided by the academic progress of students" (NCEE, 1983, p. 30) and proposes "alternative classrooms, programs, and schools" for those students who don't conform to expected standards of behavior (p. 29). *Making the Grade* calls for federal stipends to allow those "unable to learn in public schools" to attend "small-scale academies." "Such an experiment. . .would free up the substantial resources now being spent on remediation with so little to show for it" (p. 20).

Little attention is paid to rethinking classroom instruction or school organization in such a way as to promote the achievement of poor children. The only concern raised about the race/class consequences of tracking or testing criteria as standards of excellence is in a footnote of *Making the Grade* (TCF, 1983, p. 20). No concern is evidenced regarding the "dead-end" educational experiences of segregated groups of poor students with curricula aimed at passing minimum competency exams (see Darling-

Hammond & Wise, 1985, for a review of this literature). Providing different curricula for different students, as at the turn of the century, is seen as the appropriate way of meeting "individual needs." These are individual needs seen in terms of intellectual limits, not as means of enabling students to develop higher-order knowledge and skills. One commission member contributing to *Making the Grade* asserts, "I believe the mixing in the same class of students with vastly differing abilities in the name of equality has been a retrogressive step" (TCF, 1983, p. 21). Funding for children with special needs—poverty or handicaps—is to be used to support separate programs. No provisions for special access to the best educational programs—such as open admission to enriched programs, cultural criteria for placement in special programs for the gifted and talented, or affirmative action programs—are suggested.

The retreat to this narrowly meritocratic approach to the allocation of school opportunities and rewards is justified in part by the perceived successes of prior equality efforts. Both *A Nation at Risk* and *Action for Excellence* laud the gains in opportunity and achievement over the last 30 years. It is as if past wrongs have been redressed and it is now fair to return to the real purpose of education: excellence.

Reform and Equality

Of course, all of the current reform proposals acknowledge educational equity as a national interest. *Educating Americans for the 21st Century,* the report of the National Science Board (NSB, 1983), has equity as a major theme. But little in the current discussion suggests an interest in reaching beyond turn-of-the-century conceptions of social Darwinism and meritocracy to equality in access to knowledge, skills, and educational experiences. Where the reports call for equality as well as excellence, they seem to lack conviction, and they provide no strategies toward this end. As with the emergence in the '80s of economic policies of a much earlier era, the school reforms exhibit a retrenchment into the values of an earlier time. Priorities are set according to prevailing economic interests—which value most highly the kind of human capital development likely to lead to the biggest payoff in the current economic crisis. At the same time, these priorities are also consistent with the interests of the professional elite that dominates educational institutions. It would be a mistake to doubt the sincerity of most educational reformers. It is clearly too crass to suggest that they are setting out deliberately to perpetuate privilege. If overt, villainous intent were the culprit, these problems would be more easily solved. It is harder to engage the well-intended in the critical scrutiny of prevailing assumptions than to oust rascals from positions of influence.

Given the educational "reforms" of the '60s and early '70s (which may have been of considerable benefit to many minority and poor individuals, but did little to change their relative educational or economic position), we may conclude that in times of prosperity a good bit of money may be spent in efforts to create illusions of the fairest possible meritocracy. To the extent that disadvantaged individuals can be helped without jeopardizing the overall structure or control of society, so much the better. (In fact, whatever their motivation, such programs can and do change lives; they deserve a hard fight to retain even if the ground in which they are sown is so infertile as to produce only marginal yields.) In times of scarcity, however, the costs of these "equalizing" programs are deemed intolerable. Recipients of special help are perceived as responsible for the decline of not only their own well-being, but the well-being of the socio-economic classes they supposedly aspire to join.

Only three years have passed since the nation's interest turned to educational reform, and it is too early for a full assessment. But reform has become national policy and the themes of the 1983 reports are sounded repeatedly in the statements of both the President and the Secretary of Education. Several states and hundreds of local school districts have rushed to implement reforms, and a number of scholars have assessed their likely effects. And, of course, many of the specific reforms were well underway at the time of the 1983 reports. In many respects the commissions only heralded and reiterated changes conceived in the economic crises and tax revolts of the 1970s.

Time adds conviction to the suspicion that the reforms will work largely to the advantage of those who are already well-off. Through differentiated schooling experiences, attention will be turned from the difficulties of those served less well by schools. Highly motivated, able students will be offered every opportunity to achieve in ways that will strengthen the US quest for technological, economic, and military supremacy. That the distribution of school achievement has racial and socio-economic dimensions is regrettable, but, as a consequence, there is little expectation that poor and minority children will contribute greatly to the national self-interest. While our humane and democratic ideology requires extending educaticnal resources and opportunity to poor and minority children, the most pressing need at present is to cultivate those children with superior abilities, since they are seen as most likely to provide some relief from our national troubles.

All indications are that the current reform movement will produce success defined in its own terms: Children will spend more hours and days in school, more coursework will be taken in mathematics, science, and technology, and mean achievement test scores will probably rise. But beyond indicators of movement toward "excellence" (higher numbers) lies evidence of an ominous side of reform. We can already see a declining college attendance rate for minorities, increased underrepresentation of minorities in postgraduate and professional education, limited access of minority students to computers in schools and to instruction in programming, disproportionately large enrollment of minority students in low-track classes and high enrollment of whites in programs for the gifted, and disproportionately high failure rates on minimum competency tests for minority students.

The lack of evidence of advantages having "trickled-down" is not unique to education. While those at the top have declared the recovery to be in full swing, those at the bottom of the economic hierarchy experience a different reality. Today 20 million Americans—two thirds of whom are children—are estimated to be hungry, a dramatic shift from the "virtual elimination" of hunger in the 1970s (Physicians Task Force on Hunger, 1985). In current policies, social justice programs are seen as harmful to economic growth, just as equitable schooling policies are seen as destructive to educational excellence. For tangible benefits in either sphere, children who are poor and nonwhite must continue to wait.

Notes

1. A Study of Schooling was a comprehensive inquiry into a national sample of schools. Results of the study are reported in Goodlad (1984).
2. As an aside, it should be noted that "scientifically" normed intelligence tests spearheaded the rationale for *all* testing even to the point of schoolwide testing and grade-level testing—even into the classroom. So, much of the "real work" of intelligence testing quickly passed down to schools and teachers, where poorer performance on tests, "scientific" or otherwise, justified the daily reinforcement of merit.
3. See Kuttner (1984) for a fascinating counter-argument to the negative influence of social justice programs on economic health.
4. It needs to be noted, however, that the College Board's Equality Project, from which the report came, pays far more attention to the provision of both opportunities and improved educational treatment for minority students than do most current proposals. See, for example, the report *Equality and Excellence: The Educational Status of Black Americans* (College Board, 1985).

References

Bailey, A. Y. (1983). The educational equality project: Focus on results. *Kappan, 65* (September), 22–25.

Banks, J. R. (Ed.). (1981). *Education in the 80's: Multiethnic education.* Washington, DC: National Education Association.

Bell, D. (1973). *The coming of post-industrial society.* New York: Basic Books.

Bennett says he is "consumer advocate." (1985). *Los Angeles Times,* March 3, p. 1.

Boulding, K. E. (1973). The shadow of a stationary state. *Daedalus,* 102, 93.

Cagan, E. (1978). Individualism, collectivism, and radical educational reform. *Harvard Educational Review, 48,* 227–266.

Cheng, C. W., Brizendine, E., & Oakes, J. (1979). What is an "equal chance" for minority children. *Journal of Negro Education, 48*, 267–287.

College Board. (1983). *Academic preparation for college: What students need to know and be able to do.* New York: College Board.

College Board. (1985). *Equality and excellence: The educational status of black Americans.* New York: College Board.

Commoner, B. (1977). *The Poverty of Power.* New York: Bantam.

Cremin, L. A. (1964). *The Transformation of the school.* New York: Random House.

Darling-Hammond, L., & Wise, A. (1985). Beyond standardization: State standards and school improvement. *Elementary School Journal, 85*, 315–336.

Edson, C. H. (1982). Schooling for work and working at school: Perspectives on immigrant and working-class education in urban America, 1880–1920. In R. B. Everhart (Ed.), *The public school monopoly.* Cambridge, MA: Ballinger.

Goodlad, J. I. (1984). *A place called school.* New York: McGraw-Hill.

Gould, S. J. (1981). *The mismeasure of man.* New York: W. W. Norton.

Grant, C. (Ed.) (1977). *Multicultural education: Commitments, issues, and applications.* Washington, DC: ASCD.

Hall, G. S. (1905). *Adolescence: Its psychology and its relations to physiology, anthropology, sociology, sex, crime, religion, and education.* New York: D. Appleton.

Heilbroner, R. L. (1974). *An inquiry into the human prospect.* New York: W. W. Norton.

Heller, K., Holtzman, W., & Messick, S. (Eds.) (1983). *Placing children in special education: Strategies for equity.* Washington, DC: National Academy Press.

Kahn, H., Brown, W., & Martel, L. (1976). *The next 200 years: A scenario for America and the world.* New York: Morrow.

Kuttner, R. (1984). *The economic illusion: False choices between prosperity and social justice.* Boston: Houghton-Mifflin.

Larabee, D. F. (1984). Setting the standard: Alternative policies for student promotion. *Harvard Educational Review, 54*, 67–87.

Lazerson, M. (1974). *Origins of the urban school.* Cambridge: Harvard University Press.

Lipset, S. M. (1978). Growth, affluence, and the limits of futurology. In *From abundance to scarcity: Implications for the American tradition.* Columbus: Ohio State University Press.

Macrae, N. (1972). The future of international business. *Economist, 22* (January), 5–7.

NCEE [National Commission on Excellence in Education]. (1983). *A nation at risk: The imperative for educational reform.* Washington, DC: Government Printing Office.

NSB [National Science Board Commission on Precollege Education in Mathematics, Science, and Technology]. (1983). *Educating Americans for the 21st century.* Washington, DC: National Science Foundation.

Nelson, D. (1980). *Frederick W. Taylor and the rise of scientific management.* Madison: University of Wisconsin Press.

Oakes, J. (1985). *Keeping track: How schools structure inequality.* New Haven: Yale University Press.

Physicians Task Force on Hunger Report. (1985). Cambridge, MA: Harvard University Press.

Ryan, W. (1976). *Blaming the victim.* New York: Vintage Books.

Sarason, S. B. (1983). *Schooling in America: Scapegoat and salvation.* New York: The Free Press.

Schumacher, E. F. (1973). *Small is beautiful.* New York: Harper & Row.

Sirotnik, K. A., & Goodlad, J. I. (1985). The quest for reason amidst the rhetoric of reform: Improving instead of testing our schools. In W. J. Johnson (Ed.), *Education on trial: A midterm report.* San Francisco: Institute for Contemporary Studies.

Slaughter, S. (1985). *The pedagogy of profit: National commission reports on education.* Unpublished manuscript, State University of New York, Buffalo.

TCF [Twentieth Century Fund]. (1983). *Making the grade: Report of the task force on federal elementary and secondary education policy.* New York: Twentieth Century Fund.

TFEEG [Task Force on Education and Economic Growth]. (1983). *Action for excellence.* Washington, DC: Economic Commission of the States.

Wigder, S. (1982). *Ability-testing, uses and consequences.* Washington, DC: National Academy Press.

From *Educational Record*, Fall 1987/Winter 1988, pp. 9-14. © by American Council on Education. Reprinted by permission.

Minorities in Higher Education: Confronting a Time Bomb

BY REGINALD WILSON AND MANUEL J. JUSTIZ

America is no stranger to demographic challenges. Our history is marked by a series of immigration waves that have molded and shaped our society. We have turned the "tired, poor and huddled masses" into the humanpower and mindpower that are our nation's greatest strengths.

Higher education, too, has had its share of demographic challenges, most of them in the more recent past. Where not so long ago, the typical undergraduate was white, male, and between the ages of 18 and 24, that student today is likely to be older, female, minority, part-time, and a commuter.

But these demographic changes are relatively miniscule compared to what lays ahead. The overall college-age population (18-to-24-year-olds) will continue to decrease in the coming decades, and that decline will result mainly from the shrinking white population. The black, American Indian, and Hispanic population is younger than the white population and growing at a faster rate. Thus, in contrast to whites, the proportion of minority college-age persons will rise, and dramatically so in the case of Hispanics.

And, if the influx of Hispanic immigrants continues at current rates, we will have to concurrently integrate the second largest wave of immigrants in the nation's history into our culture.

Reginald Wilson is director of the Office of Minority Concerns at the American Council on Education and 1988 Martin Luther King-Rosa Parks-Cesar Chavez Visiting Professor at the University of Michigan. Manuel Justiz, who was the first Martin Luther King-Rosa Parks-Cesar Chavez Visiting Professor, is chaired professor of educational leadership at the University of South Carolina.

According to Harold Hodgkinson, author of *All One System: Demographics of Education, Kindergarten through Graduate School,* by the year 2000, America will be a nation in which one out of every three people will be non-white. The growth of minorities in the youth population, Hodkinson predicts, "will change the [education] system faster than anything except nuclear war." The newspaper *Education Week* called these demographics higher education's "time bomb."

Minority participation in higher education is stalling as minority birth rates are rising. A business-as-usual approach may well be our undoing.

The clock is ticking

The changing demographics are an explosive issue for higher education because colleges and universities have not brought minorities onto their campuses in numbers comparable to their representation in society. In the words of a 1986 report from the Education Commission of the States, "progress toward full participation of minorities in higher education has become distressingly stalled." Although high school graduation rates for all racial/ethnic groups have risen in the past 10 years, college-going rates for minorities have risen little since 1976, and in the case of blacks, have actually declined.

This lack of progress is reflected at every subsequent stage of the pipeline. Attrition is a major problem on many campuses, so fewer minorities are receiving undergraduate degrees. An inhospitable environment and prohibitive costs with questionable benefits deter minorities from pursuing graduate degrees. The insufficient pool of doctorates combined with a lack of commitment to affirmative action has produced the most minimal representation of minorities in the faculties and administrations of predominantly white institutions.

Left unchecked, the declining participation of minorities in higher education will have severe repercussions for future genera-

JAY FULLER/THE KENTUCKY COLONEL

Mexican students cross the border to attend classes at a Texas college. If the influx of Hispanic immigrants continues at its present rate, the U. S. will absorb the second largest wave of immigrants in its history.

Legal Immigration: Where They Are Coming From—Top 10 Countries of Origin, 1984

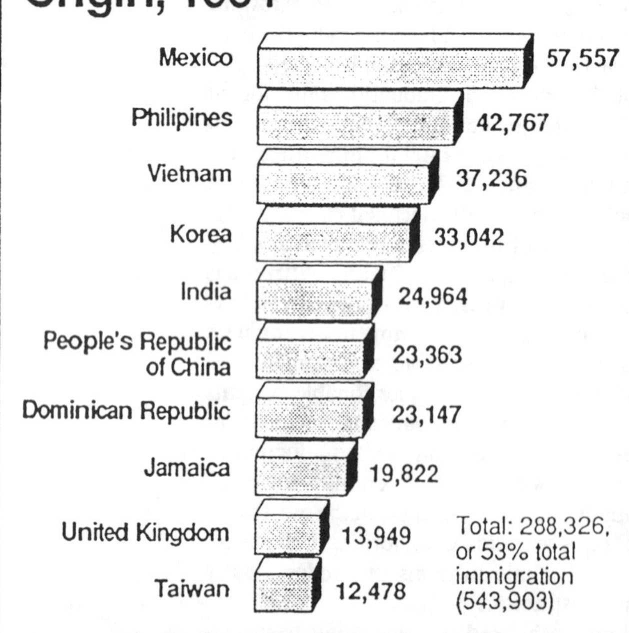

Source: Immigration and Naturalization Service

tions of Americans. We risk developing an educational and economic underclass whose contributions to society will be limited and whose dependency on others will grow. We also risk creating a culture and an economy that ignores the talents of a large number of its citizens.

This neglect occurs at a time when our nation clearly needs more, not fewer, highly educated individuals to sustain our competitiveness in a world economy. As the population rapidly ages, a heavy burden is being placed on youth to pay retirement bills. As Harold Hodgkinson points out, in 1950 there were 17 workers paying the benefits of each retiree. Four years from now, there will only be three workers providing funds for each retiree. One of the three will be minority.

Economically, we are shifting from an industrial to an information- and technology-based society. The sophisticated demands of our changing world will require higher literacy for all our citizens to be successful parents, adaptable workers, and conscientious participants in the democratic process.

The decline in commitment

Twelve years ago, after a decade of concerted effort, minority participation in higher education was at an all-time high. Unfortunately, there has been a decline in commitment to raising the attainments of minorities in education. While many programs established during the past 25 years have addressed the need to increase minority undergraduate and graduate enrollments, hire more minority faculty and administrators, and add courses to the curriculum that reflect the diversity of the student population, they have not accomplished their goals.

For one thing, many of the programs were ushered in through mandates of U. S. presidents, Congress, and the courts and have required serious enforcement from outside academe. Some have seen the federal presence as an intrusion into the academic community; yet, with the decline in federal enforcement during the Reagan era has come a decline in commitment to the goals of equal opportunity and access. At the same time, higher education is engaged in a struggle to keep costs down and raise standards. By and large, institutions are fighting to stave off losses, not working to promote new initiatives. This state of affairs has hurt minority participation in higher education.

As a result, once promising gains in minority recruitment at all levels of higher education have evaporated.

GROWTH SPURTS: The growth of minorities in the youth population, says demographer Harold Hodgkinson, "will change the [education] system faster than anything except nuclear war."

College participation

According to Bureau of the Census data, college enrollment rates for blacks dropped from 33.5 percent of high school graduates in 1976 to 26.1 percent in 1985. In this same period, the percentage of blacks completing high school increased from 67.5 percent to 75.6 percent.

For Hispanics the situation is not much better. While high school graduation rates increased from 51.9 percent in 1976 to 62.9 percent in 1985, the participation rate for 18-to24-year-old Hispanic high school graduates declined from a high of 35.8 percent in 1976 to 26.9 percent in 1985.

Meanwhile, the armed services have been steadily increasing their share of minority high school graduates. Students are told they can "be all they can be"; they are given emotional and financial support, while academe often promises an unfriendly environment at skyrocketing costs that many lower-income students simply cannot afford.

The intention of the Reagan Administration to reduce many student-aid programs and its efforts to shift more of the burden of payment to students and their families has seriously affected low-income students and hit minority students especially hard. The results of a study by the American Association of State Colleges and Universities bear out the deepest concerns of the minority community. The study, "A Call for Clarity: Income, Loans, Cost," published in 1988 shows that dependent individuals from families with incomes under $20,000 were less likely to enroll in college in 1982 than they had been in 1978, while those from families with incomes above $20,000 had increased enrollments in the same period. From 1978 to 1982, the number of students from families with incomes under $10,000 enrolling in college for the first time decreased by 16.8 percent. This decrease affected blacks most severely; they experienced a 30.6 percent reduction. Families with incomes between $10,000 and $20,000 experienced a decrease in first-time enrollment of 8.6 percent, of which Hispanics suffered the greatest decrease—21.1 percent.

As a result of financial limitations, many minority students who go on to college attend two-year rather than four-year institutions. Over half of all American Indian and Hispanic students and some 43 percent of all black and Asian students attend community colleges, compared to about 36 percent of white students.

Further declines at the graduate level

The percentage of degrees awarded to minorities declines with each successive level of education. Those minority students who leave school do not easily come back. And

RICCI BONANNO

ON THE DEFENSE: In the aftermath of a brawl between hundreds of white students and 40 blacks at the University of Massachusetts at Amherst, students demonstrate for action against racism on campus. For minority students on many campuses, the campus climate continues to be a chilly one.

those who graduate do not often go on. In 1984-85, minorities earned 11.7 percent of all bachelor's degrees, 10.4 percent of all master's, 9.5 percent of all doctorates, and 9.8 percent of all first professional degrees. These declines result in an extremely limited pool for faculty recruiting.

The world of graduate study is not an accessible one for minority students. Black and Hispanic Ph.D. recipients are disproportionately concentrated in a small number of institutions. Sixty percent of the doctoral degrees awarded to blacks in 1980-81 were awarded by 10 percent of the doctorate-granting institutions. Hispanic doctorates were even more highly concentrated than black doctorates, with 59 percent of all Hispanic doctorates emanating from 8 percent of doctorate-granting institutions. Moreover, in 1980-81, the majority of predominantly white doctorate-granting institutions awarded no degrees at all to any blacks or Hispanics. Ineffectual recruitment, limited financial assistance, and admission criteria that place undue emphasis on standardized test results are factors in this institutional disparity.

Research provides incontrovertable evidence that blacks and Hispanics are grossly underrepresented among advanced degree holders in mathematics, biology, physical science, and engineering. Meanwhile, blacks and Hispanics are overrepresented among advanced degree holders in education and the social sciences.

Faculty and administration

Higher education officials complain that the pool of minority scholars available to become faculty members and administrators just isn't big enough. In fact, more candidates are available than are finding appointments. Only 9.6 percent of all full-time faculty members are minorities. Since many of these are located at historically black institutions, the representation at predominantly white institutions is actually much lower. Minorities make up only 8 percent of the full-time faculty at white institutions, and just 2.3 percent of these faculty are black. Many of these minority faculty members are to be found in ethnic studies, equity, remedial and compensatory programs, and bilingual education.

In 1983, minorities constituted approximately 10 percent of all administrators, only a slight increase over 1977. Blacks comprise about 7.2 percent of administrators while Hispanics comprise about 1.7 percent. Minority administrators are severely underrepresented in academic positions such as department chair, dean, and vice president for academic affairs.

During the next decade, nearly half of the current faculty in American colleges and universities will be replaced because of retirement or other attrition. The makeup and quality of those replacing retiring faculty will influence the ability of institutions to assimilate increasing numbers of ethnic minorities into the economic and social mainstream of the nation.

Qualitative issues

The problem of declining minority participation in higher education goes beyond the numbers and statistics; it is qualitative as well as quantitative. The poor quality of education at earlier stages of the educational pipeline available to minority students may limit their desire and ability to achieve. The quality of the environment on many campuses is a similarly negative influence on minority attainment.

Minority high school students are likely to live and attend school in poor districts, where less money is spent per student; where teachers are the least experienced and sometimes the least prepared; and where guidance counselors are in scarce supply. Those black, Hispanic, and American Indian students who do persist through high school are less likely than white students to be in a college preparatory program. They spend fewer years studying academic subjects, take fewer years of science and mathematics courses, and are less likely to take the SAT or ACT exams. The average SAT scores for American Indian, black, Chicano, and Puerto Rican students, respectively are 798, 722, 808, and 778 compared to 939 for white students.

When minority students arrive on campus, the institutional atmosphere unduly interferes with their academic achievement and personal development. Minority students often feel isolated from campus life. One consequence of isolation is attrition. Of the 1980 high school seniors who entered postsecondary education, 28 percent of American Indians, 31 percent of blacks, 28 percent of Mexican-Americans, 42 percent of Puerto Ricans, and 26 percent of white students had dropped out by February of 1984.

Other consequences of isolation are even more disturbing for minorities and for the institutions they attend.

We risk developing an economic and educational underclass whose contributions to society will be limited and whose dependency on others will grow.

The rise of racial incidents

As recent reports in *The Chronicle of Higher Education* indicate, there has been an alarming rise in the number and intensity of racial incidents on campuses, culminating in the need to work anew on relations between black and white students.

The most publicized incident was a brawl at the University of Massachusetts at Amherst involving hundreds of white students attacking about 40 black students after the final game of the 1986 World Series. Other racial incidents have been reported at the Citadel, Fairleigh Dickinson University's Teaneck, N.J. campus, Manhattanville College, New Jersey Institute of Technology, the University of Wisconsin at Madison, Rutgers University, and the University of California at Berkeley. The list goes on.

In the wake of these incidents, many institutions are examining their institutional policies and practices to actively support the improvement of campus climate and to send a message to minority students about the commitment of the institutional leaders to their success and well-being. Specific policies on racial harassment and consequences for violations; mechanisms to hear and investigate complaints; and the presence of high-level administration with responsibility for minority affairs are all demonstrations of institutional commitment that are often lacking on campuses.

Federal and state policy shifts

Unprecedented shifts in federal policy in the past decade have been a factor in the numbers of decline we see today. The federal government has neglected its responsibilities in ensuring compliance with affirmative action legislation and minority policy issues that are of overriding national importance. These shifts are forcing states to assume increased responsibility for financing education. It is possible that in the future the federal government will play a decidedly lesser role in supporting the participation of minorities in higher education and in increasing their representation on college faculties.

Because of the withdrawal of federal commitment, an important opportunity may be lost: the opportunity to take substantial corrective action to bring the nation's colleges and universities more closely into concert with the society they serve. If recent projections of population trends and federal policy shifts are ignored, the fortuitous circumstances for increasing the numbers of minority faculty will pass. The alarming discontinuity between federal education policy and minority population trends is one of the most critical issues currently facing policymakers and institutional leaders.

Higher education's role

The American higher education system is not solely to blame for the situation of minorities in the nation's colleges and universities, nor can it eliminate by its own efforts the barriers that prohibit minorities from participating fully in education, the professions, the sciences, and so on. There must be coordinated action taken uniformly at every stage of the education system—from early childhood programs to graduate school. At the same time, colleges and universities must respond immediately with improvements in policies, programs, and practices and with a significant movement from good intentions to actions.

The key to reversing poor minority participation in higher education is not a mystery. We know the reasons for minority attrition —limited financing, a hostile campus environment, racism, lack of relevance of curriculum, and academic difficulties. In the past, we have created recruitment and retention programs and seen impressive gains. What has been lacking in the past decade is commitment from higher education's leadership and faculties to sustain the gains of the early 1970s. This commitment must be expressed in the priority we give to programs on our campuses, in the seriousness with which we set goals and use timetables to monitor progress, and in funding levels.

Improving the campus climate is a long-term goal and requires a far-reaching agenda which can be more easily accomplished by taking some clearly defined steps. Administrators and presidents should bear in mind that institutions that are effective in retaining minority students take an active posture in seeking minority students out, in incorporating counseling and remediation into their programs, and in requiring faculty and staff to be responsive to their needs.

As far as finding minority faculty is concerned, there is a large cadre of bright minority college graduates that is escaping from the pipeline. These are not the "superstars" but individuals with potential for success as graduate students and faculty. While there must be national fellowship programs to encourage the most gifted to stay in academe, there must also be strong institutional commitment to "growing their own."

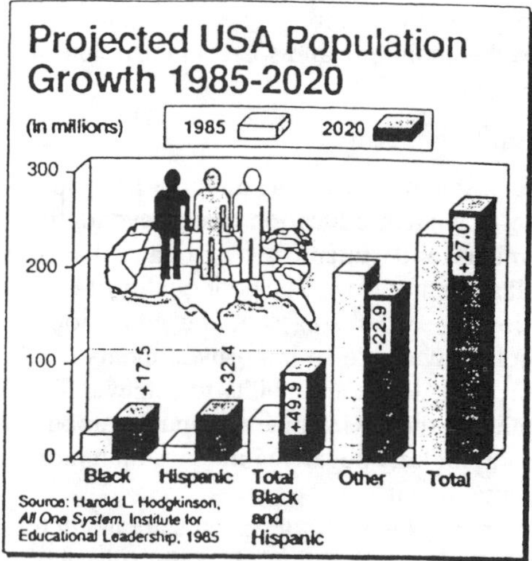

By the same token, national programs designed to increase the number of minority administrators through talent search, training and skills development, and networking opportunities are not enough. Initiatives such as the ACE Fellows Program or Harvard's Institute for Education Management must work in concert with efforts on campus to improve the episodic and ad hoc leadership development programs they offer. Campus leaders must actively adopt both an institutional philosophy and a practical plan for developing new leadership to include minorities. Moreover, challenging job opportunities must be available to minority leaders or their training will be wasted.

Another part of the unfinished agenda for higher education lies in challenging the institution to expand its understanding of what is appropriate in the production and transmittal of knowledge. Our ability to understand, appreciate, and encourage the diversity of our students depends in part on the knowledge we have about their cultures, histories, values, and beliefs. Yet very few attempts have been made to see that the curriculum is transformed to include such material. We must support scholars in ethnic and women's studies and be willing to look at new methods, new questions, new areas of inquiry, new ways of thinking and looking at the world if we are to continue to develop a curriculum that not only responds to the new majority in higher education but also educates the dominant culture for a new age.

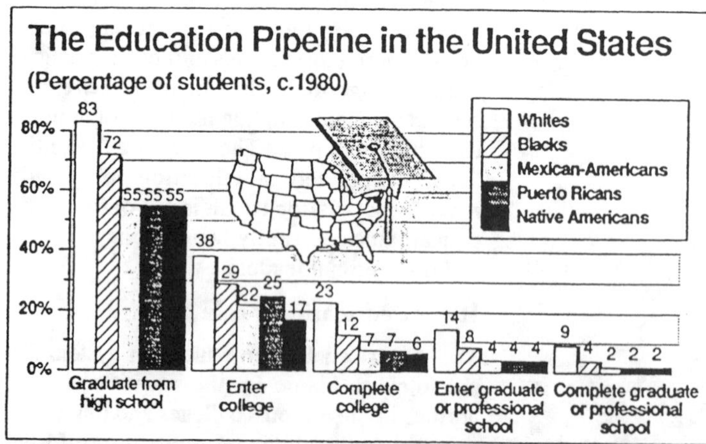

Source: Astin A. *Minorities in Higher Education*. San Francisco: Jossey-Bass, 1982. Cited in *Equality and Excellence: The Educational Status of Black Americans*. New York: College Entrance Examination Board, 1985

From *Journal of Negro Education*, vol. 55, no. 3, 1986, pp. 347-357. © by Bureau of Educational Research, Howard University. Reprinted by permission.

*The Impact of National Testing on Ethnic Minorities: With Proposed Solutions**

Peter A. Garcia, *Dean, Extended Education and Governmental Relations, Pan American University*

The national concern about the condition of public education has generated steadfast support for accountability in the education establishment. State and national policy makers have undertaken the task of mandating examinations intended to improve the quality of teacher education in United States since a series of education commissions have indicated that the manner in which teachers are trained is inadequate. However, the negative impact that teacher testing has had on the depletion of ethnic minority candidates has caused great concern.

Widespread reports that education majors are not as academically able today as compared to those of the past led to numerous commission reports citing the shortcomings of educators. Partially in response to the April 1983 release of the report *A Nation at Risk*,[1] the American Association of State Colleges and Universities (AASCU) conducted a survey of state colleges and universities to learn how those institutions worked with elementary and secondary schools to solve problems in the schools. Among the 64 percent responding to the survey, requirements for entry into teacher-education programs varied considerably—for example: "a mean grade-point average of 2.4 . . . ; 13 percent required a preprofessional exam; 34

*This article is based on research conducted for *A Study on Teaching Competency Testing and Test Validity with Implications for Minorities and the Results and Implications of the Use of the Pre-Professional Skills Test as a Screening Device for Entrance into Teacher Education Programs in Texas*. Final Report. NIE Grant No. G-85-0004. August 1985. The opinions expressed herein do not necessarily express those of the National Institute of Education.

[1]National Commission on Excellence in Education, *A Nation at Risk: The Imperative for Educational Reform* (Washington, D.C.: U.S. Government Printing Office, 1983).

percent required an orientation course; 73 percent required an English competency exam. Recommendations, interviews, and a physical examination were also necessary for admittance into several programs."[2]

A survey conducted by the author in spring 1985[3] of the directors of teacher certification and selected deans of education in each of the fifty states found that multiple criteria are still being used for admission into teacher education. Only one state reported use of a single cutoff score on a test as the sole criterion for admission. Sixteen of the states reported data on failure rates of ethnic minorities. These responses indicate that the present use of cutoff scores on stated-mandated tests prevent entry into or continuation in teacher-education programs. In some instances, the scores may be used to withhold certification. Multiple criteria notwithstanding, single cutoff scores are very powerful because applicants then are not considered on the remaining criteria.

Some states reported a limited number of attempts are accorded examinees to pass an examination with an acceptable cutoff score, while others provided unlimited opportunities to achieve the cutoff scores. However, retake data on tests such as the Pre-Professional Skills Test (PPST) show little improvement on retake of standardized examinations, with diminished pass rates after the third try.

Tests and test scores have become strong political weapons. Evidence that can be cited with numerical indicators provides great support to politicians wishing to show better schools through testing. Because educators depend on the public for support, they have been reluctant to oppose the use of tests. There is also strong indication that teachers do not fully understand the competency tests and the application of testing. According to Salganik,[4] there is a concern on the part of educators that testing for solutions to problems in education will be viewed as being mechanistic with input/output processes that are unnatural and technical in nature, with proposed solutions becoming self-defeating.

Several researchers have indicated that testing policies in most states have been mandated by legislators responding to the "excel-

[2] "AACTE Board Meets," *AACTE Briefs*, 6 (March 1985), 7.

[3] P. A. Garcia, *A Study on Teacher Competency Testing and Test Validity with Implications for Minorities and the Results and Implications of the Use of the Pre-Professional Skills Test (PPST) as a Screening Device for Entrance into Teacher Education Programs in Texas* (Grant No. NIE-G-85-0004) (Washington, D.C.: National Institute of Education, 1985).

[4] L. H. Salganik, "Why Testing Reforms Are So Popular and How They Are Changing Education," *Phi Delta Kappan*, 66 (May 1985), 607–610.

lence in education" movement.[5] A review of actions taken by legislative bodies suggests that state policies are shortsighted and do not reflect awareness of the impact they will have on teacher supply and ethnic minority representation in American education.[6] Testing continues to be the cheapest way to evaluate teachers, but it is not likely to improve the caliber of those wishing to enter the profession. Instead, it simply denies access to those who score low on competency examinations.[7] Because large numbers of Blacks and Hispanics score low on competency tests, these groups are more adversely affected than others by legislative actions concerning testing.

In 1980, the National Center for Education Statistics projected a teacher shortage. Only 3 percent of the college-bound males reported their intended major to be education, as compared to 6 percent in 1972. The number of females interested in teaching also dropped—from 19 percent to 10 percent.[8] Stewig reported that each year 8 percent of all United States teachers leave the profession permanently and that 70 percent express dissatisfaction with their jobs.[9] In addition, there is a severe shortage of prospective minority teacher candidates, other than Asians. The number of minority students enrolled in college is far below the percentage of college-age minorities in the general population.[10] If the under-representation trends continue, the future looks bleak for Hispanics, Blacks, and Native Americans. Census Bureau data for 1980 show that,

> . . . Hispanics represented 7.5 percent of all 18- to 24-year-olds counted . . . , but only 2.9 percent of the college population that year. Similarly, the black college-age population of 13 percent translates to 8.4 percent of college enrollments, and Native Americans were 0.5 percent of the college population that year compared to 0.7 percent of the population in the age group.

[5]See R. B. Ekstrom and M. E. Goertz, "The Teacher Supply Pipeline: The View from Four States" (Paper presented at the annual meeting of the Educational Research Association, Chicago, March 1985); M. E. Goertz and B. Pitcher, *The Impact of NTE Use by States on Teacher Selection* (Princeton, N.J.: Educational Testing Service, 1985); M. E. Goertz, R. B. Ekstrom, and R. J. Coley, *The Impact of State Policy on Entrance into the Teaching Profession*. Final report submitted to the National Institute of Education, (NIE Grant No. G83-0073) (Princeton, N.J.: Educational Testing Service, 1984); G. P. Smith, "The Impact of Competency Tests on Teacher Education: Ethical and Legal Issues in Selection and Certifying Teachers," in M. Haberman, ed., *Research in Teacher Education* (Norwood, N.J.: ABLEX, in press); G. P. Smith, "Unresolved Issues and New Developments in Teacher Competency Testing," *Urban Education*, forthcoming; and J. L. Kidd, "Crossing the Rubicon: The Impact of Teacher Testing," *Teacher Education and Practice*, 1 (1984), 27–33.

[6]Ekstrom and Goertz, "The Teacher Supply Pipeline."

[7]"Teacher Exams: The New Rage," *Education USA*, 27 (January 7, 1985), 291.

[8]J. P. Sikula and R. A. Roth, *Teacher Preparation and Certification: The Call for Reform* (Bloomington, Ind.: Phi Delta Kappa Educational Foundation, 1984).

[9]J. W. Stewig, "Reaching for Links that Foster Strength and Stability," *Phi Delta Kappan*, 66 (May 1985), 640–642.

[10]See Newsnotes, "Asian Americans Lead the Way in Educational Attainment," *Phi Delta Kappan*, 67 (March 1986), 546; and U.S. Department of Education, *Indicators of Education Status and Trends* (Washington, D.C.: Government Printing Office, 1985).

> Conversely, the white and Asian college enrollment percentages exceeded their proportions in the population for 18- to 24-year-olds. Whites made up 80.9 percent of the age group and represented 82.9 percent of the college students, and Asian teens were 1.5 percent of the age group and 2.1 percent of the college population.[11]

This combination of decreasing proportions of black and Hispanic students choosing teaching careers, coupled with their lower rates of college attendance, will result in proportionally fewer prospective teachers emerging from teacher-education programs to even seek certification.

Teacher Competence

Short states that the term "competence" is one of the most misused and overused concepts in the reform movement.[12] The ability of a teacher to pass a basic-skills test or to perform a highly developed teaching skill is often referred to as teacher competence. Competence and incompetence are often referred to as if they are distinctly identifiable, like dark and light. Politicians, the media, the public, and even many educators talk about competency as being clearly defined and measurable. In truth, there is a great difference between demonstrated teacher competence which is observable in the classroom and what many current tests measure.

Of great concern in the reform movement is the use of tests to dismiss teachers. Bridges and Groves studied dismissal for incompetence of tenured teachers over a forty-three-year period.[13] Their research shows a clear difference between the content of tests being used to filter prospective teachers from entering teacher-education programs and evaluation for teacher retention.

The administration of teacher competency tests is likely to bring about contract terminations without regard for proven teacher effectiveness. Kelleher describes the incompetent teacher as one "who has demonstrated his or her inability to meet minimum standard of performance *over a number of years*."[14] Teachers need an extended period of time to demonstrate competence with measurable behaviors as well as other validated criteria.

When testing is used in an accountability framework, it becomes basically punitive, demoralizing, and sends insidious and erro-

[11] "Minority Education Trends: A Mixed Bag," *Hispanic Business*, (July 1985), 45–46; and Newsnotes, "Asian Americans Lead the Way in Educational Attainment."

[12] E. C. Short, "The Concept of Competence: Its Use and Misuse in Education," *Journal of Teacher Education*, 36 (1985), 2–6.

[13] E. M. Bridges and B. Groves, *Managing the Incompetent Teacher* (NIE Grant No. 400-83-0013) (Eugene: University of Oregon, ERIC Clearinghouse on Educational Management, 1984).

[14] P. Kelleher, "Inducing Incompetent Teachers to Resign," *Phi Delta Kappan*, 66 (1985), 362–364.

neous messages to people about ways of educating human beings. Evaluation is not synonymous with testing. Accountability calls for a higher order of ethical responsibility on the part of those who mandate. Demanding more time, more courses, more testing, more standards, and greater accountability in a mechanized fashion is foreign to educating America's youth.[15]

The question is, What is teaching effectiveness and can it be *measured* accurately? The complex teaching process can be described as a practical art which requires cognitive awareness, practice, and dedication. Gage states:

> As an instrumental art, teaching departs from recipes, formulas, and algorithms. It requires improvisation, spontaneity, the handling of a vast array of considerations of form, style, pace, rhythm, and appropriateness in ways so complex that even computers must lose the way, just as they cannot achieve what a mother does with a 5-year-old.[16]

Wisniewski states:

> If we avoid dealing with personality variables, we concurrently miss the rich social dynamics that are the heart of teaching. Teaching is essentially a balancing act involving teachers and students. Whatever the subject or grade level, the balance between expectations and behaviors include give and take, command and response, goad and reaction, fear and praise, respect and hate, participation and withdrawal, passion and boredom, and every other characteristic of human interaction.[17]

Needless to say, standardized, paper-and-pencil tests do not measure these dynamics.

WHAT TESTS MEASURE

The predictive validity of a test rests with its ability to show a significant relationship between the test score and actual performance. Stedman[18] criticizes test developers and examiners for disregarding the importance of the predictive validity of tests. He states:

> . . . The true value of tests lies in their predictive power or their ability to estimate success in whatever it is they are to measure. . . . Predictive validity relates to the accuracy of determining who is likely to succeed or fail in professional practices based upon data collected from some form of evaluation (i.e., a test). It may also be applied to establishing evidence that a given

[15]K. A. Sirotnik, "Responsibility vs. Accountability: Towards a Profession," in E. Silva (Chair), *The Pedagogy of Profit: A Critical Appraisal of Current Proposals for Educational Reform* (Symposium conducted at the annual meeting of the American Educational Research Association, Chicago, March 1985).

[16]N. L. Gage, "What Do We Know about Teaching Effectiveness?" *Phi Delta Kappan*, 66 (October 1984), 87–93.

[17]R. Wisniewski, "The Competence Muddle," *Teacher Education and Practice*, 1 (1984), 35–38.

[18]C. H. Stedman, "Testing for Competency: A Pyrrhic Victory?" *Journal of Teacher Education*, 35 (1984), 2–5.

> program or set of experiences will produce necessary skills to improve practice. Unfortunately, few professions have been successful in establishing predictive validity for their basic programs, entry exams, licensing exams, or continuing education activities. There is some concern that current psychometric theory is inept as providing guidance for such determinations. . . . No data exist to support either the choice of test or the level of competency required regarding potential for success in teacher education programs.[19]

There are many problems involved in the correlation and predictive power of tests. Hunter[20] has done extensive work on the generalizability of validities with meta-analysis of knowledge based on previous work by Glass and Schmidt. The improvement in data gathering and organization of measurement information for evaluation is also encouraging from research on credentialing examinations in the health professions.[21] However, teaching performance and the applications of mandated tests in use in the teaching profession are strikingly different in scope and application from those mentioned. Therefore, care should be taken by educational professionals when applying related research from other employment areas to teaching. Educational pencil-and-paper tests present the examinee with primarily cognitive tasks and have no predictive value.

The two main problems of standardized testing involve scientific and ethical decisions. Standardized tests are inadequate measures of the capabilities of minorities.[22] In 1975, the idea that a culture-free test of general learning ability would be practical simply had not been developed.[23] According to Woolever, standardized rating forms used for teacher evaluation are assumed to measure elements of quality teaching and to be reliable. He states, "This is clearly not the case."[24] The accurate measurement of teaching performance is beyond our current ability to measure.[25] With reference to the impact of the current testing reform on minorities, Smith states: "Clearly, any professional practice that excludes disproportionate numbers of minorities represents neither excellence nor equity. If this nation

[19]Ibid.

[20]J. E. Hunter, "Are Validities Generalizable? An Empirical Assessment" (Paper presented at the annual meeting of the American Educational Research Association, Chicago, 1985).

[21]R. K. Hambleton and H. J. Rogers, *Technical Advances in Credentialing Examinations* (Amherst: University of Massachusetts, 1986).

[22]S. Messick and S. Anderson, *Educational Testing, Individual Development, and Social Responsibility* (Princeton, N.J.: Educational Testing Service, 1970).

[23]P. A. Young, "A Culture-Free Performance Test of General Learning Ability" (Master's thesis, Naval Postgraduate School; Springfield, Va.: National Technical Information Service, 1975).

[24]R. M. Woolever, "State-mandated Performance Evaluation of Beginning Teachers: Implications for Teacher Educators," *Journal of Teacher Education*, 36 (1985), 22–25.

[25]R. S. Soar, D. M. Medley, and H. Coker, "Teacher Evaluation: A Critique of Currently Used Methods," *Phi Delta Kappan*, 65 (December 1983), 239–246.

is considered at risk now, a decade of willful elimination of minority teachers will result in a nation lost."[26]

TEACHER TEST USE

Tests such as the National Teacher Examinations (NTE), California Basic Educational Skills Test (CBEST), and the Pre-Professional Skills Test (PPST) measure knowledge and certain abilities such as reading, writing, and mathematics. They do not measure teacher performance, classroom control, motivation techniques, application of knowledge in a teaching situation, personality, or stress. Tests such as the NTE were never intended to predict teaching performance, and there are very low correlations between measures of teacher effectiveness and test scores.[27]

Remediation for these tests becomes nearly impossible. The PPST, CBEST, and California Achievement Test (CAT) are difficult to teach because institutions cannot specify deficiencies within each basic-skills subtest. There is no evidence to indicate that institutions are coordinating their efforts to provide needed remediation.[28] Based on its data base of PPST test results, the Educational Testing Service (ETS) predicts only minor remediation is possible. Forty percent of the retakes on the PPST fail to change their scores.[29]

Declining Scholastic Aptitude Test (SAT) scores often are cited with regard to teacher candidates. SAT scores are valid predictors only for the first year of college. The first year of academic performance does not predict performance for the fourth year because of the adjustments made during this period. Most college faculties prefer that students also possess such other characteristics as honesty and open-mindedness and be altruistic and highly motivated. Ed Morante, director of testing at New Jersey Institute of Technology, has raised serious questions about the usability of the SAT and ACT for admission purposes and as predictors.[30]

From a practical viewpoint, most colleges could ignore their applicants' SAT scores without appreciably altering the overall accuracy of their admissions decision. This is contrary to the advice offered to colleges by the College Board and ETS that they should

[26]Smith, "The Impact of Competency Tests on Teacher Education."

[27]R. E. Peterson, "CBEST, NTE, and Other Mensurations: Notes on Testing Would-be Teachers in California and Elsewhere" (Address delivered at the Spring Conference of the California Council on Education of Teachers, San Diego, April 1984).

[28]Ekstrom and Goertz, "The Teacher Supply Pipeline."

[29]M. Goodison, "Testing the Basic Competencies of Teacher Education Candidates with the Pre-Professional Skills Test (PPST)" (Paper presented at the annual meeting of the American Educational Research Association, Chicago, 1985).

[30]E. Morante, "Testing for Basic Skills: A Guide to the Maze" (Paper presented at conference sponsored by Miami-Dade Community College, Miami, Florida, February 1986).

use an applicant's scores to make better academic selection decisions from their pool of applicants. The College Board and ETS might argue that, even though most colleges could ignore their applicant's SAT scores without appreciably altering their admissions outcomes, they would nonetheless sacrifice *small but worthwhile gains* in student quality.[31]

The credibility of the testing movement in the name of educational accountability is adamantly criticized by journalist David Owen in his book, *None of the Above: Behind the Myth of Scholastic Aptitude*.[32] Owen points out that Carl Campbell Brigham, the creator of the SAT, was known for his studies on the so-called inferiority of blacks. Owen charges that the SAT is based on a white, upper-middle class, suburban point of view, thus penalizing Blacks and other urban minorities. Despite the shortcomings in the tests, however, the testing of educators is likely to continue unabated for quite some time.

Proposed Solutions

Recommendations and solutions to the problems associated with the national testing movement and its negative impact on ethnic minorities have not been convincing. The cries to raise standards and provide greater opportunities for ethnic minorities through recruitment, fiscal support, and tutoring programs fail to address the basic cause of the problem. The national testing movement has not recognized the limited usability of tests in making career decisions of students. The issue of depletion of ethnic minorities from inclusion in education programs and related vocations can only be addressed when it is recognized that tests have limited ability to measure a sufficient number of desirable tracts (domains) of any given occupation.

The following are presented as proposed solutions to the teacher-testing problems:

1. A single cutoff score on any examination which prevents admission, continuance in any teacher-training programs, or for certification should be avoided.
2. States making career decisions on prospective or practicing teachers based on a single cutoff score from any test should end the practice. The myth that a single standardized pencil-

[31]Garcia, *A Study on Teacher Competency Testing and Test Validity*.

[32]D. Owen, *None of the Above: Behind the Myth of Scholastic Aptitude* (Boston, Mass.: Houghton Mifflin, 1985).

and-paper examination costing twenty-five dollars can evaluate a prospective or practicing teacher should be placed to rest.

3. The use of tests should be avoided in making career decisions despite the additional costs that will become necessary to establish more acceptable and accurate testing practices. Local customized tests are likely to be better measures than national standardized tests.
4. It should be recognized that the testing movement is political in nature, and that teachers, unions, lawmakers, the public, and the teaching profession as a whole can develop, together, the finest educational system without sacrificing equity for assumed quality.
5. In the public interest, local and state educators should work closely with state legislators in the development and approval of teacher competency testing programs. Conversely, legislators should not mandate changes that in effect "handcuff" professional educators from productive involvement.
6. Experts on testing from institutions of higher education should be playing a major role in the enlightenment of their fellow professionals, legislators, and the public on testing appropriateness and examination use. Examinations should be reviewed by psychometric experts and professional educators before adoption by states to ensure that professional standards are met.
7. National and interstate agreement should exist on what constitutes desirable teacher competencies.
8. Multiple criteria, weighted separately, should be used in evaluation for entry into teacher-education programs at every stage through certification. Decisions from cumulative evidence (different domains) over a period of time will result in the best teacher-selection procedure.
9. Complete data collection on pass/fail rates, including those of ethnic minorities, should be required of all states and examiners to provide information necessary to ensure that informed decisions are made by lawmakers. The main purpose of tests should be for diagnostic and remediation purposes; and adequate time should be provided for teachers who fail examinations to meet minimum requirements by relearning or remediation.
10. The testing mandate should make a provision for the talents, such as language and cultural knowledge, which ethnic minorities bring into teaching but which are *not* measured through standardized tests.
11. Teachers should be required to study the applicability of testing, test development, ethical use of tests, especially as it relates to

their students and themselves, in order to ensure that children and adults learn the dangers of stigmatization, misclassification, and of possibly damaging people unconsciously, perpetrating a false belief about what tests measure. States should establish policies that will include ethnic minorities as a representative part of the teaching profession to ensure the availability of role models consistent with the American way of life.

12. The legal profession should become versed and knowledgeable about the application of examinations to ensure that examinations are used accurately and fairly through the courts. Lawmakers must come to the realization that a test may be systematically declared valid and still be unfair.
13. As a priority, and in order to be responsible to the American public, the U.S. Secretary of Education should appoint a permanent commission with broad responsibility to review and make recommendations to states on current testing practices and examinations in use.
14. National funding for research in testing should be provided to independent researchers and institutions of higher education rather than to commercial test developers in order to bring about a better balance and greater integrity in research practices on testing teacher competency.
15. The PPST, CBEST, and NTE should not be used for admission into teacher-education programs.

The proposals listed above, if adopted, will serve to limit dependence on testing and provide teachers, students, and others with more complete information about the limitations of tests. Emphasis should be put on development of more appropriate criteria in the evaluation of teachers than presently obtains.

Conclusion

Teacher education testing is having a devastating effect on ethnic minorities in this country.[33] The pass rates of ethnic minority groups on tests for entry into teacher-education programs, credentialing, and certification continue to restrict the numbers of ethnic minorities entering and remaining in the teaching profession. Teacher

[33]G. R. Anrig, "Educational Standards, Testing, and Equity," *Phi Delta Kappan*, 66 (May 1985), 623–625; G. R. Anrig, "Teacher Education and Teacher Testing: The Rush to Mandate," ibid, 67 (February 1986), 447–451; J. F. Brown, "Implications of Basic Skills Testing for the Ethnic Group Composition of Professional School Staffs" (Memorandum to members of the Executive Committee of the Commission on Teacher Credentialing, by R. W. Watkins, Consultant, Examinations, Sacramento, Calif., February 6, 1985); Ekstrom and Goertz, "The Teacher Supply Pipeline"; Goertz and Pitcher, *The Impact of NTE Use*; W. J. Popham, "Teacher Competency Testing: The Devil's Dilemma," *Teacher Education and Practice*, 1 (1984), 5–9; and "Teacher Exams: The New Rage," *Education USA*.

shortages in certain types of inner-city school districts have already been noted. If not curtailed, teacher shortages will continue to work against inclusion of ethnic minorities in the nation's teaching corps.[34]

Policy makers must come to realize that currently used standardized measures for testing teacher competence do not predict performance in the classroom. They must realize that competencies other than test scores are necessary for effective teaching. The unique qualities that ethnic minorities bring to the classroom, such as language and cultural knowledge, must be viewed as attributes. New, more realistic criteria must be established if ethnic minority teachers are to enter and remain in the teaching force in numbers sufficient to meet the needs of all children in this pluralistic society.

[34]Ekstrom and Goertz, "The Teacher Supply Pipeline"; and Smith, "The Impact of Competency Tests on Teacher Education."

Teacher Education Admission Requirements: Alternatives for Black Prospective Teachers and Other Minorities

Walter A. Mercer

We live in a multicultural/multiracial society. Therefore, we need representation in all of the professions from all the racial and cultural groups. The teaching profession is no exception. Such representation in any profession should approximate a particular racial or cultural group's presence in the total American population. However, the fact that a racial or cultural group *should* be adequately represented does not automatically mean that this is currently the case. If Blacks are seriously under represented among the nation's teachers, for example, it would seem logical to establish ambitious programs for the recruitment of higher proportions of Blacks among our teacher education students. But all too often we encounter talented, committed black students who are unable to gain admission to teacher education programs because of inadequate entrance examination scores.

Commenting on indicators of talent, Dr. Benjamin Payton, President of Tuskegee Institute, asserted:

> We can't act as if we are a Harvard or a Dartmouth. We can only rely on test scores as the primary indicators of talent, or as indicators of what is likely to contribute to society. The Tuskegee mission is different — to educate those who need it most. We must address them where they are and turn them out as highly qualified, competitive individuals. (Middleton, 1975, p. 7)

Dr. Stephen J. Wright, former President of Fisk University and former Vice President of the College Entrance Examination Board, expressed his position on the mission of teacher education in the following statement:

> The survival of black public school teachers just has to be a part of the very reason for being of departments and schools of education in our black colleges and universities. . . . The far greater challenge, it seems to me, is to prepare teachers who can lift the horizons of inner city black children, who can teach them to see the relationship between success in school and large life opportunity, and who can motivate them to realize their potential and take pride in achieving their potential. (Norfolk State University, 1980, p. 70)

College Entrance Examinations and the Future Teacher

The release of data by the College Board (Jacobson, 1980) shows that Blacks lag in Scholastic Achievement Test scores. These data reveal that black students who took the SAT during the five-year period 1972-73 to 1976-77 scored a cumulative average of 199 points lower than Whites on the verbal section and 134 points lower than Whites on the mathematics section. The Black/White test-score gap comes as no surprise to those familiar with the historically unequal education available to Blacks as compared with Whites and the corresponding differences in economics, social position, and occupational areas of American life. Coupled with these data is the release of test results (Florida Times Union, 1982) regarding the 75,000 Black high school seniors who took the SAT in 1980-81. For the one million seniors who took the test during this period, the national average scores were 424 in verbal and 466 in mathematics on a scale of 200 to 800. Blacks scored an average of 100 points lower than the national norm.

Twenty-one states (American Association of Colleges for Teacher Education, 1982) are implementing or planning to have testing requirements as part of the criteria for admission to teacher education programs. State legislatures or state departments of education mandate such requirements. Standardized tests appear to be more widely used at the admission level than institutionally administered tests (AACTE, 1981).

Reliance on SAT scores as a teacher education admission requirement hurts future black teacher production (Mercer, 1981). The state of Florida is an example of what is taking place in other states. Its State Board of Education mandates that a prospective teacher possess a minimum score of 835 on the SAT or an equivalent score on any other nationally normed standardized college entrance examination approved by the Commissioner of Education.

Table 1 provides SAT average scores of entering college students who were registered at Florida public universities with lower divisions, Fall 1981 (State University System of Florida, 1981-82).

Table 1

SAT Average Scores at Florida's Public Universities With Lower Divisions, Fall 1981

Institution	Racial Composition	Average SAT Score
University of Florida	Majority White	1,055
Florida State University	Majority White	959
Florida A & M University	Majority Black	749
University of South Florida	Majority White	942
University of Central Florida	Majority White	959
Florida International Univ.	Majority White	1,052
State University System (Mean Score, All Institutions)		976

Since Florida's Board of Education permits either a score of 835 on the SAT or 17 on the American College Test, let us also examine the average ACT score of entering college students who were registered at Florida public universities with lower divisions in the Fall of 1981. Such data are presented in Table 2 (State University System, 1981).

Mercer is a Professor of Education at Florida A & M University, Tallahassee.

Table 2

ACT Average Scores at Florida's Public Universities With Lower Divisions, Fall 1981

Institution	Racial Composition	Average ACT Score
University of Florida	Majority White	24.2
Florida State University	Majority White	21.5
Florida A & M University	Majority Black	14.3
University of South Florida	Majority White	20.5
University of Central Florida	Majority White	21.5
Florida International Univ.	Majority White	23.0
State University System (Mean Score, All Institutions)		21.7

Data in Tables 1 and 2 show that Florida A & M University, historically a black state-supported institution, has a lower average SAT score and a lower average ACT score than do the other, predominantly white, state-supported universities. Yet, the State Board of Education requires that all prospective teachers present either a score of 835 on the SAT or 17 on the ACT as a basis for admission to a teacher education program. It is obvious that such admission requirements adversely affect the admission of prospective black teachers to teacher education programs.

All too often we encounter talented, committed black students who are unable to gain admission to teacher education programs because of inadequate entrance examination scores.

Commenting on the performance of minority students on the SAT, Samuda (1975) stated:

> The significant point to remember, when considering the performance of minority students, is that the average minority score on tests of aptitude and achievement has been demonstrated to fall one standard deviation below the mean of the white student as a whole. (p. 122)

As a consequence, noted Samuda, "the strict application of test scores must, necessarily, result in the systematic exclusion of the vast majority of students of minority ethnic background from the educational opportunities of professional training" (p. 122).

It may be seen from this discussion of college entrance examinations, teacher education admission requirements, and test scores of Blacks that, unless other valid criteria are used, there will be a declining number of future black teachers.

Alternative Admission Criteria

Standardized test scores serve as the major criterion by which students are admitted — or denied admission — to most American colleges and universities, but alternative criteria exist and should receive serious consideration. Alternative standards for admission into teacher education programs include (a) a consideration of the student's past accomplishments, (b) variables related to the success of black students, (c) the Ford Foundation's Value-Added Model, and (d) a competencies/assessment mastery model.

Past Accomplishments

It has been asserted by Baird (1979) that Educational Testing Service (ETS) ranks people by individual merit. However, such an assertion does not stand up to the hard facts of student performance. In a massive study of 36,581 students, Astin (1971) found that, unlike the SAT scores, first-year grades did not correlate with parental income. In 1969, Educational Testing Service studied 15,535 college-bound students and found that actual accomplishments such as leadership in organizations and extra curricular activities outside the classroom did not correlate with income either. While educational ambitions were significantly related to accomplishment in several areas, family income was not. For example, students from families with different incomes did not significantly differ in the number or level of accomplishments they reported. In a summary of research in the field, Baird (1979) stated that the lack of relationship between accomplishments and family background is supported by the National Merit studies which reported no significant correlation between these two variables in their samples. Although disadvantaged students do score lower on academic ability tests (ETS aptitude tests), these results suggest that the accomplishment measures do not discriminate against disadvantaged students. Further, Baird found that these measures were actually better predictors of college and graduate school success than were test scores. He wrote:

> Since the consensus of the studies indicated that information about past accomplishments is the best predictor of later accomplishments . . . admission committees who wish to select students with the greatest potential for future accomplishments should look for evidence of students' past accomplishments. (p. 23)

Commenting on past accomplishments as the best predictor, Allan Nairn (1980) had this to say:

> In sum, it (SAT) is advertised as a test of 'scholastic aptitude' and although it is used by colleges to accept and reject applicants ostensibly on the basis of merit, for many students, the SAT may be more a reflection of their social class than of their potential for accomplishment inside or beyond the classroom. (p. 652)

The lack of relationship between accomplishments and family background is supported by the National Merit studies which reported no significant correlation between these two variables in their samples.

Variables Related to Success

In a study of the characteristics of successful and unsuccessful black students at the University of Florida, Grant (1975) inquired into similarities and differences among the successful black students admitted through the Expanded Educational Opportunities Program (EEOP) of the University of Florida. Specifically, the investigator

Photo by ITS Photography, University of Wisconsin-Stout, Menomonie

sought to identify and describe characteristics and variables possibly related to the success of black students.

The variables examined were early decision on goals, motivation, type of high school curriculum, participation in high school activities and organizations, study habits, students' employment and work hours, and student attitudes and perceptions. Recommendations made by the investigator include the following: (a) that further studies be conducted to determine the usefulness of the identified variables as predictive measures, and (b) that empirical studies be conducted to establish a measurable standard of admission using the identified variables as alternatives to those used in traditional admission policies (Grant, 1975).

Ford Foundation's Value-Added Model

A value-added admission system is one in which students are admitted and evaluated on the basis of their potential for learning and growth rather than on their past achievements as indicated by grades and test scores. The Ford Foundation Commission has recommended that educational institutions revise their testing and grading procedures to reflect and enhance the value-added system. Such a revision would require, first, that current normative or relativistic measures be replaced by measures that assess the learning and growth of the individual student, and second, that these measures be administered periodically to assess the individual's growth over time. The individual students and their teachers should routinely receive results from both local and national tests. By providing students, teachers, institutions, and policy makers with this feedback, such revised testing and grading procedures will better serve the educational process. Not only will this feedback be useful in evaluating the effectiveness of educational programs, but it will also provide valuable data in diagnosing the educational progress of individual students (Middleton, 1982).

A value-added admission system is one in which students are admitted and evaluated on the basis of their potential for learning and growth rather than on their past achievements as indicated by grades and test scores.

Another recommendation of the commission is that educational institutions enlarge their concept of competency measures to include the assessment of growth in the non-cognitive realm: personal development, interpersonal skills, and self-esteem. The commission has also recommended that educational institutions use standardized tests for course placement, evaluation, and counseling in addition to the selection and screening of students.

Competencies Assessment/Mastery Model

A competencies assessment/mastery model as an alternative teacher education admission criterion is outlined in a proposal by the Florida A & M University College of Education in conjunction with the University Career Counseling and Placement Office (1982). The rationale for the proposal is that empirical evidence suggests strongly that those who desire to teach should possess a combination of stated qualities and characteristics if they are to become competent teachers. Consequently, this proposal advances the position that such qualities and characteristics must be given equal weight in the admission process to the attainment of stated levels of test scores.

An assessment center would be established which would be responsible for developing learning experiences designed to measure agreed-upon competencies which prospective teachers should possess for a successful career in teaching. Students applying for admission to teacher education who scored lower than 835 on the SAT or 17 on the ACT would have to successfully complete a set of exercises based on the competencies/qualities listed in Table 3. The exercises would be completed in two days with an additional day used by an assessment team (serving as evaluators) to make recommendations. Students who are denied admission to the teacher education program based on their performance in the exercises would receive a written report noting deficiencies and containing suggestions for improvement. Such students would be given one more chance, after a period of one year, to complete the assessment exercises satisfactorily.

Table 3
A Listing of Competencies/Qualities
To Be Measured in the Exercises

Leadership
The ability to take charge, to direct and coordinate the activities of others. To maintain control of situations and others.

Sensitivity
The ability to be sensitive to the needs and feelings of others, to develop rapport and trust and accept interpersonal differences.

Oral and Written Communication
The ability to clearly express and present information both orally and through written means.

Organizing and Planning
The ability to systematically structure tasks, plans, and objectives, to establish priorities, and to classify and categorize information.

Perception and Analytical
The ability to identify, assimilate, and comprehend the critical elements of a situation and to attend to details of a problem.

Decision Making
The ability to use logical and sound judgment in choosing a particular course of action.

Flexibility and Adaptability
The ability to alter normal posture with the presentation of additional information and to appropriately change courses of action dictated by changes in the situation.

Structure of the Assessment Center

Many exercises are available that would serve as measuring tools for the assessment program. However, the most important measuring instrument would be the members of the assessment team themselves. The team would observe the students as they perform on group and individual exercises designed to measure the above qualities. The assessment team would include faculty from the College of Education, counselors from the University Career Counseling Center and the Placement Office, administrators from the local high schools, and representatives from the Department of Education. The students would be divided into groups of six for the group exercises, which could be completed during one session of approximately four hours. The written and other individual exercises would require an additional eight hour day.

Despite barriers, continuous efforts must be made to ensure that the teaching profession reflects the racial and cultural diversity which has made America great.

Conclusion

In response to the public's demand for increased quality in the preparation of teachers, many colleges and universities are using minimum cut-off scores on standardized tests as part of the teacher education admission requirements. Since Blacks and other minorities, as groups, tend to score lower on standardized tests, fewer teachers from the present pool of these groups are likely to qualify for admission to teacher education programs. Consequently, future teachers from these groups could become vanishing breeds. In some states, as is the case in Florida, state legislatures would have to amend existing laws regarding teacher education admission requirements and grant approval to colleges and universities to use alternative teacher education admission requirements. Despite barriers, continuous efforts must be made to ensure that the teaching profession reflects the racial and cultural diversity which has made America great. ✓

References

American Association of Colleges for Teacher Education. (1981, December). Teacher education admissions assessed in 12 states. *AACTE Briefs.*

American Association of Colleges for Teacher Education. (1982, November). Teacher competency assessment plans little short of phenomenal. *AACTE Briefs.*

Astin, A. W. (1971). *Predicting academic performance in college.* New York: Free Press.

Baird, L. L. (1979, June). *Development of an inventory cf documented accomplishments for graduate admissions.* Princeton, NJ: Education Testing Service.

Florida A & M University College of Education and University Career Counseling and Placement Office. (1982). *Competencies assessment/mastery model: A proposal.* Tallahassee, FL: Florida A & M University.

Florida Times-Union (Jacksonville, Florida). (1982, October 5), pp. A-1, A-2.

Grant, M. L. (1975). *Characteristics of successful and unsuccessful black students at the University of Florida.* Doctoral Dissertation, University of Florida.

Jacobson, R. L. (1980, January 7). Blacks lag in SAT scores. *The Chronicle of Higher Education,* 5.

Mercer, W. A. (1981, November 26-December 2). Future black teachers hurt by SAT score requirement. *Capital City Outlook,* Tallahassee, FL, p. 1.

Middleton, L. (1981, December 9). Booker T. Washington Tuskegee 100. *Chronicle of Higher Education,* p. 7.

Middleton, L. (1982, February 3). Colleges urged to alter tests, grading for benefit of minority-group students. *Chronicle of Higher Education,* pp. 1 & 10.

Nairn, A. (1980). Class in the guise of merit. *Educational Leadership, 37,* 651-653.

Norfolk State University, School of Education. (1980, June 26-27). *Proceedings: National conference on problems, issues, plans, and strategies related to preparation and survival of black public school teachers.*

Samuda, R. J. (1975). *Psychological testing of American minorities: Issues and consequences.* New York: Dodd & Mead.

State University System of Florida. *Fact Book 1981-1982.* Tallahassee, FL: Florida Board of Regents, 26-27.

Factors that Affect or Influence the Decision to Enter the Teaching Profession

OVERVIEW

The influences reducing the number of minorities entering the teaching profession are also factors motivating minority students toward other professional careers.

In the first article, opportunities indicate that for women and minorities other career opportunities have resulted from the women's movement and the civil rights movement respectively. In the second article, the authors describe the working conditions teachers face. Little attention has been given to the stresses in the internal environment of urban schools, resulting in the promotion of two major themes that characterize working conditions for teachers: the no-respect syndrome and barriers to teaching.

POTPOURRI

Freshmen Interest in Teaching: Recent Trends

Ronald D. Opp

Opp analyzes changes in freshmen interest in teaching using Cooperative Institutional Research Program data from 1966 to 1988. The changes in freshmen interest in teaching by sex, race, high school grade point average, level of schooling, probable major, and type of institution are examined.

Opp is Research Analyst, Higher Education Research Institute, UCLA.

Three recent teacher education reform reports have expressed serious concerns about both the quality and quantity of the present teaching force (National Commission for Excellence in Teacher Education, 1985; Carnegie Forum on Education and the Economy, 1986; Holmes Group, 1986). There has been less attention focused on the characteristics of prospective teachers — those students still in the "educational pipeline" who are interested in pursuing an elementary or secondary teaching career. These students make up much of the talent pool from which teaching traditionally has recruited. Reformers need to focus on changes in this talent pool in assessing the impact of recent teacher education reforms.

Any effort to assess impact needs data on how interest in teaching has changed over time and the resultant changes in the characteristics of prospective teachers. The annual Cooperative Institutional Research Program (CIRP) freshman survey provides a unique resource for monitoring changes among freshmen interested in teaching. Since 1966, the CIRP, sponsored by the American Council on Education and UCLA, has surveyed some 6,000,000 first-time, full-time students as they enter postsecondary institutions. Each year, some 275,000 students in roughly 550 two-year and four-year colleges participate in the CIRP freshman survey program. This study analyzed CIRP data from 1966 to 1988 to provide new information about how freshmen interest in teaching has changed and to draw inferences about the consequences of these changes for the future teaching force.

The Supply of Future Teachers

Several recent teacher education reform reports predict a serious shortage of elementary and secondary teachers during the next decade. One report estimates that nearly 1.3 million new teachers will be needed by the 1990s, or nearly one out of every four new college graduates by 1992 (Carnegie Forum on Education and the Economy, 1986). Another report notes that between 1980 and 1990 the number of 18-year-olds will drop by some 800,000 persons, reducing the overall pool from which education traditionally has recruited teachers (National Commission for Excellence in Teacher Education, 1985). Furthermore, there has been a dramatic decline over the past 15 years in the proportion of freshmen interested in teaching careers (Astin, Green, and Korn, 1987). The declining interest in teaching careers among freshmen, coupled with the drop in the overall size of the college-age cohort, suggests a significant decrease in the population of prospective teachers.

However, these projections of the supply of prospective teachers depend on a number of assumptions. One reason projections of the supply of future teachers are difficult is that the effect of changing conditions on student interest in teaching is not known (Hecker, 1986). For example, CIRP data indicate a 4.1 percent point increase since 1982 in freshman interest in teaching. This modest increase no doubt reflects, in part, well-publicized increases in the starting salaries of teachers in many states, along with perceptions of an improving teacher labor market. Depending on the assumptions one makes, these economic incentives may or may not attract enough college students to teaching to meet the projected demand for classroom teachers in the 1990s.

Another factor complicating the

prediction of the supply of prospective teachers is that the "talent pool" of prospective teachers is actually composed of at least two pools. One pool, recent college graduates with teaching certificates, is the major source of entrants to teaching. Data from the U.S. Department of Education's *1984 Survey of Teacher Demand and Shortage* found that 89 percent of the total national demand for teachers in that year was filled by new teacher graduates (Carnegie Foundation, 1987). The other pool is a reserve composed of college graduates with teaching certificates who either are not currently teaching or have never taught. The National Educational Association has estimated that the reserve pool consists of 4,000,000 people, twice the number of active teachers (NEA, 1986). In theory, sufficient numbers from this reserve pool could be enticed back into teaching to meet the anticipated need for classroom teachers. However, the Metropolitan Life Survey of Former Teachers in America found that only 26 percent of the women in the sample thought it was very likely or fairly likely that they would return to teaching within the next five years, while only 12 percent of the men thought so (Harris, 1985).

A third potential pool from which prospective teachers might be drawn is the pool of all baccalaureate recipients (Feistrizer, 1987). This pool of talent depends on the implementation of alternative routes of certification, such as that recently implemented in New Jersey. In that state, B.A. degree recipients with a major in the subject they want to teach who can pass the appropriate subject area NTE test can be hired as classroom teachers. These teachers are then provided intensive training during their first year of teaching. Twenty-three states have recently adopted such alternative routes to teacher certification (Darling-Hammond and Berry, 1988). Depending on the numbers utilizing such alternative routes to certification, there may or may not be enough B.A. recipients who could be recruited into teaching to meet the projected demand.

The prediction of changes in the characteristics of future teachers using freshmen data also assumes that some of the freshmen interested in teaching will maintain this interest over their college years. Certainly it is well-known that the career choices of college freshmen can (and often do) change many times before graduation. Thus, any trends about prospective teachers based on freshmen data must be viewed as only a partial picture of the total pool of prospective teachers. Nevertheless, previous research in the area of career choice suggests that a relatively high percentage (56 percent) of freshmen maintain an interest in a teaching career over their college years (Astin and Panos, 1969).

Freshmen Interest in Teaching

National projections of all first-time, full-time freshmen based on annual CIRP freshmen surveys provide the following data about freshmen interested in teaching. First, the actual number of freshmen interested in teaching careers has declined precipitiously. In the fall of 1988, an estimated 144,300 freshmen hoped to pursue careers in teaching, down from an estimated 252,400 freshmen in 1966. This estimate reflects a drop of 43 percent in the number interested in teaching between 1966 and 1988. The magnitude of this drop is masked by the substantial increase in the number of first-time, full-time freshmen over this 23-year period. A level of freshmen interest in teaching comparable to that of 1966 would require 355,900 freshmen in 1988, or an increase of 147 percent over the present number.

Second, the percentage of first-time, full-time freshmen interested in teaching careers has declined by over one-half since 1966 (from 21.7 percent in 1966 to 8.8 percent in 1988). Since 1982, however, the percentage of freshmen interested in teaching has increased by over four-fifths (from 4.7 percent to 8.8 percent).

Third, the correlation between freshmen interest in education majors (as measured by the CIRP survey) and the actual number of undergraduate degrees earned in education (as reported in Higher Education General Information Survey data) is high (.827). This high correlation provides evidence that the CIRP data on freshmen preference for education majors is an accurate predictor of the actual numbers of seniors graduating each year with education as their undergraduate major.

Results and Policy Implications

Sex

Freshmen interest in teaching has declined for both male and female college students. Among all freshmen females, the percentage interested in teaching has decreased by over one-half (from 33.4 percent in 1966 to 13.3 percent in 1988). Among all freshmen males, the percentage interested in teaching has decreased by over two-thirds (from 10.9 percent in 1966 to 3.4 percent in 1988).

The steep decline in interest in teaching among freshmen women reflects, among other things, the increase in other career opportunities for women as a result of the women's movement. For example, CIRP data indicate that the percentage of freshmen women interested in business has increased by six times the level recorded in 1966 (from 3.3 percent in 1966 to 22.7 percent in 1988). These trends suggest that teaching can no longer count on a "captive" labor force of talented women to ease the impending shortage of teachers (Sedlak and Schlossman, 1986). Moreover, the even steeper decline in interest in teaching careers among freshmen men suggests that there will be even fewer male role models in classrooms in the future.

Race

Freshmen interested in teaching has declined for both minority and white students. Among white freshmen, the percentage interested in teaching careers has declined by over one-half (from 21.4 percent in 1966 to 9.5 percent in 1988). Among minority freshmen, the percentage interested in teaching has declined by over three-quarters (from 20.6 percent in 1966 to 4.9 percent in 1988).

The significant decline in interest in teaching among minority freshmen is due in part to the increase in their career opportunities as a result of the civil rights movement. The substantial decline in interest in teaching among minorities lends credence to the projections of one teacher education reform report that predicts the percentage of

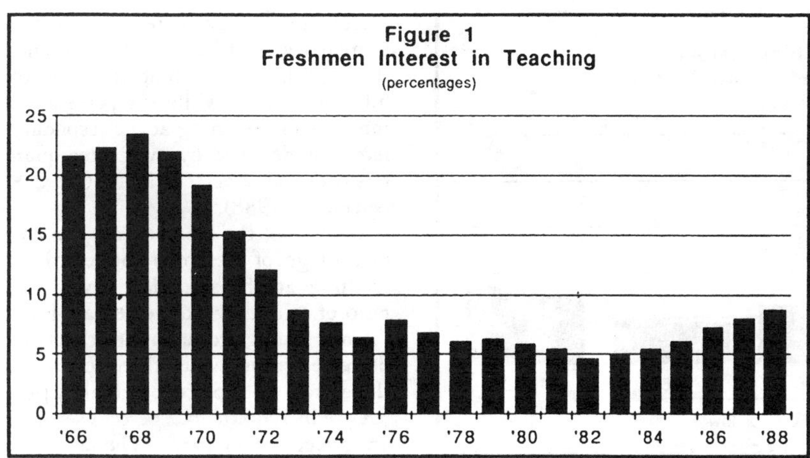

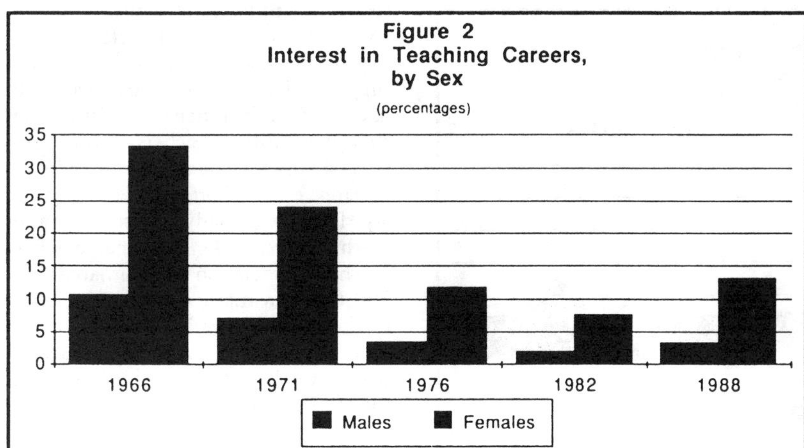

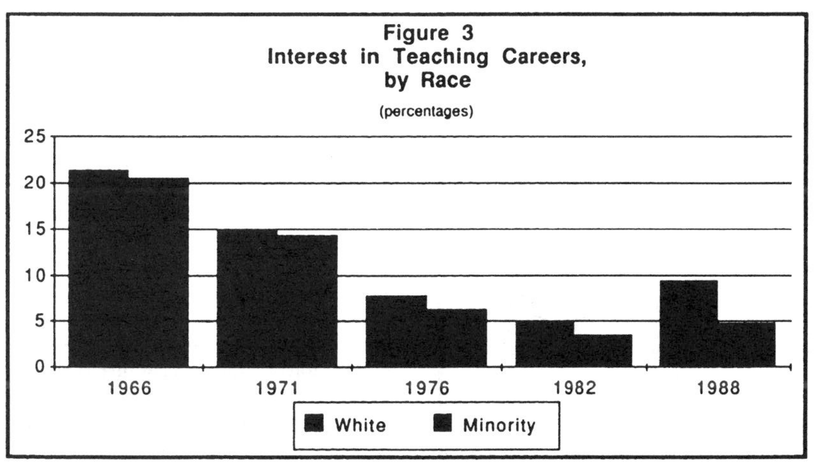

minorities in the K-12 teaching force will drop by nearly two-thirds in the next decade (from 12.5 percent to 5 percent), even as the minority student population increases (from 26 percent to 30 percent) by the 1990s (National Commission for Excellence in Teacher Education, 1985). This trend portends an acute shortage of minority teachers who are needed to reflect the diversity of the nation's racial and cultural heritage.

High School Grade Point Average

Freshmen interest in teaching has declined for both academically well-prepared and less well-prepared students. Among freshmen with an A- or higher high school grade point average, the percentage interested in teaching has declined by two-thirds (from 22.1 percent in 1966 to 7.4 percent in 1988). Among freshmen with a C or lower high school grade point average, the percentage interested in teaching has declined by almost one-half (from 16.1 percent in 1966 to 8.6 percent in 1988).

Despite a significant decline in interest in teaching among freshmen with an A- or higher high school grade point average, the percentage of prospective teachers with this high school grade point average has actually increased by almost one-quarter (from 15.9 percent in 1966 to 20.9 percent in 1988). However, much of this increase can be attributed to well-publicized grade inflation during these years. To try to take into account this grade inflation, researchers rank-ordered the 44 probable careers on the CIRP by mean high school grade point average. Relative to the mean high school grade point average of all probable careers, the mean high school grade point average of teaching has declined from 13th place in 1966 to 26th place in 1988. This decline in the rank order of the mean grade point average in teaching suggests that teaching is attracting a smaller portion of well-prepared freshmen now than in previous years.

Level of Schooling

Freshmen interest in teaching has declined for students interested in teaching both at the elementary and secondary levels. Among all freshmen, the

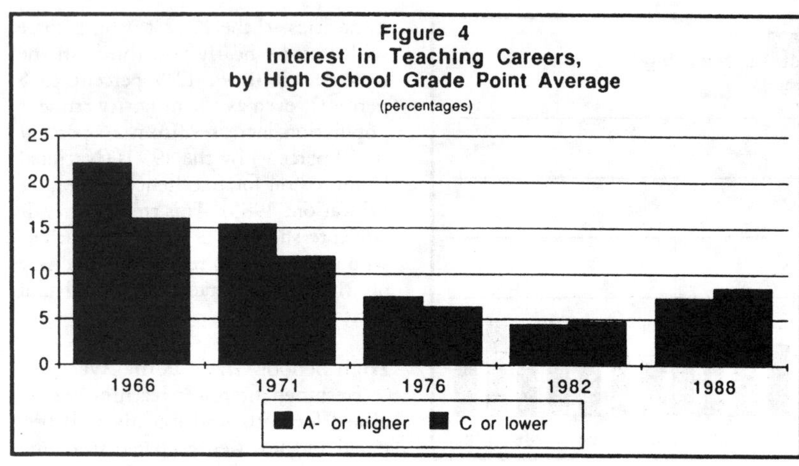

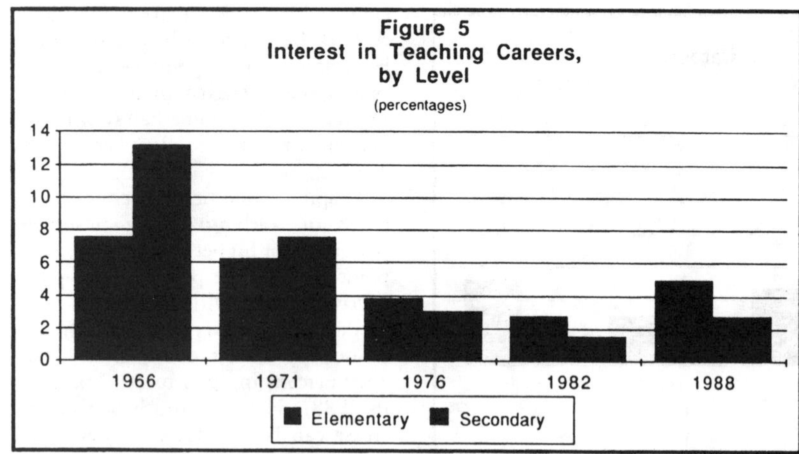

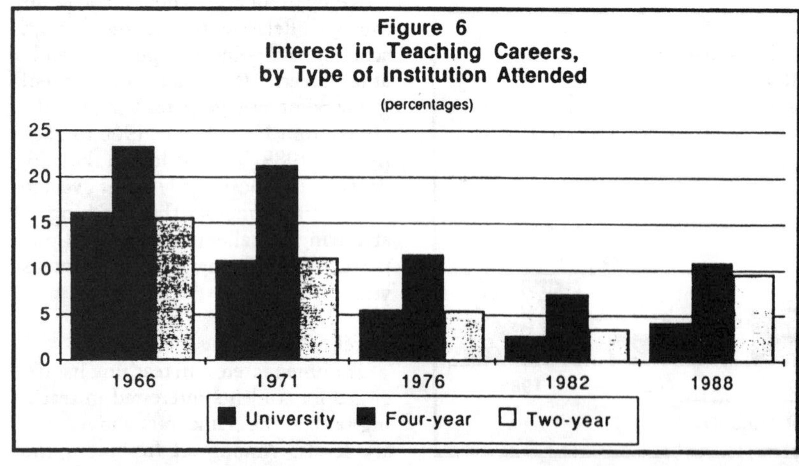

percentage interest in teaching at the elementary level has declined by one-third (from 7.6 percent in 1966 to 5.0% in 1988), while the percentage interested in teaching at the secondary level has declined by over three-quarters (from 13.2 percent in 1966 to 2.8 percent in 1988).

Because of the dramatic drop in the percentage of freshmen interested in teaching at the secondary level, the ratio of secondary- to elementary-level interest among prospective teachers has decreased from two in three to one in three (from 63.4 percent secondary preference in 1966 to 36.2 percent secondary preference in 1988). The fact that teaching at the elementary level is now favored by freshmen over teaching at the secondary level is surprising, given the greater comparative prestige associated with teaching at the secondary level. This disparity in preference between the two levels of schooling suggests that the secondary level will have particular difficulty in attracting enough qualified teachers. School districts across the country are already reporting teacher shortages at the secondary level, especially in science and math. Indeed, the National Science Teachers Association has estimated that 300,000 new mathematics and science teachers will be needed by 1995, more than the total number of math and science teachers currently in classrooms today (Darling-Hammond, 1984).

The increasing preference of freshmen interested in teaching at the elementary level is no doubt related to the precipitous decline in freshmen interest in teaching among men. Males interested in teaching have traditionally preferred to teach at the secondary level. As the ratio of male to female freshmen interested in teaching has decreased, so has the ratio of secondary- to elementary-level preference. The declining interest in teaching among freshmen males will undoubtedly exacerbate the shortage of teachers at the secondary level.

Type of Institution Attended

Freshmen interest in teaching has declined for students attending two-year institutions, four-year institutions, and universities. Among freshmen attending universities, the percentage interested in teaching has declined by

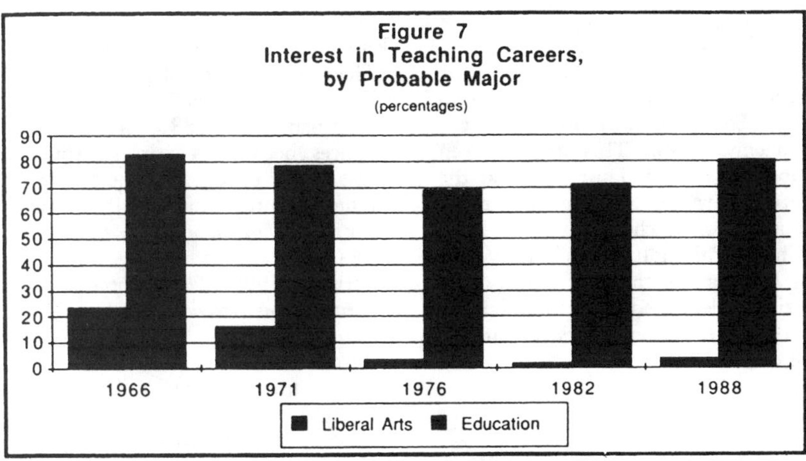

almost three-quarters (from 16.2 percent in 1966 to 4.3 percent in 1988). Among freshmen attending four-year colleges, the percentage interested in teaching has declined by over one-half (from 23.3 percent in 1966 to 10.9 percent in 1988). Finally, among freshmen attending two-year institutions, the percentage interested in teaching has declined by over one-third (from 15.6 percent in 1966 to 9.6 percent in 1988).

Although there has been a significant decline in the proportion of prospective teachers attending four-year colleges, the four-year sector continues to be where the majority of freshmen interested in teaching are being educated. Clearly, the preeminent role of four-year colleges in teacher education needs to be taken into account by the teacher education reform movement. Teacher education is a mission in which many of these institutions continue to have a considerable vested interest. Both the educational and fiscal impact of shifting teacher education from the four-year institutions to the graduate level must be researched.

The dramatic decline in interest in teaching among freshmen attending universities is a cause for some concern. Perhaps this trend is simply a reflection of Weaver's finding that "talent follows opportunity" (Weaver, 1981). Nevertheless, finding ways to reverse this trend would certainly help teaching recruit its fair share of well-prepared students. The Holmes Group, a consortium of major research universities interested in teacher education, might research ways to recruit more well-prepared students into teaching careers. The Campus Compact, a consortium of 150 institutions joined together to promote community service activities for their students, might be able to recruit talented students into teaching through their placement of student volunteers in local schools. Through such contact with local schools (ideally coupled with follow-up coursework in education), students who might not otherwise consider a career in teaching might be encouraged to do so.

Finally, the comparatively small decline in interest in teaching among freshmen attending two-year colleges underscores the importance of developing alliances between two- and four-year colleges. This trend is particularly important, since 54 percent of all Hispanic students and 45 percent of all Black students attend this sector (Haberman, 1988). If teaching is going to recruit a larger percentage of minorities successfully, institutions of teacher education need to work closely with two-year colleges to ensure that more minorities interested in teaching careers successfully transfer to their programs. At minimum, this will require that teacher education programs at four-year colleges provide academic counseling to minority two-year college students about general education and admissions requirements at their institutions. One such statewide model is operating in Wisconsin, which has instituted a pilot program in which two-year college students who have completed a specific general studies program are guaranteed admission to teacher education programs at selected four-year colleges (Haberman, 1988). More programs similar to this one are needed to help recruit more minority students into teaching.

Changes in Probable Major

Finally, freshmen interest in teaching has declined both for probable education and arts or science majors. Among freshmen with probable majors in education, the percentage interested in teaching has declined very little (from 83.3 percent in 1966 to 81.1 percent in 1988). Among freshmen with probable majors in an arts or science, the percentage interested in teaching has declined by over four-fifths (from 24 percent in 1966 to 4.1 percent in 1988).

The dramatic decrease in the percentage of arts or science majors interested in teaching has profound implications for the profession, particularly since both the Holmes Group and the Carnegie Forum have called for the elimination of the undergraduate major in education (Holmes Group, 1986; Carnegie Forum on Education and the Economy, 1986). Conventional wisdom suggests that majoring in an arts or science major is better subject-matter preparation than majoring in education. Some teacher educators argue, however, that there is little difference between the education and an arts or science major in subject-matter preparation (Jacobson, 1986). Clearly, the best major for teacher education students should be viewed as an empirical question rather than as a revealed truth. Empirical research is needed to measure the differential impact (if any) of arts or science majors versus education majors on subject-matter preparation.

There is also concern among some teacher educators that eliminating the undergraduate education major may serve to exacerbate the impending shortage of teachers. Previous research has indicated that students who major in education tend to remain in education from the freshman to senior year (Astin and Panos, 1969). If teacher education students are forced to major in an arts or science major rather than education, this may have an influence on the number of college students interested in pursuing a teaching career.

Research is also needed on how the elimination of the undergraduate education major will affect the supply of students interested in teaching.

Conclusions

Freshmen trends in interest in teaching over the last 23 years illuminate a number of areas of concern for policy makers, institutions, and educators interested in teacher education. The CIRP freshmen data clearly indicate that there is cause for concern about both the quantity and the quality of the prospective teaching force. Changes in freshmen interest in teaching by sex, race, high school grade point average, teaching level preference, type of institution, and probable major reveal some of the causes of this concern.

For example, the trends in freshmen data over the last 23 years suggest that the future teaching force will probably be more female, more white, with a mean high-school grade point average below the median high school grade point average for all careers. Furthermore, the data suggest that future teachers will probably favor the elementary over the secondary level by a two-to-one margin and will very likely major in education rather than in arts or sciences. Finally, the freshmen data suggest that the majority of these future teachers will be educated in two- and four-year colleges rather than in universities.

In addition, the 8.8 percent of freshmen interested in teaching careers in 1988 is well below the estimate of the Carnegie Forum that 23 percent of all college graduates will be needed to fulfill the demand for teachers for the nation's classrooms in the 1990s (Carnegie Forum on Education and the Economy, 1986). This gap between supply and demand suggests that the nation may be facing a substantial shortfall of teachers in the 1990s. Whether this shortfall can be alleviated by tapping into the reserve pool or by hiring college graduates through alternative certification routes remains to be seen.

References

Astin, A. W., Green, K. C., & Korn, W. S. (1987). *The American freshman: Twenty year trends.* Los Angeles: Cooperative Institutional Research Program.

Astin, A. W., & Panos, R. J. (1969). *The educational and vocational development of college students.* Washington, DC: American Council on Education.

Carnegie Forum on Education and the Economy, Task Force on Teaching as a Profession. (1986). *A nation prepared: Teachers for the 21st Century.* Hyattsville, MD: Author.

Carnegie Foundation for the Advancement of Teaching. (1987). Prospective teachers: Career choices. *Change, 19* (2), 31-34.

Darling-Hammond, L. (1984). *Beyond the commission reports: The coming crisis in teaching.* Santa Monica, CA: The RAND Corporation.

Darling-Hammond, L., & Berry, B. (1988). *The evaluation of teacher policy.* Santa Monica, CA: The RAND Corporation.

Feistrizer, C. (1987, February 17). There's no shortage of good teachers. *The Wall Street Journal,* p. 32.

Haberman, M. (1988, July 27). Alliances between 4-year institutions and 2-year colleges can help recruit more minority students into teaching. *The Chronicle of Higher Education, 34* (46), A28.

Harris, L. (1985). *The Metropolitan Life Survey of the American Teacher, 1985: Strengthening the Profession.* [Conducted for Metropolitan Life Insurance Company]. New York: Author.

Hecker, D. (1986). Teacher's job outlook: Is Chicken Little wrong again? *Occupational Outlook Quarterly, 30* (4), 13-17.

The Holmes Group (1986). *Tomorrow's teachers: A report of the Holmes Group.* East Lansing, MI: Author.

Jacobson, R. (1986, June 18). Some college officials balk at proposal to drop education major. *Chronicle of Higher Education, 32* (16), p. 23.

National Commission for Excellence in Teacher Education (1985). *A call for change in teacher education.* Washington, DC: American Association of Colleges for Teacher Education.

National Education Association (1986). *Teacher supply and demand.* Washington, DC: NEA Research.

Sedlak, M., & Schlossman, S. (1986). *Who will teach? Historical perspectives on the changing appeal of teaching as a profession.* Santa Monica, CA: The RAND Corporation.

Weaver, W. (1981). The talent pool in teacher education. *Journal of Teacher Education, 32* (3), 32-36.

From *Urban Review*, vol. 19, no. 1, 1987, pp. 3-23. © by Plenum Publishing Corporation. Reprinted by permission.

Working Conditions in Urban Schools

Rick Ginsberg, Henrietta Schwartz, George Olson, and Albert Bennett

The recent wave of reform reports in education promulgated a wide variety of recommendations to address identified concerns. This research explores an issue mostly ignored by the reform reports, the working conditions teachers face. Utilizing ethnographic techniques and multisite analyses of in-depth case studies of six schools in two large urban areas, the authors identify five broad categories of stressors in the work environment, including governance/leadership, budget cuts, security, staff relations, and student issues. In addition, two major themes characterizing working conditions for teachers are specified, the no respect syndrome and barriers to teaching. The need to address these issues before attempting to implement the major reforms in the national reports is highlighted.

The recent spate of national reform reports in education identified a broad set of problems with schools and set out a host of proposals as solutions. The resulting reform movement in America aimed at improving the performance of schools has reached most every state and local community (*Education Week*, Feb. 6, 1985, p. 11). The majority of recommendations are being directed at what the National Commission on Excellence in Education (NCEE) report, *A Nation at Risk* (NCEE, 1983), called, "disturbing inadequacies in the way the educational process itself is often conducted" (p. 18). The bulk of reform measures in all the reports emphasize the educational process, including areas such as curriculum content, teaching practices, and use of time in the classroom, as well as fiscal support for schools.

The purpose of this paper is to emphasize an aspect of teaching only briefly touched upon in the various commission reports. We believe it is so central to improving classroom performance that unless it becomes an integral part of current reform agendas, all other well-intended improvements are doomed to failure. We are referring to the working conditions teachers are exposed to, especially in urban school districts. Several reports did mention working conditions but only very briefly and generally. For example, in its findings regarding "Teaching," *A Nation at Risk* stated, "that the professional working life of teachers is on the whole unacceptable." (p. 22). Yet, the only related discussion regarding this point refers to salary prob-

Rick Ginsberg, Department of Educational Leadership and Policies, University of South Carolina, Columbia, SC 29208. Henrietta Schwartz, School of Education, San Francisco State University; George Olson and Albert Bennett, College of Education, Roosevelt University.

lems and the fact that teachers have little influence on professional decisions. Similarly, *The Paideia Proposal* (Adler, 1982), in a single paragraph, laments the poor working atmosphere, suggesting it is no surprise "that the level of achievement in many of our public schools falls below the comparable minimum" (p. 57). But here again, no recommendations or lengthly discussion follow. *Making the Grade* (Twenieth Century Fund, 1983) discusses a number of changing social conditions confronting schools in its section entitled *Excessive Burdens,* though the whole area of working conditions for teachers is only implicitly discussed and completely disregarded in recommendations.

We conclude that the problems associated with urban working conditions for teachers are not examined in much detail in the reports; and recommendations usually ignore this issue as if it didn't exist. Boyer's *High School* (1983) is an exception, in that he highlights the point by offering five recommendations to improve work life and recognition problems confronting teachers. His words are informative:

> The working conditions of teachers must improve. Many people think teachers have soft, undemanding jobs. The reality is different. Teachers are expected to work miracles day after day then often get only silence from students, pressure from the principal, and criticism from the irate parent. (p. 307)

Yet even Boyer's intelligent insights ignore much of the harsh reality of the daily working conditions that exist in our city schools. And how can we really expect any proposals for improving student performance to succeed—the inadequacies in the educational process so pictorally identified in all the reports—before we make the school and classroom atmosphere more conducive for teaching and learning?

In this paper we hope to enlighten current reform and policy discussions by describing in some detail the conditions teachers in urban schools face on a daily basis. Recent research supports our contention that working conditions are integral factors associated with effective teaching (*Education Week,* April 16, 1986, p. 1; McLaughlin et al., 1986). We have examined six urban schools in great detail, and given similar results in related research, we believe that our findings represent conditions in urban areas. Our purpose is to place the reform movement in some perspective given the need we depict for improving working conditions.

We are aware that other research has examined working conditions in schools (Lortie, 1975; *Education Week,* loc. cit.). Our data, however, are especially significant for two reasons. First, our study involved six case studies of schools in two large cities. We thus have very in-depth descriptions of about six schools and draw conclusions from multisite analyses. Second, our data were collected at about the same time when most of the data from the recent reform reports were collected. Thus, our findings are based on material taken from the same time period—and perhaps even the same systems and schools—as that used to prepare the reform reports. This makes our findings particularly interesting given the dearth of attention to working conditions presented in the reports' findings and recommendations.

The study reported here involved a multisite analysis of three schools in a large northeastern city and three schools in a large midwestern city. An elementary, junior, and senior high school were chosen from each city based on a variety of variables, such as enrollment, student composition, faculty size and composition, number of reported grievances, achievement levels, etc. The goal was to try to get schools that represented each level of schooling and to avoid outlier schools that might present a skewed image of the working atmosphere. The purpose of the study was to gather information about working conditions in order to better understand the causes of teacher stress. Previous stress research mostly involved survey type self-report measures, and our aim was to use ethnographic techniques in order to expand the understanding of working conditions as they relate to teacher stress. Given the fact that research on stress suggests that it causes a variety of negative consequences related to teacher performance and productivity (see, e.g., Kyriacou and Sutcliffe, 1979), an examination of underlying conditions affecting stress is particularly relevant for current reform debates.

The rich description of working conditions produced by the study were compiled following data collection between 1980 and 1982. These are the same years that most of the data in the reform reports were collected. The six case studies utilized ethnographic techniques of interviews, observations, analysis of memos and documents, as well as several quantitative measures administered in each school. Two researchers spent a minimum of fifteen days in every school spread out over an entire school year, to avoid time bound conclusions. In addition, numerous telephone calls and after school discussions were held. Following the formal data collection period, follow-up visits were made to each school and lengthy interviews with principals were conducted. Data gathering in the schools was guided by Hershkovitz's (1948) universal aspects of cultures, which included collecting information on values, technology, economics, governance, socialization processes, social organization, language, and cosmology in each site. A final case study describing working conditions for every school was compiled, and multisite analyses were undertaken to identify the working conditions affecting teacher stress (Miles and Huberman, 1984).

What follows is a very brief synopsis of each of the six case studies describing working conditions in the schools. Next the findings and conclusions regarding how working conditions affect teacher stress are presented. This information is especially relevant because it highlights specific problems in urban schools that affect teacher conduct and performance. Finally, implications of the analysis of working conditions are related to the commission reports and reform movement in education today.

THE SCHOOLS

Elementary School—No. 1

Located in a large northeastern city, elementary school #1 borders a high rent district and a predominantly Hispanic low income area. The surrounding neighborhoods reflect these differences, with a methadone clinic a block away in one direction and expensive high-rise buildings in another. Although the building capacity is listed as 1,163, enrollment is currently 468, with 60% Hispanic, 30% black, 7% white, and 3% other. Annual attendance rate is just under 90%. The 28 member faculty differs in racial composition from the student body, with 93% white, 4% hispanic, and 3% black. The majority are female and married with 75% falling in the 31-50 age bracket. The principal is a white male who had been a teacher and assistant principal before becoming principal in this school.

The school is surrounded on two sides with major thoroughfares. The grounds include large playground areas which are posted as off limits to outsiders during school hours, although holes in fences make access very easy. Teachers and parents regard the neighborhood as dangerous and protect themselves and students accordingly. Teachers constantly talk about the need for greater security, and point to large amounts of graffiti as adding to a norm of "dirt and disorder." Parents tend to walk their children to and from school and keep their children at home after school because of the dangers in the neighborhoods. Adults who gather in playgounds near the school are described as pimps, prostitutes, and drug addicts. Teachers mentioned how easy it is for outsiders to enter the school building, and how safeguards such as student escorts and locked classroom doors are helpful in protecting one another during the day.

Teachers described parents in mixed terms, though the general consensus of teachers was that most parents are interfering and apathetic. Several parents work in the school daily as volunteers. Perhaps the root of teachers' attitudes comes from the enrollment decline in recent years, with white students leaving the school while replacement programs are geared towards minority populations. Indeed, there is an apparent split amongst faculty as the new program staff are viewed negatively by the older "regular" teachers.

When discussing outside forces that affect their performance, teachers constantly cite an ominous "they," referring to the school board, superintendent, and other high level administrators. They are the ones who send the teachers incorrect computer printouts, require duplicate information from week to week, send out new forms to replace old ones recently submitted, and demand that all rollbooks be sent on three hours notice because school board officals misplaced their own records. The principal sympathizes with the teachers but explains that, "it is confusing, but there is nothing I can do about it, that's the Board's system."

The principal in elementary school #1 is well liked by his staff, who find him very supportive. One described him as, "real supportive and doesn't harass the teachers." He contributes his own money to support teacher activities such as a yearly "welcome back" breakfast, and he writes each teacher a personal note at the end of the year thanking him or her for specific ways he or she helped the school. The principal must run the school by himself, as he has been without his two assistant principals or a secretary for over a year. Nonetheless, the principal strives to run an open operation, giving teachers great input into his decisions. His biggest problem revolves around the split between his regular staff and the new program faculty who have joined the school in recent years. Otherwise, the teachers like him but are angered by the paperwork and the severe lack of supplies and support personnel which "they" at the school board allow. As one teacher explained, the school board is "inept, inconsistent and unsupportive."

Teachers in the school are also disturbed by the lack of support they get from parents and society in general. They see parents of the students as poor role models, who often keep their children at home for no reason. Many children miss school to accompany parents to welfare offices because the parents speak poor English. One teacher suggested that "one third of the parents have as much or more difficulty facing the world as do their kids. They are drug addicts, alcoholics, and child abusers." When the media criticizes teachers, the frustrations are intensified. One teacher clearly described this attitude:

> So many things are impinging on teachers. Teachers are an easy mark. Snide remarks all of the time . . . the public wouldn't criticize a doctor or lawyer the way it criticizes teachers. It's demeaning; the profession doesn't deserve that.

Middle School—No. 2

School #2 was originally erected as an elementary school in 1908 before being converted into a junior high school. The building is old and in poor condition, with a leaky rook, falling paint and plaster, and floors which are coming up. Located in a large northeastern city, the school has an enrollment of 641, less than half of the citywide average for junior high schools. The attendance rate in the school is about 85%. The neighborhood, located in the central city, is run-down, although parts are being renovated. It is mostly Hispanic, as is the student body (55% Hispanic, 25% black, 15% white).

School #2 has a large Title I program in reading and math using the pull out model where students leave regular classes to attend those programs. Regular classes average about 30 students, though several special education classes were considerably smaller. Students are grouped in this school based primarily on reading scores. Of the 39 faculty on staff, 82% are white, 10% black, 5% Hispanic. Nearly 75% are in the 31-50 age group with gender broken down evenly. The school had six incidents related to intruders and one assault in the past year, and six union grievancies were filed related to class size.

To offer protection to students and staff, aides and teachers patrol every floor. The front door is also carefully guarded. Nonauthorized persons are confronted throughout the building. Parents cannot enter the building without signing in and being approved in the main office. Teachers report feeling safe within the school. It is outside, in the local area, that danger abounds. Thus, few leave the school for lunch. Last year, an aide was hit in the head by a doorknob on the playground, thrown from a tenement across the street. Teachers appeared very frustrated with the difficult task of teaching the students in this school. Teachers reported that they never see parents unless there is a problem. After observing classrooms throughout the year, we asked teachers what they disliked. Their responses are alarming:

> "The uselessness of my position. . . . I feel that way every morning."
>
> "It's punishment to be in a school like this."
>
> "I often ask myself, why am I here?"
>
> "I'm getting very fed up."
>
> "Bad kids are hell to teach."

The principal, a white male, has served as a teacher and assistant principal in this school. Several of the old-timers seemed jealous of the principal, and resented him. One explained, "if he didn't follow all the rules when he was a teacher, then I won't." Yet most are supportive of the principal in school #2. They see him as supportive, a strong leader and fair supervisor. He works hard to help teachers who are full of ideas—in his words, "connecting with kids." One teacher said that despite the problems, the school has an atmosphere that is "conducive to experimentation because the principal gives help when one needs it," while others talked about how the principal supports opportunities and experiences for faculty that help careers and relieve boredom.

The principal and teachers are upset by school board interference and unresponsiveness. The principal complained of interference cutting away from his time. He ignores board decrees and refuses to call faculty meetings unless there are instructionally related issues involved. Teachers feel that the board is not really interested in children or education. One complained that "the board dehumanizes us." Another explained how she tried to call the board to help solve a problem, but nobody answered the phone after it rang for 29 minutes. Others agreed that clerks and staff at the board just sit around all day drinking coffee and talking.

The school stresses order and discipline for students. We observed youngsters snapping to attention when the principal walked by. During class changes, children all walked to the right, observing the white lines printed down the middle of halls. One teacher described that the school administration takes an active part in enforcing student behavioral standards.

Supply shortages are a major problem in this school. The $2,000 budget for supplies (including funds for postage) does not cover even necessary items. Last year midterm exams were not given because of paper shortages. All assignments were written on blackboards for students to copy, and old scrap paper had to be used for quizzes. Audio-visual equipment lay idle for lack of repairs. Some reading teachers had no books and used donated magazines in their place.

Similarly, the building is in constant need of repair. For example, damage due to a fire in one wing of the building was left unfixed by simply boarding off the entrance to the wing; a carpentry shop bench was not secured to the floor so one student held it while another worked on it; the pay phone in the school was out of order during most our visits; classroom radiators were very noisy though they produced little heat; and several students had been hit by falling plaster. One teacher said, "I begin to feel as if the school and children don't matter anymore." Another complained, "It's a dreary place to work because the building is decaying."

A final obvious problem in this school is language related. Most parents and children speak only Spanish, most teachers only English. A teacher told us he lets his pupils out to play baseball every day because he can't communicate with them in Spanish. Another explained his buddy-system, where a translator is placed next to a Spanish speaker, and he uses simple phrases and large gestures to explain material. As one flustered teacher told us, "I want to learn Spanish, but I have too much paperwork, so I can't."

High School—No. 3

School #3 is a five story structure erected in 1924 with a current enrollment of 2,621. Located in a large northeastern city, the majority of students are white (73%), with blacks (18%) and Hispanics (8%) bussed in. Average attendance is 73%. The neighborhood surrounding the school is completely white, mostly Italian in ethnic origin. The area is considered safe by most, with many small retail businesses nearby. There is no public housing in the area; black and Hispanic students attending the school travel as much as an hour each way from poor neighborhoods to attend under an open enrollment plan.

The faculty consists of 107 members, 94% white, 3% black, and 3% Hispanic. A little over half are female, while nearly 75% fall in the 31-50 age group. The school has a long and rich tradition, including among its graduates several prominent actors and many doctors, judges, lawyers, and other professionals. The school is run by a white male principal, two assistant principals, and eight department heads given the title of assistant principal.

This group makes up the school's "cabinet." The school houses numerous programs, including an ESEA Title VII Italian bilingual program, a program for severe and profound handicapped, an alternative program for potential dropouts, and an academy for gifted. The school has an academic and career track.

Teachers reported a disparity in goals for schooling between themselves and the local community. Parents tend to take the position that children should folow them in their perspective—traditional domestic roles for women, working class jobs for men. Teachers value academics and school experiences as a means of broadening potential for improving future opportunities. As a result, teachers and administrators view parents as provincial and limited in their aspirations for their children. Teachers reported little parent support with things like homework. Parental involvement in the school has been limited, except when proposals have been brought up like reorganizing, which would have integrated the school and changed its makeup. There is a strong community desire to maintain the ethnic traditional way of life.

Department heads are required to submit to the principal and the school board fifty written teacher observations each year, including at least three for each new teacher. Principals must submit forty to the board. Yearly, each teacher is evaluated, with poor reviews leading to efforts to help the teacher improve. The faculty overwhelmingly supported this method of evaluation.

Teachers in school #3 had several complaints about their principal. Many found him lax on enforcing behavior codes. Many students were observed roaming the halls and smoking, both strictly prohibited. Comments from teachers included, "I don't think he gives a damn," "he isn't an educator," "(he) doesn't realize what we are faced with." One teacher explained that if the administration would get more concerned, "it would filter down."

Another common complaint about the principal related to decision making. Teachers do not feel they have much input or are encouraged to speak up. Most agreed that "whatever he (the principal) feels should be done is done." Related to these feelings are similar gripes about the school board. They described the board as incompetent, its lack of concern exhibited by the slow reaction to building and equipment repair requests. The board's system for teacher absenteeism was described as fostering poor attendance, as the incentives are designed in such a way that there is no reward for accumulating sick days not taken. Teachers were also upset because the school board imposes mandates without consulting teachers. For example, an MBO system of lesson plans was imposed, which teachers experience as a very time consuming extension of what was previously done.

Additional concerns of teachers in this school are the confusing program and bell schedules. Students are assigned to classes without consulting teachers, and homeroom teachers are left with loads of paperwork to finalize class schedules. The school operates under several bell schedules, and teachers are not always aware which schedule is in effect. During our visitation, the bell system was out of operation on several occasions, rendering a state of great confusion.

Teacher counselors exert much influence in this school. They assign students their programs, which influences the school's governance structure since every department is required to have at least twenty teachers to stay in existence. Placement in a course at the freshman level can affect the course's continuance, as there is a 45% dropout rate, and courses assigned to earlier grades are more likely to attract necessary numbers of students.

Citywide budget cuts add to unhappiness with the condition of the school building. Throughout the school, paint is peeling from walls, lights are burned out, garbage is not picked up, window shades are torn, windows are broken, and those areas which were painted never matched other areas. In one room we observed, a large hole in the ceiling was obvious, and the room was cold and uncomfortable. One teacher complained, "How can you teach in conditions like this?" Teachers also related other complaints to budget constraints, including the lack of secretarial support, too much paperwork, lack of time to help young teachers get started, and little money to repair audio-visual and other equipment.

Several teachers described the school as a safe place to work. This apparently adds to the school's prestige. For black students bussed into the school, however, security is a big concern. Teachers explained that blacks can't participate in many extracurricular activities because it is not safe for them at night. One teacher described the time before Christmas as especially tense. White students aim for what they call "a White Christmas"; they try to scare away all blacks in the school for the Christmas season.

Elementary School—No. 4

Located in a major midwestern city, school #4 houses students in kindergarten through fifth grade. The school, built in 1971, is a carpeted, air-conditioned two story modular unit. The local community is low income black, as is the 99% black student population. Average daily attendance is about 90%. The building capacity is 480 with 456 students currently in attendance. The school has 18 teachers, all women, split evenly racially. The principal is a white female who had been in the school for six years. Two teachers had reportedly gone to the district superintendent with complaints about the principal.

The school was originally built as a branch to help relieve overcrowded conditions nearby, and the teachers believed they were here because of "the ability to perform their responsibility without constant supervision." When the school was given independent status, the assistant principal in charge of the branch was not elevated to principal. The present principal and the staff have been in conflict ever since. She is a strict disciplinarian, and her ordered and structured approach is appropriate for students, according to faculty, but very detrimental for staff morale. The principal's use of the public address system is a good example of this point. One teacher who had just been interrupted by the PA system asked, "What is it, 9:30 and I've already been buzzed three times? If you want to do something that will help, then do something about that thing." Another cautioned us, "I'll talk to you, but if I hear a click from that (pointing to the intercom), then I'm going to stop. I can't have the principal accidently hear what I have to say."

Teachers felt that they had no input in decision making. According to teachers, the principal uses "intimidation and implied threat" and "an unrelenting resolve to win any confrontation." Teachers said that when they were asked for their opinions, it was "pro forma" and that the principal had already made the decision. When we interviewed the principal, she explained that she was not afraid to take the responsibility that goes with making unpopular decisions. She also made frequent classroom visitations, as many as five or six a day according to some.

Entry into the school is tightly controlled and students come and go in an orderly fashion. The relative tranquility in the school is a contrast to conditions in the local neighborhood. We were warned where to park and what streets to avoid. A nearby school yard/parking lot is frequented by groups of high school dropouts. The local high school, about 3 blocks away, has street gangs that affect school #4 through their recruitment activities and intergang wars that take place in the neighborhood.

Several high level administrators and school board directives created problems for teachers. A new district superintendent seemed foolish to teachers. When several teachers approached him about problems with the principal, he avoided helping them by merely suggesting that they try to get along. One of his first orders concerned the visibility and placement of wastepaper baskets in classrooms. One teacher who was ordered by this superintendent not to wear her hat after the entry bell, was dismayed because she used hats in an educational way. "They help to set a mood," she explained. "The kids come in, they see that the teacher has a funny hat on, they laugh and I laugh. We start the day out laughing. I think I ought to be able to wear hats if I think they are of some educational value." Eventually, the district superintendent rescinded his antihat rule.

Similarly, school board regulations are often seen as unnecessary and excessive. The board instituted an open campus/closed campus schedule without any teacher input. Parents and teachers complained about this. One teacher confided, "If this is how democracy works, I don't want any part of it. We (parents and teachers) voted for open campus, then they took it away without explanation." Paperwork and time demands are similar sources of conflict, as teachers feel burdened by paperwork associated with a new mastery learning type program. The forms to be filled out for student medical records are also a concern, along with attendance records, meal subsidy reports, and frequent board mandated head counts.

Supply shortages are another source of disgust for teachers, and the additional $28 per teacher for supplies recently won by the union is appreciated but seen as too little. Although the building itself is in good condition, the size of the physical plant is disturbing to some. There is no place for any privacy in the building, no gymnasium, so when inclement weather forces physical education classes indoors, classes have to double up to make room.

Finally, teachers in this school are concerned about budget cuts. Not only does this affect the supplies, it closes off possible career opportunities by decreasing numbers of new administrative positions. The principal felt obliged to eliminate recess and to use auxiliary personnel as substitutes, depriving teachers of their preparation time. Thus, planning time was cut, and little time exists during the day for teachers to be away from students. In addition, the custodial staff was reduced causing some questions as to the future upkeep of the plant.

Middle School—No. 5

Located in a large midwestern city, this upper grade center houses students in grades 5-8. The building is about twenty years old, with no grass around it, and with halls frequently littered with paper and other rubbish. There were no grievances filed with the teachers union in the past year. The neighborhood surrounding the school is 99% black, with about 70% considered low income. There are 36 teachers; over half are black, and three quarters have 6-12 years experience. The principal is a white male who has been in the school for six years. Of the 743 students in the school, 99% are black, and the average daily attendance is approximately 90%.

Tension between white and black teachers was obvious in school #5. One black teacher said, "when I first came here, I would speak to white teachers and almost none would speak back. I began to wonder if it was me. It was only after I spoke with other teachers that I discovered that this was just the way things were around here. I was not prepared for this kind of environment." A white teacher who had been displaced from a position reasoned, "I would have never been moved by the principal had I been black. He's a political animal who reports to his major constituency." Even the principal commented, "It's sad, but you know, I've been around a long time and it just doesn't seem to work—black teachers and white teachers . . . once I even had someone from the Human Relations Department of the school board come in. It didn't help."

The principal boasted that he is supported by the community because he is a strict disciplinarian. Yet, teachers, both blacks and whites, have a different view of him, finding him punitive sometimes and preferential at other times. His governance style was characterized as "benign neglect." The principal suggested that his governance style is "loose as a goose," but teachers interpreted this in a very negative way. They recognized that there are no structures or formal committees to involve teachers in decision making. The principal never interacts with teachers in the cafeteria, and only twice was he seen out of his office during all our observations. Lesson books are not collected, and classes are only rarely visited by the principal. Some teachers joked privately that the principal so often changed his mind that they were unsure if decisions reached in his office would remain in force long enough for them to reach their classrooms. One teacher described the situation in somewhat Dantesque terms: "It seems that I can't plug into the school because someone is always moving the outlets."

An incident we observed clarifies some of the issues teachers raised concerning their input. Following a day when several teachers' cars had been vandalized in a parking lot which mistakenly was not locked, angry teachers came to a faculty meeting anxious to discuss their concerns. The meeting began with teachers asking for an opportunity to talk. The principal agreed, but nonetheless began by reviewing other information. Then he read a 25 minute prepared speech on the incident and time ran out as students began to enter. Teachers called his speech a lot of "nothing," as their time for input was completely shut down.

Budget cuts are another major cause of concern for teachers, as many areas have been affected. The state of the physical plant is depressing. A teacher explained, "This place is terrible. It used to be mopped and waxed twice a year . . . but now with budget cuts it won't even get that. Still, it could be better than this." We observed garbage strewn throughout the halls, and floors were rarely swept and seemingly never mopped. Budget cuts have also affected supplies; for example, duplicating paper, a mainstay for many teachers' curricula, is in very short supply. Other items like construction paper, scissors, and art materials are also very limited. The cuts affected personnel, as several teachers were bumped and shuttled in and out during the year. Repairs were left undone, stolen or damaged goods never replaced, and security personnel were cut back.

The overriding concerns expressed by teachers in school #5 were related to security and discipline. Teachers are upset with violence and vandalism, and seemed to grudgingly accept nonteaching assignments like hall duty to protect the building and keep order. Hall duty consists of standing in the hall at one's classroom door while students pass from class to class. After the bell sounds, teachers are expected to "sweep the halls" and make sure all students are in class and no outsiders are around. In one instance we observed, several youngsters remained in the hall after the tardy bell. Observing all the students, a young female teacher yelled out to a female student:

Teacher: O.K. Helen, you heard the bell, get to class and stop playing in the hall.

Student (laughing): All right, Miss X, cool out, I'm going.

Teacher (agitated): Don't tell me to wait, do what I tell you now! You heard the bell.

Student: Look, don't yell at me, you're not my mother and I'll go to class when I'm ready.

Teacher (closing her classroom door): We'll see about that, won't we Miss Harris.

Teachers in school #5 are disturbed with these kinds of circumstances which they have had to endure. And they are perplexed that their principal, other administrators, and the public find it so easy to censure and blame teachers whenever something goes wrong.

High School—No. 6

School #6 serves students from ninth to twelfth grades. In a large midwestern city, the building has an academic wing with a recreational structure attached by a tunnel. The building was constructed in 1972 on an experimental "school within a school" concept. Four groups or houses of approximately 500 students and staff would operate in the building, bringing the advantages of a small school along with those of a larger operation. Recent budget cuts, however, brought the experiment to an end, along with the cutting of a variety of programs.

The community is predominantly low income, made up of approximately 71% black, 24% Hispanic, and 5% white. The teaching staff is 60% white and 40% minority, while the principal is a white male who has been in this school for five years. Student enrollment is 2,224 with about 80% black, 19% Hispanic, 2% white. Average daily attendance is 82%.

The current principal is credited by staff as turning the school around. Before he arrived, the school had students constantly wandering halls, many disturbances, false fire alarms, and the like. Now, the school is able to maintain calm, discipline, and order. Indeed, a strong sense of us (the school) against them (everyone else) pervades the environment. All members of the school community wear easily visible ID cards with pictures. Youngsters without them are sent to the attendance office for "blocking," a form of in-school suspension which requires a parent or guardian to come to the school to reinstate the student. One teacher explained, "I'm sure you won't find a teacher who would recommend abandoning it (ID policy). It's important to the school."

We often saw police officers in the school. Local gang warfare created the need for visible law enforcement officials. The threat of gang warfare, although not a physical danger in the school, bothers teachers because of the emotional effects on students who are the targets of gang recruitment. To avoid confrontations, many students stayed home. As a teacher described it, "It breaks my heart. I have a freshman division and during the big gang recruitment periods you can see the fear in their faces."

The principal tries to involve as many faculty as feasible in the decision making process. The principal utilizes the formal mechanism of a Professional Problems Committee extensively, with active faculty involvement in the regularly scheduled meetings. We also observed the principal to be very visible and accessible. He seems to go out of his way to insure that teachers are informed of decisions, especially those that could create distress for teachers who would be affected. His main goal was to keep as much "administration" as possible out of the classrooms so that teachers can concentrate on teaching.

School system financial troubles are a major problem. School grounds are littered and garbage cans not emptied as cutbacks have affected housekeeping. In classrooms, shades are often torn, with cracked windows simply boarded up. Video equipment was left unused as staff to run it were cut. Books are in short supply, and teachers have little input into decisions about which books and supplies are ordered. Materials simply come from "downtown." Library purchases were stopped. Teachers are also concerned about the lack of mobility in the system as the principal described the possibility of new positions opening as being "almost futile."

There is no parental support apparent in the school. Teachers and administrators mentioned how a strong PTA might help the school with fund raising activities, but there is no active PTA. In fact, parents are not seen in the school except for disciplinary matters. Teachers felt that parents place little stock and show little interest in their children's education. Indeed, over one third of the students were initially refused admission because parents didn't bring their children in for required innoculations.

Teachers in school #6 are burdened with numerous other disadvantages. Because of the school's reputation as a trouble ground with gang problems, many academically superior students go elsewhere. One teacher told us she wouldn't allow her child into a school like this. This attitude left teachers with a predominance of weak students mostly from disadvantaged backgrounds.

The teachers also complained of tedious amounts of paperwork forced on them from "downtown." One teacher's comments epitomized this feeling:

> I don't mind grading the kids' papers, that's part of the job. But if I see one more grid that I have to fill out and turn in by yesterday, I'll scream. I'm not a clerk, I'm not a secretary. What I am when I am left alone is a pretty good teacher. Ask around, paperwork is a really big problem around here.

Similarly, many teachers are dismayed that they find themselves teaching at levels well below high school. Sometimes as low as third, fourth, fifth grade level. One teacher responded, "who wouldn't like to have challenging students?" Another sighed, "I wasn't trained to teach kids at the elementary level. I don't know how to teach reading and at the high school level, I don't think I should have to." Another confided to us, "Sure, I'm surprised at some of the things they don't know ... but I never let them know it."

STRESSORS AND THEMES IN THE WORK ENVIRONMENT

The case study prepared for each school revealed a considerable amount of information about working conditions for teachers. Using multisite analytic techniques (Miles and Huberman, 1984), we grouped those conditons affecting teachers' stress into broad categories, and then reanalyzed our categories to pinpoint key themes descriptive of the work environment. Below we discuss very briefly each of the categories of stressors and present the themes we derived.

Governance/Leadership

The stressor of governance/leadership was identified in each of the six schools. This category referred to dissatisfaction or unhappiness with the leadership of the principal, as well as the operation of higher levels of administration as this affected teachers. The principal, quite clearly, is the most significant actor in the school, in terms of influence over the working climate. The principal has the power to alter working conditions and control material and resource allocations, security procedures, evaluations of performance, and discipline measures. As a result, the principal can have a major impact on the levels of stress in a school. Teachers want a principal who has a clear set of expectations, who is consistent and treats everyone equally, and who allows for teacher input into decision making. The further a principal departs from these ideals, the more stressful the situation becomes for teachers.

Problems with higher levels of administration were also identified, with either the board of education or district office as the main source of difficulty. The board is seen as causing duplication of effort and excessive amounts of paperwork; of forcing top down orders and mandates which ignore any teacher input; of being unreasonable in demands yet unavailable when needed or simply insensitive and uncaring. Certain rules and regulations cause teachers to feel that those who run the system do not support them. The actions of higher levels of governance add to teachers' feelings of isolation, and the sense that nobody cares. Teachers believe they are the ones who perform the basic task of any school system, the teaching; they perceive their wishes and concerns to be unacknowledged by policy makers.

Budget Cuts

In an era of financial retrenchment for all levels of government, many school systems face large cutbacks. Problems associated with budget cuts were identified in all of the case studies. The most serious areas which were altered include personnel, supplies, maintenance, and repairs. Teachers witness their colleagues being transferred or fired, and often have to accept intrusions on their turf from outsiders from new programs which are brought in to increase enrollments. Along with this, security personnel are being cut, as well as support staff such as paraprofessionals, teacher aides, clerks and secretaries, who are all vital parts in the operation of a school.

Lack of supplies, poor condition of equipment, few repairs and inadequate maintenance make the teacher's primary task extremely difficult. Teachers lack rudimentary materials like books and paper, special equipment often does not work, and the condition of the buildings is often depressing—with cracked walls, roaches and mice, and no toilet tissue in bathrooms. Several teachers commented that this all has negative psychological effects on them and the children. Add to these problems the fact that in a period of retrenchment most avenues for upward career mobility are closed, and teachers are left with an additional sense of helplessness.

Security

Security, identified in five of the six case studies, includes a number of issues: personal safety and protection of property, as well as job security. The most prevalent security concern relates to individual safety. In areas where neighborhoods are dangerous or perceived as dangerous, teachers feel continually threatened. Especially outside of the school plant, they fear assault and crime. Such fears are exacerbated in schools with poorly organized and inefficient security procedures. This heightens anxiety within the building, often characterized by intrusion from outsiders and classroom interruptions.

Similarly, teachers are concerned with vandalism and theft. School property is often damaged or stolen, as well as personal property. This is disheartening to teachers, and adds to security related frustrations.

Finally, the schools we studied have experienced large budget deficits and cuts in recent years, and teachers witness colleagues either being transferred involuntarily or losing their jobs. The problem of job security arises due to financial difficulties and shrinking enrollments. Teachers feel relative degrees of stress concerning their seniority and their chance of being fired or bumped. Teachers not only must fear that jobs won't be protected, but some teachers feel trapped, as many avenues for career advancement have been closed due to oversupply of personnel.

Student Issues

Student issues were identified as a category of stressors only in the two high schools. The older age students affect teachers in two ways. The students are bigger, stronger, and pose a greater threat than younger, smaller children in terms of personal safety. The proliferation of gangs and the concommitant problems are prevalent in one site, while poor attitudes, a lack of respect, verbal abuse, and fears of violence characterize the other school. Since the majority of students in one high school are black, and in the other high school the majority of the students are white, these concerns seem to transcend racial differences.

Similarly, teachers in both sites are concerned about the low academic ability of students. In one school, teachers lamented the decline in ability over the years, and the fact that these students probably are better suited for a more vocationally oriented curriculum. The other school also has low ability students, and teachers complained of being unprepared to teach high school students with such poor skills. This combination of older and stronger students with low ability poses a physical threat and places a further teaching burden on the respective high school faculties.

Staff Relations

Three schools were characterized as having stress due to staff relations. This meant that whatever the site specific causes, relationships amongst teachers are either hostile, unfriendly, or simply uncooperative. At these schools, groups of teachers simply coexist with one another much of the time, with limited interaction professionally and socially. In each case, groups of teachers were pitted against each other. In one school, regular teachers were threatened by the influx of new and competing programs, and jealousies resulted with no forum for discussion and/or resolution. In another school, a group of older, experienced faculty banded together to oppose the principal and union representative, who each emphasized the importance of a close knit faculty. Mutual respect and cooperation between teachers was lacking here. Finally, groups were formed along racial lines in a third school and a segregated system flourished. In each instance, the relations of the staff which had developed over time undermined the development of a cohesive working environment, and made these schools less pleasant places to work.

Themes

The "I Don't Get No Respect" Syndrome

All of the categories of stressors added to a sense that teachers are held in low esteem by students, parents, administrators, and the general public. Teachers felt they have little input into decision making, no upward mobility opportunities, are forced to work in unsafe, deteriorating conditions without much job security, often are faced with great shortages of necessary materials, and have disrepectful parents and students. Comments by teachers such as, "You see and hear only the bad, seldom good"; "No one cares or is able to effect change"; and "The lack of power to make the job better makes it stressful" characterize the feeling of no respect which was prevalent.

Barriers to Teaching

Teachers in all six schools appeared anxious to teach, but felt that various pressures in the school impinge upon this central task of their job, teaching, the task for which they trained. This *barriers to teaching* is a constant theme we found in the workplace. Administrators of all levels expect teachers to perform many nonteaching functions (i.e., lunch and hall duty) while at the same time demanding large amounts of paperwork, which is often repetitive, such as lesson plans and curriculum guidelines. Teachers are faced with acting as security personnel when actual security forces are being cut, while classroom intrusions by outsiders are common. The lack of requisite supplies such as textbooks and paper for tests are seen as barriers to properly conducting classes, and low-ability level students cause new concerns for teachers, now stuck on remedial subjects, unable to teach appropriate grade-level materials. Teachers in the schools clearly depicted a number of barriers to the teaching function as surmountable, but revealed that these barriers act as deterrants to performing their job.

CONCLUSIONS

Our findings regarding the working conditions that teachers in urban schools confront are supported by other survey and self-report research on institutional variables affecting teacher stress and burnout. Concerning what we call governance, other studies have identified a variety of factors, including lack of teacher involvement in decision making, no control over job environment, including involuntary transfer, denial of transfer, and principal harassment (Cichon and Koff, 1978; Newell, 1979; Reed, 1979; Young, 1978; Walsh, 1979; Cacha, 1981; Farber and Miller, 1981). Related to our category of budget cuts, others report factors such as lack of mobility, budget reversals, long hours, lack of supplies, large classes, and too much paperwork (Reed, 1979; Sullivan, 1979; Coates and Thorenson, 1976; Feshback and Campbell, 1978; Walsh, 1979; Cacha, 1981; Farber and Miller, 1981). Security problems are similarly reported such as management of disruptive youngsters, threats of violence, assaults on colleagues, and verbal abuse (Cichon and Koff, 1978, Coates and Thorenson, 1976; Feshback and Campbell, 1978; Walsh, 1979; Farber and Miller, 1981). Finally, our categories of staff relations and student issues are supported by variables such as teaching below average students, little chance to interact with others, teacher isolation, self-centered students, no sense of community among teachers, and students who don't want to learn (Bardo, 1979; Reed, 1979; Scriven, 1979; Walsh, 1979; Farber and Miller, 1981; Koff and Cichon, 1980; Newell, 1979).

While we make no claims of originality in our findings, the in-depth nature of our case studies and analyses provides vivid examples of the findings in self-report studies and thus great insight for understanding the work environment of teachers. More important, given that we observed schools when most of the data in the highly publicized commission reports were being collected, we believe that their recommendations erred by promoting solutions for educational problems before addressing the issues of working conditions. If there are inadequacies in the way the educational process is conducted, as *A Nation at Risk* (NCEE, 1983) so poignantly tells us, our data suggest that no solutions for improvements can be successful unless the work environment is drastically altered. For example, can recommendations like a strengthened curriculum, longer school day and school year, performance based pay, and the like realistically be expected to change anything when teachers often work in unsafe conditons with students who don't care or are unprepared for their grade level, and with administrators and policy makers making decisions with little teacher input? We don't believe so. While certain of the commission report recommendations would address some of the problems we identify, the main thrust is on altering the delivery and various components of services before first improving the work environment. We believe this is faulty logic.

In fact, our themes of "no respect" and "barriers to teaching" imply an underlying fallacy in the reasoning employed by the reform reports. The questions shouldn't focus first on problems in the educational process, but rather on how our society could allow the workplace for our teachers to exist as we describe. The NCEE report chides the country by suggesting that the nation would consider it an act of war if another country had caused the educational process to erode as it has. We believe a more fundamental concern should be how the public, policy makers, and school officials have allowed teacher working conditions to erode to their current state. The question the educational reports should be asking, then, changes from, "Why are schools doing so poorly?" to, "How have schools performed so well?" given the environment teachers must face each day!

Our findings also imply certain areas for improvement that we believe would help teachers' performance. These recommendations should receive equal attention to other popular reform initiatives, as improving working conditions should be a prerequisite to other changes directed at the teaching process itself. Concerning governance, school principals should be strongly encouraged to focus their self-development activities on the improvement of their leadership ability and management and communication skills. Programs for administrators should include components emphasizing skills in assessment of the climate and structure of learning environments through use of multiple research methodologies. Boards of Education, school administrators, and teacher unions should cooperatively explore the ramifications of new reward systems and career ladders for teachers, to make teaching more attractive and open up new avenues for career mobility. We believe that greater decision-making authority for instructional matters should exist at the school building level, with teachers having significant input. Boards of Education should be more thorough in exploring the impact of their decisions on daily life in classrooms and schools and on the teaching/learning process. Finally, principals and teachers must collaboratively develop strategies to improve the public image of teachers in the community.

The ramifications of budget cuts must be understood by policy makers before slashing materials or personnel significant for effective teaching. At a minimum, school systems should be required to assure that basic materials and equipment necessary for teaching are available to all teachers throughout the school year. Related to this, new revenue sources to increase funding for schools should be explored. In addition, school systems should assess the amount of paperwork they require of teachers, and devise new systems to accomodate record keeping needs, to give teachers ample time to teach.

Security problems have a debilitating affect on teachers and can severely hurt classroom performance. We feel that Boards of Education and city governments should develop a means for assessing school needs related to protection from physical harm and the psychological strain the fear of it engenders, and cooperatively take action to eliminate this threat from the schools. Teachers must be protected from outside disturbances, vandalism of property must be curtailed, and staff and students must feel safe on school grounds.

Finally, teachers should be given regularly scheduled time outside the classroom to increase opportunities for collegial interactions which enhance professional skills, promote the sharing of ideas, and minimize the isolation of the classroom. This should help improve staff relations among teachers. We also believe that to minimize what we call student issues, teacher preservice and inservice programs must prepare teachers for underachieving students, to foster realistic expectations of student performance, and offer teachers methods to instruct this population.

Improvement of work conditions must be a first step in reforming American education. Other content, process, and structural changes will probably fail unless the work environment is conducive to teaching and learning. If indeed the nation is at risk because of educational performance, working conditions for teachers have been a part of the cause. Reforms must address these problems.

Acknowledgments. This research is based on work presented to the National Institute of Education, Report No. G-80-0011. The opinions, conclusions, and recommendations are those of the authors.

REFERENCES

Adler, M. (1982). *The Paideia Proposal.* New York: Macmillan.

Bardo, P. (1979). The pain of teacher burnout: a case history. *Phi Delta Kappan* 6(Dec.): 252-254.

Boyer, E.L. (1983). *High School: A Report on Secondary Education in America.* New York: Harper & Row.

Cacha, F.B. (1981). Teacher burnout: causes and solutions. *Phi Delta Pi Record* 18(Fall): 26-27.

Cichon, D., and Koff, R.H. (1978). The Teaching Events Stress Inventory. Paper presented at American Educational Research Association Annual Conference, Toronto.

Coates, T.J., and Thoreson, C.D. (1976). Teacher anxiety: a review with recommendations. *Review of Educational Research* 465(Spring): 159-184.

Farber, B., and Miller, J. (1981). Teacher burnout: a psychoeducational perspective. *Teachers College Record* 83(Winter): 235-243.

Feshback, N., and Campbell, M. (1978). Teacher stress and disciplinary practices in schools. Paper presented at the annual meeting of the American Orthopsychiatric Association, San Francisco.

Hershkovitz, M. (1948). *Man and His Works.* New York: Knopf.

Kyriacou, C., and Sutcliffe, J. (1979). Teacher stress and satisfaction. *Educational Research* 21: 89-96.

Lortie, D. (1975). *Schoolteacher.* Chicago: University of Chicago Press.

McLaughlin, M. W., Pfeifer, R.S., Swanson-Owens, D., and Yee, S. (1986). Why teachers won't teach. *Phi Delta Kappan* 67(Feb.): 420-425.

Miles, M., and Huberman, A. M. (1984). *Qualitative Data Analysis.* Beverly Hills, CA: Sage.

National Commission on Excellence in Education (1983). *A Nation at Risk: The Imperative for Educational Reform.* Washington, DC: U.S. Department of Education.

Newell, R. (1979). Teacher stress warning: teaching maybe hazardous to your health. *American Teacher* (Dec 1978-Jan. 1979): 16-17.

Reed, S. (1979). What you can do to prevent teacher burnout. *The National Elementary Principal* 58(March): 67-70.

Scriven, R. (1979). The big click. *Today's Education* 68(Nov/Dec): 34-35.

Sullivan, C. (1979). Sources of anxiety within the school setting as reported by Emory University pre-service and in-Service teachers: a descriptive study. Emory University.

The Twentieth Century Fund Task Force on Elementary and Secondary Education Policy (1983). *Making the Grade.* New York.

Walsh, D. (1979). Classroom stress and teacher burnout. *Phi Delta Kappan* 61(Dec.): 253.

Young, B.B. (1978). Anxiety and stress: how they affect teacher teaching. *NASSP Bulletin* 62(Nov.): 78-83.

Programs and Strategies for Increasing Minority Student Enrollment in Teacher Preparation Programs

OVERVIEW

This chapter introduces a variety of strategy models to redress the minority teacher shortage. The strategies range from state level activities to two-year college activities, to activities for the college of education. Alston, Jackson, and Pressman describe ways in which various states have begun to take the lead in demonstrating what can be done to deal with the various aspects of the minority teacher shortage problem. A seminal model developed at the 1987 National Invitational Conference on the Recruitment and Retention of Minority Students in Teacher Education is also included in this chapter. This model designates teacher education programs as the lead facilitator in establishing a collaborative relationship with school districts and community representatives in order to recruit minorities into teacher education. Other models are discussed that have particular implications for increasing the number of Hispanic and Native American teacher educators. The remaining articles represent case studies of activities currently being implemented at both historically black and historically white institutions of higher education.

3. STATE ACTION TO INCREASE THE SUPPLY OF MINORITY TEACHERS

by Denise Alston, Nathaniel Jackson, and Harvey Pressman

INTRODUCTION

In the fall of 1987, the Southern Education Foundation (SEF) convened a five-state task force to address the problem of minority teacher shortages. Supported by matching funds from the National Governors' Association (NGA) and SEF, the Southern Regional Task Force on the Supply of Minority Teachers was organized to facilitate the work of five separate state task forces appointed by the governors to address the problem: What can our state do to increase the supply of minority teachers (especially Blacks), in both the immediate future and the long run?

The regional task force, made up of representatives from Arkansas, Georgia, North Carolina, Tennessee, and Virginia, met five times between November 1987, and May 1988. Delegates discussed alternate strategies by which states could increase public awareness of the need for more minority teachers and develop new practices that could slow the precipitous decline in their numbers. Each state task force developed a concrete plan to deal with this problem, and made specific recommendations to their respective governors. The background of these efforts, and the specific results follow.

IN-STATE ACTIVITIES

Over the past five years, individual states have begun to take the lead in demonstrating what can be done to deal with various aspects of the minority teacher shortage problem. In data collection and analysis, Illinois and Florida might show the way. In terms of planning for the future, Missouri and Maryland took some interesting early steps. With respect to "pipeline" strategies, Alabama and South Carolina initiated promising programs. In developing financial aid incentives, North Carolina and Florida have organized new approaches. In reinforcing support for the historically Black colleges and universities, which have traditionally produced the bulk of the Black teaching force in America, South Carolina and North Carolina have provided funding for interesting new initiatives. In terms of promoting strategies designed to have some immediate impact on the problem in the short term, Maryland and, again, South Carolina have devised innovative new steps. And all of these activities have served as a base on which the five task forces in the states involved in the SEF/NGA project have tried to build. Let's look at some examples.

Minority Teacher Development and Recruitment Activities

Information Gathering. The most important initial step a state can take is to study teacher supply and demand taking into account the race and ethnicity of the current and projected teaching force. Collecting reliable statewide data on minority teachers and teacher candidates was found to be the most difficult task encountered by the fifteen states. Several states did not collect or report teacher (or student) data by race.

A good example of data gathering is the Illinois State Board of Education and State Teacher Certification Board's report, "A Study of Teacher Trends and Traits." The report was required by the 1985 Illinois educational reform legislation, and presented a thorough analysis of the gender and minority distribution of students enrolled in colleges of education and teachers. These data were analyzed in the context of the past and current minority student enrollment. The data showed parts of the state where minority teachers were working, where minority students were enrolled, and the size of the pool of future minority teachers.

Florida's Education Standards Commission produced a similar report on meeting the challenge of providing minority teachers to their public schools. This 1987 report also included specific recommendations on how the state could increase the supply of minority teachers and improve data collection on teachers. The recommendations include a statewide study on the causes of teacher attrition and the systematic follow-up of college of education graduates.

Planning. In South Carolina, in 1984, the deans of several colleges of education provided leadership for forming a task force to plan for a teacher recruitment center. The task force developed a proposal and submitted it to the Higher Education Commission, where it was turned into successful legislation that resulted in the formation of the South Carolina Center for Teacher Recruitment. The Center's initial annual budget was $250,000. The Center is a consortium of representatives from twenty-six teacher training institutes, public school educators, legislators, business people, and representatives from state education agencies and professional associations. Through the Center, the state intends to make a concerted effort to compete with business, industry, and the professions for talented people. The Center focuses its recruitment efforts on individuals of above-average academic ability who feel some inclination to teach, but may be discouraged by peers, parents, or teachers.

Illinois has begun its planning process with a different approach. Last year, the State Board of Education and State Higher Education Board created a joint committee of educators, business people, and community activists who will create recommendations for improving minority student achievement and recruiting and retaining minority teachers. They will consider existing research findings and presentations by institutional and program representatives in developing the recommendations.

The Missouri Department of Education has created an internal task force that is exploring ways to increase minority recruitment. The task force members represent teacher education, urban education, desegregation technical assistance, and the deputy commissioner of public instruction.

The state school superintendent in Maryland appointed a task force on minority teacher recruitment and promotion. The task force's charge is to submit an action plan to the superintendent that reflects its assessment of minority teacher recruitment strategies and local systems' promotion policies. The action plan may result in recommendations for programs and practices or requests to the legislature for funds. The report was released in spring 1988.

Strategies to Improve the Pipeline. Planning activities informed by the needs and resources of individual states can focus minority teacher recruitment efforts on a variety of target groups. Some states have begun by targeting young adolescents still in the middle grades to raise aspirations and to provide academic assistance. Other states provide students with early exposure to teaching experiences in order to recruit them into the profession. Still others have started by focusing on access to higher education by providing financial aid or other incentives. Some states have begun by building on the importance of historically Black colleges in preparing Black teachers and, thus, committing additional resources to these institutions to help them better prepare their students. Most of these activities have been instituted so recently that sufficient time has not passed to evaluate their effectiveness.

In targeting early adolescents, Alabama State University conducts a partnership program with local high schools that targets ninth-graders interested in teaching. The students are provided with remedial services, guidance in curriculum selection, and test-taking skills to better prepare them for college.

South Carolina has one of the most organized statewide recruitment programs operating through its Teacher Recruitment Center. Its central activity is to interest talented students in teaching. Finding minority students with high academic achievement is a top priority for its Teacher Cadet Program. High school juniors and seniors with a B+ or better average take a course on teaching, have field experiences that introduce them to a range of of teaching opportunities, and take a close look at the challenges and rewards of the teaching profession. The course is offered with support from college teacher education faculty. The Cadet Program has grown from 28 high schools serving 400 students in 1986-87 to 55 high schools and 900 students in 1987-88.

The Maryland Teacher Education and Certification Office helps local school districts, colleges, and universities build local chapters of Future Teachers of America. These chapters encourage young minority students to enter teaching. A statewide network to support the chapters is being developed and several individual schools and districts are moving ahead in establishing chapters.

In a unique venture, Los Angeles, California, Unified School District has a magnet school in a predominantly Black neighborhood that prepares high school students for teaching careers. In addition to pedagogical instruction, the students receive teaching experience.

Fiscal Support for Improving Participation. In an effort to ensure that minority high school graduates have full access to higher education in general, and teacher education in particular, a few states support programs that provide financial and other assistance to interested students. One challenge is to offer amounts large enough to lure students away from more prestigious and potentially more lucrative careers.

The Public School Forum of North Carolina's Project Teach encourages Black and American Indian high school students to consider teaching as a career and to apply for a North Carolina Teaching Fellowship to finance their college educations. The Teaching Fellows Program is a loan forgiveness plan that provides $5,000 per year for up to four years of college in exchange for up to four years of teaching after graduation. Project Teach, which started in fall 1987, employs community-based teams who carry information about the fellowship to students and parents. The teams also expose students to what is necessary to get into and stay in college, such as standardized test-taking skills and guidance counseling.

In summer 1987, Florida's Department of Education asked the legislature to double its promising teacher scholarships program to allow each high school to be eligible for two awards, one of which would be earmarked for a minority student. If there are minority students at each of Florida's eligible secondary schools, 317 scholarships would be available to minority students.

Beginning in the fall of 1987, the Georgia advisory committee funded a pilot program through Georgia Southern College to identify high school students interested in teacher education, provide them with financial and academic assistance to get into the college, and social support once they are on campus. Georgia Southern is a traditionally white institution that has suffered high attrition rates among Black students. The social support aspect of the program responds to reports that for Blacks, a key factor in attrition from the college of teacher education has been their sense of alienation from campus life.

Supporting Schools that Minorities Attend. South Carolina's historically Black colleges and universities received state funding from the 1987 legislature to cultivate qualified teacher candidates from Black high school students with average and below-average grades, primarily from small and rural school districts.

Governor James G. Martin's North Carolina Consortium to Improve Teacher Education has made a commitment to improve the preparation of Black teacher candidates. The consortium made a one-time grant of $700,000 in 1987 to the state's historically Black colleges and universities to purchase computers and National Teachers' Examination software. This effort is intended to improve the pass rates of these candidates on the state teacher exam.

Florida is considering pilot programs at community colleges where minority students are highly represented. The programs would recruit, provide initial training, and increase the retention of students who would then be eligible for teaching scholarships for their upper division coursework. This proposal presumes an increase in the two-year to four-year articulation of minority students at community and junior colleges.

Immediate Strategies. For the most part, the programs and activities described above represent long-term commitments to preparing minority students for teaching careers. Whether grooming intermediate and high school students or providing financial assistance and social support to college students, the outcomes of these practices will not be seen for at least five years. Several states have such a shortfall of qualified minority teachers and so few students in the pipeline, that more immediate action should be instituted as well. One possible solution is to develop pools of minority professionals to be brought into teaching.

The Florida legislature recently received a recommendation from the State Department of Education to declare a critical shortage of minority teachers. In so doing, funds would be available for retraining candidates drawn from alternative pools of professionals, and for scholarships, loan reimbursements, and summer institute training of high school students.

The South Carolina Teacher Recruitment Center has made alternative pool recruitment one of its goals for 1987-88. The Center hopes to recruit minorities from business and the military, both in and outside of South Carolina, for alternative route certification in critical shortage areas. A summer program to prepare alternative pool candidates for the professional standards section of the state teacher certification examination is under consideration.

Maryland's Teacher Recruitment Office has a well-developed military recruitment and preparation program targeted at three military bases in its state. At Fort Meade, for example, a teacher certification program has been designed by two institutions of higher education and delivered to officers before retirement who wish to pursue second careers in the classroom. Approximately a dozen minority military personnel and their dependents participate. In addition, the recruitment office is involved in a collaborative project that reaches out to early retirees from government and private industry. It has approached government laboratories and research centers, utility companies, and manufacturers as sources of math and science teachers. Much of the publicity in both the military and government/private industry campaigns is directed to attracting minorities.

THE REGIONAL TASK FORCE

The preceding examples were selected from a survey limited to fifteen states. No doubt other important experiments are being tried in other states, though our information suggests these tend usually to be pilot or local programs. The five task-force states involved in the SEF/NGA project set out to build on these kinds of examples, but within a framework of planning for comprehensive, statewide action.

Delegates to the regional task force reflected the diversity and variety of players and power centers within the educational decision-making processes of the states involved. Some states sent policy specialists from the governor's office; others sent key members of state legislatures, state department of education officials, and/or members of boards of education or higher education. A college president, the dean of a major graduate school of education, and members of SEF's own education advisory committee added to the mix.

Each state's delegates accepted as their charge responding to the Carnegie Report's call for state-level policies to address the minority teacher shortage, on a state-by-state level. The Regional Task Force meetings were set up to facilitate the local planning processes by examining existing state policies and initiatives, considering new ideas, and exploring the political strategies that would be required to implement new state policies successfully. No monolithic strategy or model was sought. Rather, the delegates were encouraged to take from the Regional Task Force's deliberations those ideas and strategies that lent themselves most effectively to getting the job done in their states.

Nonetheless, the opportunity to hear from experts about what was already happening in some forward-looking states, and to talk to each other about what was already going on in their respective states, inevitably produced some shared strategies as well as some individualistic ideas that fit the experience and needs of only one of the states. A look at these various shared and individual strategies will perhaps provide the best evidence of how far the group progressed in a relatively short span of time.

SHARED STRATEGIES

Not surprisingly, about half of the specific strategies developed through this process have been adopted in one form or another by more than one state. Examples include Teacher Cadet programs, "forgivable" college loans and fellowships for people who make commitments to teach in certain areas and/or certain fields, Young Educator clubs that give greater emphasis to minority participation, and Teacher Recruitment campaigns that pursue a similar emphasis.

Forgivable Loans and Fellowships

Tennessee plans to design and initiate a new Teaching Fellows Service Award Program to provide fellowships for minority students, which would include a pay-back arrangement based on teaching service within the state. Colleges and universities participating as Teaching Fellow sites would incorporate a variety of specific training experiences and mentoring relationships in their program. (Virginia, North Carolina, and Georgia have also developed variations of this kind of program.)

Teacher Cadet Programs

Virginia would create a variation on the Teacher Cadet model, specifically targeted at the middle school student. Teacher Cadet programs (also slated for Arkansas, Georgia, and Tennessee) recruit academically able secondary students to study the skills of teaching, observe master teachers, tutor younger students, and enter into mentor relationships with successful teachers.

Young Educator/Future Teacher Clubs

Arkansas proposes to develop a statewide program of Future Teacher clubs to encourage minority students and others to consider teaching, to take the necessary precollegiate academic work, and to tutor other students. Georgia and Tennessee plan variations on this model, with features designed to increase the number of minority students preparing for college, to improve their capacity to complete test requirements for entry into teacher education programs, and to assist school systems in geographic locations that have difficulty in attracting new teachers to "grow their own" teachers for future needs.

Statewide Recruitment Campaigns for the Teaching Profession

The North Carolina Initiative on the Supply of Minority Teachers seeks to encourage persons to enter or reenter the teaching profession through a variety of methods, including (1) establishing multiethnic advisory committees at both state and local levels to assist in recruiting minorities; (2) involving the media, civic and community organizations, and industry in recruiting minorities for the teaching profession; (3) identifying competent minority students as prospective teachers; and (4) providing widened exposure to teacher education programs. Virginia will design a series of programs to enhance the image of the teaching profession and encourage talented young people to consider a teaching career.

Revised Certification Regulations

Arkansas will explore alternative certification as a way to encourage adults who did not originally prepare to be teachers to become teachers. Virginia will identify the elements of certification that may have a negative impact on the supply of qualified teachers and will devise effective alternatives to these regulations.

Statewide Teacher Job Banks

Tennessee will (1) invite local school systems to list open teaching positions, (2) encourage teachers searching for positions to place resumes on file, (3) enhance the ability of qualified minority teachers to respond to the competitive environment, (4) track the placement of minority graduates from in-state teacher education programs, and (5) seek private funds to support recruitment incentives that will attract minority Tennesseans trained out of state back to the state to teach. Virginia proposes to establish a job-matching service as part of a broader state support system.

Publicize Teacher Recruitment Initiatives Among Minority Students

Two states propose to make extra efforts to stimulate increased participation of minority students in programs already in place. The Georgia task force will provide more publicity regarding funds available to students interested in teaching in critical teaching fields. North Carolina will utilize an extensive financial incentive structure already in place to increase the number of minorities entering teaching.

Improve Data Collection and Analysis

Georgia and Arkansas will take steps to improve the quality of available information about the supply of minority teachers, the minority composition of the current teaching force, and the attitudes of prospective students toward careers in teaching.

INDIVIDUAL STRATEGIES

Tennessee's task force agenda calls for the establishment of transition programs that would function as a bridge between high school and college by providing ways for minority high school students to become acculturated to the expectations of college life, in an "Upward Bound" experience for prospective teachers. Programs for members of minority groups who are presently teacher aides, substitute teachers, or community college students, but do not hold four-year degrees would be established through a matching grant program to consortia of local school systems and higher education institutions. Tennessee would also establish a matching grant program to attract minority candidates for teacher education from among graduates of four-year colleges who hold credentials in fields other than education. A separate state incentive grant program would reward higher education institutions for dealing with minority students' problems of entry, retention, and completion, and would require institutions to indicate their ability to respond to the needs of this population in the areas of curriculum, advising, mentoring, tutoring, enrichment, financial support, and counseling.

Virginia proposes to establish and staff a continuing statewide support system. The staff would administer the cadet program, a high school teacher mentor program, a college/university freshman and sophomore career seminar, a job-matching service, career-switcher programs, and a variety of other initiatives. Virginia also proposes, through a competitive grant process, to reward institutions of higher education that restructure their strategies for recruiting and retaining minority students.

Georgia plans new programs designed to increase the financial resources available to prospective minority teachers. In one, the state would encourage and stimulate the development of business-education partnerships designed to increase the private financial assistance available to future minority teachers. A second would extend an existing loan-forgiveness program currently available to college juniors and seniors to minority freshmen and sophomores.

Finally, Arkansas proposes to relate current efforts to upgrade the curriculum in the schools more directly to efforts to increase the pool of potential minority teachers, by, for example, providing in-service training to counselors on how to encourage minority students to take college prep courses and on the importance of increasing student awareness of all the options available.

IMPLEMENTATION AND FUNDING

Each state delegation accepted the responsibility for developing an implementation plan dealing with the practical issues of getting its recommendations accepted in the policy arena, and seeking sufficient financial support for those elements of each state plan that require additional expenditures. To this end, continuing state task forces on the supply of minority educators were established, drawing from a broad spectrum of the business, political, and educational communities. These task forces are assuming the responsibility, in the words of the Virginia report, for the "variety of actions necessary to further conceptualize and implement" the policy agendas such as "comprehensive data gathering, policy formation, political and private support, and organizational and agencies' approval."

Methods for funding the various state plans were developed simultaneously with the creation of their content. The North Carolina delegation, for example, decided to introduce during the "short session" of its General Assembly a bill "proposing allocation of State dollars to programs that will increase the supply of minority teachers" through the implementation of new proposals in the areas of teacher recruitment, academic preparation, and financial incentives.

Virginia, on the other hand, chose to submit a budget addendum request for support of a new program, dubbed Project TREE (Teacher Recruitment for Excellence in Education). Georgia, in addition to seeking support for certain of its proposals (e.g., Future Teachers clubs and/or Teacher Cadet programs, increased funding for minority student loans) through requests in the FY '90 budget, also decided to promote private sector initiatives through local partnership arrangements with the business community. The immediate goal of these arrangements would be to increase private financial assistance to minority students interested in becoming teachers.

CONCLUSION

As the above summary should make clear, each state that was involved in the Regional Task Force managed to make very specific, concrete progress toward the implementation of a statewide plan to deal with the issue of the declining minority teaching force, in a relatively short span of time. Why was this so?

One explanation may lie simply in the process of frequently meeting with colleagues from other states to compare notes and report progress to each other. In addition to the obvious advantages of learning from each other, this process may have imposed an urgency within each state's task force to make some concrete progress before the next regional get-together in the next state capital. These meetings, occurring on a monthly basis, thus may have helped to speed up the process as well as to infuse it with ideas from outside experts and colleagues from other states.

Another spur to progress may have derived from the willingness of local educational policymakers to look to other states (rather than, for example, to federal demonstrations or university initiatives) as major sources of new ideas. Although several observers of American education have noted a shift in the locus of innovation and initiative to the states during the Reagan years, there are still relatively few mechanisms by which one state can readily learn from another in this area. The Regional Task Force provided such a structure.

Finally, the existence of an outside agency (or, in this case, two outside agencies) willing to help facilitate the discourse among states proved very helpful. The Southern Education Foundation and the National Governors' Association not only provided the funds needed to get the delegates together on a regular basis, but also provided staff to facilitate the meetings, research current innovations, and help drive the process forward. These practical supports proved, according to many of the delegates, crucial to their ability to make rapid progress within their respective states.

A Model for Recruitment and Retention of Minority Students in Teacher Preparation Programs

Minorities

Ernest J. Middleton
Emanuel J. Mason
William E. Stilwell
William C. Parker

The authors provide a comprehensive model for planning, implementing, and maintaining an institutional effort to recruit and maintain minority students in teacher education programs. Significant factors in planning a recruitment program and suggestions for making the recruitment model institution-specific are discussed. Activities are suggested for each of the eight functions in the model.

Middleton is Associate Professor, Mason is Professor, Stilwell is Professor, and Parker is Vice-Chancellor for Minority Affairs, University of Kentucky.

Educators and educational planners have become increasingly concerned about the representation of minority groups among professional teachers in the country's schools (Hackley, 1985; Graham, 1987; Kortokrax-Clark, 1986; Reed, 1986). Despite the need for greater participation of minority teachers for an increasingly diverse public school population expected in the very near future, the number of minority teachers has been declining steadily over the past ten years (Graham, 1987). Looking just at the situation for Black teachers, during the 1970s and early 1980s Blacks constituted about 8% of teachers in the public schools and about 14-16% of the students. More recently, however, the proportion of Black teachers has dropped to less than 7%, and is expected to continue to decline for a variety of reasons. At the same time the proportion of Black students in the system is on the increase, perhaps reaching 40% of the public school population by the year 2000 (Graham, 1987).

The importance of having minority representation in the corps of professional teachers has been recognized; one reason given is that teachers serve as role models for children (e.g., Barton and Osborne, 1978: Brophy and Putnam, 1979; Meichenbaum, 1977). There is a justifiable concern that minority students would benefit more directly from a teacher role model when the teacher is a member of the students' own minority group (Graham, 1987). Yet it is possible with the dwindling minority teacher representation that a minority student could complete the K-12 school experience and never meet a minority teacher.

Furthermore, non-minority students will benefit from the opportunity to experience minority teachers. Interaction with minority teachers will result in increased familiarity with minorities and experience in seeing them in professional roles. This can raise aspirations in minority group children and lead to higher expectations for minority group members in others.

Another reason for recruiting minorities into teaching is an impending shortage of qualified teachers, a shortage caused primarily by three factors: low salaries relative to industry and other occupations, reportedly difficult or depressing work conditions, and increasingly difficult and demanding standards for entry into the profession (Hawley, 1986). Many of the influences reducing the numbers of new people coming into teaching are also driving minority students toward other professions (Graham, 1987). If more students from minority populations who go to college were interested in becoming teachers, the impending shortage would be reduced. On the other hand, statistics show that at the present time fewer Blacks have been seeking higher education in general than in 1976 (Graham, 1987). For example, the number of Blacks entering graduate schools dropped 19.2% between the 1976-77 and 1984-85 academic years; at the same time, there were marked increases in the number of Hispanics (20.4%) and Asians (54.4%) (Heller, 1986). Such data suggest that large portions of the Black population will not be available for teaching careers.

Many suggestions have been offered to increase the numbers of minority students in teacher preparation programs. One approach would be to concentrate on those individuals who show interest in becoming teachers (Hanes and Hanes, 1986-87). Other suggestions have included increasing the collaboration between higher education institutions and elementary and secondary schools, increasing the attractiveness of a teaching career by raising the salary and status of teachers, increasing the funding support for minority students, enlisting mid-career professionals who are looking for a change and would like to work with children, and establishing programs to improve minority applicants' ability to score well on admissions and other tests required in teacher education programs (Graham, 1987; Hawley, 1986; Hackley, 1985). These kinds of proposals and initiatives must be recognized as programs that fit into the larger context and mission of the institution in order to thrive and be successful.

Several model programs have been developed for specific institutions or communities (e.g., Hackley, 1985; Middleton and Mason, 1987). While each of these programs has proved successful in some dimensions, a comprehensive and widely applicable model for planning, implementing, and maintaining an institution's efforts to recruit, retain, and prepare minority students to be highly qualified and motivated professional teachers is needed. Such a model would assist teacher preparation programs to respond to this important national need.

Increasing the Pool of Minority Teachers

Systems theory provides a conceptual mechanism for dealing with dynamic complex interacting elements in a systematic way (Hussain, 1973). The present paper applies a systems design originally developed by Stilwell (1976b) for managing change in dynamic educational programs and initiatives. The approach has been applied to social changes in education in various contexts; for example, passage of school law (Mason, Prus, and Stillwell, 1976), implementation of computer education (Zuk and Stilwell, 1984), provision of school psychological services (Stilwell, DeMers, and Niquette, 1985; Stilwell, Buffington, and DeMers, 1984), and affective education (Stilwell, 1976a).

A systems approach to recruitment and retention of minority students in teacher education programs seems particularly appropriate when the problem is viewed with the kind of broad perspective a successful program requires. The current low level of minority participation in the teaching profession and teacher education must be recognized as a complex problem with many origins. For example, students are deciding early in their educational careers not to seek higher education due to problems of access, academic preparation, sense of efficacy, and other influences. Colleges of education wishing to be successful in their minority recruitment efforts must seek students several years before they are ready seriously to consider higher education and a career in teaching, or the battle will be lost. This reality requires involvement with community agencies, schools, local businesses, and other groups. The Stilwell approach assumes that the resources for problem solution can be found within existing educational, governmental, and community elements, and that these resources can be best mobilized by analysis and organization of the various elements into a dynamic system (Stilwell, 1976b).

Recruitment Model

The Stilwell (1976b) approach was used to organize several hundred ideas and suggestions generated in working groups at a conference on minority recruitment and retention in teacher education (Middleton and Mason, 1987). These ideas and suggestions were analyzed, interpreted, and classified, and then organized into a systems model. Because the model was designed to represent the perspective from within a college of education, some adaptation might be required if control of the program lies elsewhere on campus, or in another agency. The model contains eight functions that are explained below. Planners can use this discussion as an outline to develop specific activities within each function that would be appropriate for the setting and program being planned. A sample of activities generated under each of the eight functions of the model is shown in Table 1.

Activities listed in Table 1 may be broken down further into subactivities depending on need and complexity. In addition, it should be pointed out that each activity shown in Table 1 implicitly has some form of evaluation

Table 1
Sampling of Activities under Eight Functions of Program for Recruitment and Retention of Minority Students in Teacher Education

1. Analysis of teacher education program systems.
- ☐ Document need for participation of minority students in TEP at an increased level.
- ☐ Describe the structure of the TEP (entry and certification requirements, course structure, faculty responsibilities, etc.).
- ☐ Organize and analyze available data on recruitment and retention in TEP, particularly those pertaining to minorities.
- ☐ Describe faculty composition.
- ☐ Detail multi-cultural issues in the curriculum.
- ☐ Study graduate employment patterns.
- ☐ Document relationship of state laws and statutes to TEP.
- ☐ Identify differential enrollment patterns under different curriculum alternatives.
- ☐ Describe support services for students.
- ☐ Describe the influence of local community and other outside agencies on potential minority applicants to the TEP.

2. Specify goals for minority participation in teacher education.
- ☐ Specify target population.
- ☐ Develop criteria for supportive environment (Academic, economic, cultural, and social).
- ☐ Develop community interest and participation in planning (Include civic, religious, business, and other interested groups).
- ☐ Establish level of participation for professional organizations and practicing teachers.
- ☐ Increase awareness of multicultural issues within teacher education programs.

3. Involve community groups.
- ☐ Establish collaborative working relationships with various community, civic, public, and professional groups.
- ☐ Establish public information plans and procedures.
- ☐ Identify potential sources of funding support in the community.
- ☐ Develop sources of incentives with organizations representing appropriate potential students (e.g., stimulate interest through workshops, contact with local media).
- ☐ Explore alternative minority recruitment possibilities (e.g., inservice teacher-, staff-, administrator-, and/or parent-training, and other potential minority recruitment programs) on campus.

4. Develop plans for recruitment and retention.
- ☐ Identify program director and someone who will assume responsibility for evaluation of the program (evaluation director).
- ☐ Establish a planning group consisting of members of the business, university, teaching profession, and civic and community groups.
- ☐ Prepare objectives for minority recruitment and retention program.

Table 1 (continued)

- ☐ Identify roles for schools, educators, administrators and educational agencies in the program.
- ☐ Establish performance criteria for objectives.
- ☐ Develop evaluation plan and schedule.
- ☐ Prepare a document covering comprehensive plan.
- ☐ Obtain approval (or commitment) of plan from constituent groups.
- ☐ Prepare a checklist or guide sheet from the planning document to include objectives, funding, resource development, leadership, progress assessment, and assignment of responsibilities.
- ☐ Disseminate plan to all concerned parties.
- ☐ Develop a plan for curriculum to include study of cultural diversity.

5. **Prepare for installation of recruitment/retention plan.**

- ☐ Assure that counseling center advisors, university minority student office, and other support services are capable of meeting needs of the new minority TEP students.
- ☐ Assure funding, space, and other resources requirements are in place for program start-up.
- ☐ Implement training for faculty and staff to provide necessary support to newly recruited minority TEP students.
- ☐ Implement a pilot test of program systems a semester or two before program start-up, evaluate the pilot study, and do revisions suggested by the results.

6. **Implement the minority recruitment and retention plan.**

- ☐ Coordinate recruitment efforts with high school teachers and guidance counselors.
- ☐ Provide a speakers bureau to discuss teaching as a career with civic and community groups (PTA or PTO, boy and girl scouts, community recreation groups, etc.).
- ☐ Identify and provide financial aid information to students.
- ☐ Provide workshops to improve test taking and study skills.
- ☐ Encourage positive interaction between faculty and minority TEP students.

7. **Evaluate program outcomes.**

- ☐ Evaluate students' interaction with curriculum.
- ☐ Collect data implied by the program objectives.
- ☐ Evaluate unintended effects (e.g., effects on high school students' attitudes toward teaching, parents' aspirations, students' use of campus services, etc.).
- ☐ Collect and disseminate suggestions for program improvement.
- ☐ Disseminate evaluation results to management and staff, and to constituent groups.
- ☐ Design and implement performance evaluation of project staff and director with ultimate responsibility assumed by the dean.

8. **Maintain recruiting and retention reference system.**

- ☐ Establish a data collection schedule for the purpose of entering information into the database (e.g., monthly, quarterly, etc., depending on type of information).
- ☐ Conduct ongoing analysis of data as received.
- ☐ Report results on ongoing analyses according to prearranged schedule (e.g. weekly, monthly, each semester's end, etc.).
- ☐ Designate a monitoring committee composed of members from TEP and constituent groups to review data and make timely recommendations to program director or dean.
- ☐ Disseminate annual recruitment and retention report as appropriate to community, TEP faculty, on-campus programs, university administration, etc., and request feedback.
- ☐ Maintain a mailing list of other similar programs at other institutions for the purpose of information sharing.

---

activity; each activity is stated in operational terms and in a manner that will permit evaluation. Through the ongoing process of evaluation, the director of a recruitment and retention program will be able to determine how the program should be revised to maintain its effectiveness. Users of the model are urged to adapt the model and suggested activities to their specific setting.

1. Analyze teacher education program system.

This analysis includes all aspects and constituencies of the teacher education process. For example, the public school student population, the community make-up, and the characteristics of the institution should be considered. Initially the level of minority participation in teaching is studied and the needs for increased participation documented. Then other aspects of the issue are studied such as certification requirements, program entry requirements, the role of other programs on campus (e.g., Arts and Sciences College, Music School, etc.). Information gathered in this function helps to set the stage for the activities conducted in other functions of the model.

2. Specify goals for minority participation in teacher education.

The college of education, working with local and state agencies, should provide guidelines for the development of goals and objectives for minority student participation in the teacher education program. These goals and objectives should be based on information obtained in Function 1. Activities in Function 2 would be most successful when a variety of institutions, agencies, and community groups interested in increasing minority participation in teacher education participate.

3. Involve community groups.

Whether or not community involvement was initiated in the previous function, certain steps should be taken to ensure support in the community. The manager of a minority recruitment program should be familiar with the concerns and interests of relevant elements in the community that might be supportive in recruiting students, generating funding support, and providing other kinds of support to students in the program. Further, involvement with prominent individuals in the community adds to the credibility and visibility of the program.

4. Develop plans for recruitment and retention.

A comprehensive plan for recruitment and retention of minority students into teacher education programs is developed in the fourth function of the model. Coordination is made with appropriate community constituencies, and program criteria and objectives are established with a concern for managing, evaluating, revising, and strengthening the program during its operation. In addition, program developers ought to be guided by the available knowledge about marketing higher education (Kotler and Fox, 1985).

5. Prepare for installation of recruitment/retention plan.

In this function of the model, preparation is made for the implementation of the program. Action is taken to meet requirements for space, resources, and human services. In addition, personnel are trained or informed about their roles in the program and the overall objectives used to guide the planning process. When staff, supporting personnel, and representatives of cooperating groups (professional groups, community agencies, etc.) are sufficiently knowledgeable about the program, effective operation is more likely.

6. Implement the minority recruitment and retention plan.

In the sixth function the plan is made operational. That is, it is put into action. The actual activities performed in this function will be determined by the objectives of the plan and local or institutional needs and conditions. For example, if the plan calls for a tutoring clinic in basic skill areas, in this function activities will involve opening the clinic and offering services. In addition, feedback from participants, schools, the community, and other sources can help to fine tune and smooth operation of the program.

7. Evaluate minority recruitment and retention program outcomes.

Both formative and summative evaluation are recommended. Formative evaluation is designed for the purpose of maximizing the success of an ongoing program or project during its operation (Rossi and Freeman, 1985). Formative evaluation is accomplished by the personnel associated with the program during its operation. It enables problems and deficiencies to be dealt with quickly and, hopefully, effectively. Consider the following example of how formative evaluation can be used to improve the effectiveness of a program:

> A tutoring center has been established in a building near campus for a student support services program. However, three weeks into the program, evaluation of the services being provided by the center suggested that students were not using the facility. The evaluator sought to determine possible reasons for this using a survey of a random sample of ten students in the program. The survey suggested that the hours of operation of the center (between 10 am and 3 pm) conflicted with the times most required courses were scheduled. As a result, the hours of operation of the tutoring center were changed, and use by the students immediately increased.

Formative evaluation should be designed into the plan and should include systematic monitoring of progress and activities through collection of data on a regular schedule.

Summative evaluation will normally be done at the end of an academic year (but no more frequently than at the end of each semester). It focuses on the effectiveness or worth of the products of the program (e.g., number of students counseled or tutored, increase in number of students from minority backgrounds in the teacher education program, faculty members trained to work with minority students, increase in fellowships awarded to minority students, etc.). However, there might be some focus on the operation of the program as well. For example, in the summative evaluation, it might be useful to determine how frequently the program director communicated with the relevant community and civic groups, or the effectiveness of the multicultural curriculum committee in offering guidance to the program. The goals and objectives of the program should relate directly to the criteria used in the summative evaluation. The specific evaluation design should be determined by local needs and program conditions and should be planned as an integral part of the overall program.

8. Maintain recruiting and retention reference system.

The reference system is an important part of a project. It permits determination of whom the program has served and when, of the length of time and staffing required to accomplish tasks, and of the progress made at various milestones within the program. If designed and executed effectively, the evaluation activities associated within each element can provide the data for the reference system. These data can be organized into a useful database using traditional data storage and cataloging methods. Activities in this function can form the basis for subsequent program design, evaluation, and decision making.

The eight functions of the model are interrelated as shown in Figure 1. The functions should be considered overlapping, dynamic, and interactive. For example, although the first function assesses the teacher education system, this system is constantly changing. New statutes may be passed requiring changes in the teacher preparation program, and, concomitantly, administrative guidelines and requirements will need to be changed. Therefore some activities concerning the first function might be implemented at various times in the project. Further, a change in teacher certification might affect the implementation or evaluation functions, or it may have an impact on planning or objectives. Last, if the program is to continue, planning for the second year under Function Four would undoubtedly be influenced by the first year data compiled in Function Seven and maintained in Function Eight. Because of the interdependency of the functions, the model should be perceived as a system rather than as a list or hierarchy of functions and activities.

Summary and Conclusions

A successful minority recruitment and retention program will require cooperation and coordination with many different groups. Some are on campus, others in the schools and community, and still others include teachers, alumni, business groups, and professional associations. In addition, the program should be designed to meet the various cultural and ethnic characteristics of the students. It requires faculty and staff training, and constant monitoring and evaluation. Further, it must be flexible to meet changing needs and conditions. The eight function model presented above offers a framework for dealing with the complexities of designing such a program.

Local setting may require consideration of different specific elements, or emphasis on other ideas or strategies. A program that plans to serve only ten students per semester (about 40 students in a four-year program at one time) will require a different design than one that expects to serve fifty students per semester (or 200 students in a four-year teacher preparation program). Additionally, a program designed to serve only one ethnic minority may be designed differently than one that expects to serve a variety of minorities (e.g., Black Americans, Mexican-Americans, Cubans, Haitians, and Asians). Thus, the model is provided to help guide planning and development of specific program objectives and design features rather than a cookbook for all minority recruitment and retention programs.

Reference Note

[1]An earlier version of this paper appears in the *Proceedings of the National Invitational Conference on Recruitment and Retention of Minority Students in Teacher Education*, Lexington, KY, March 29-31, 1987.

Figure 1
Eight Functions in the Model for Recruitment and Retention of Minority Students in Teacher Preparation Programs

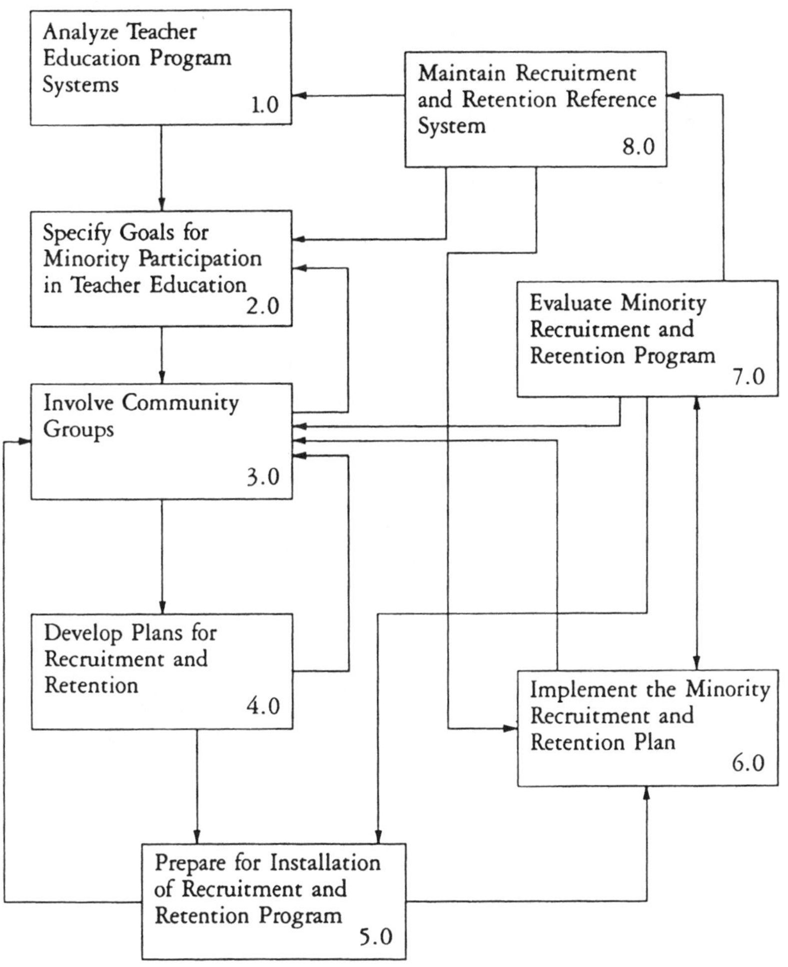

References

Barton, E. J., & Osborne, J. G. (1978). The development of classroom sharing by a teacher using positive practice. *Behavior Modification, 2,* 231-250.

Brophy, J., & Putnam, J. (1979). Classroom management in the elementary grades. In D. Duke (Ed.), *Classroom management* (The Eighty-eighth yearbook of the National Society for the Study of Education) (pp. 182-216). Chicago: University of Chicago Press.

Graham, P. A. (1987). Black teachers: A drastically scarce resource. *Phi Delta Kappan, 68,* 598-605.

Hackley, L. V. (1985). The decline in the number of black teachers can be reversed. *Educational Measurement: Theory and Practice, 4* (3), 17-19.

Hanes, M. L., & Hanes, M. L. (1986-87). Broader perspective for teacher recruitment. *Action in Teacher Education, 8* (4), 1-5.

Hawley, W. D. (1986). Toward a comprehensive strategy for addressing the teacher shortage. *Phi Delta Kappan, 67,* 712-718.

Heller, S. (1986, Sept. 10). Women flock to graduate school in record numbers, but fewer blacks are entering the pipeline. *Chronicle of Higher Education,* pp. 1, 24.

Hussain, K. M. (1973). *Development of information systems for education.* Englewood Cliffs, NJ: Prentice-Hall.

Kortokrax-Clark, D. (1986). The minority teacher shortage: An overview and a solution. *Action in Teacher Education, 8* (4), 7-13.

Kotler, P., & Fox, K. F. A. (1985). *Strategic marketing for educational institutions.* Englewood Cliffs, NJ: Prentice-Hall.

Mason, E. J., Prus, J., & Stilwell, W. E. (1976). A systems model for facilitating passage of school law. *Planning and changing, 6,* 221-230.

Meichenbaum, D. (1977). *Cognitive behavior modification.* New York: Plenum.

Middleton, E. J., & Mason, E. J. (1987). *Proceedings of the National Invitational Conference on the Recruitment and Retention of Minority Students in Teacher Education.* Lexington, KY: College of Education, University of Kentucky.

Reed, D. F. (1986). Wanted: More Black teacher education students. *Action in Teacher Education, 8* (1), 31-36.

Rossi, P. H., & Freeman, H. E. (1985). *Education: A systematic approach* (3rd Ed.). Beverly Hills, CA: Sage.

Stilwell, W. E. (1976a). A systems approach for implementing an affective education program. *Counselor Education and Supervision, 15,* 200-210.

Stilwell, W. E. (1976b). A systems approach to social-, educational-, or institutional change. In L. C. Silvern (Ed.), *Application of systems thinking to the administration of instruction.* Los Angeles: Educational and Training Consultants.

Stilwell, W. E., Buffington, P. W., DeMers, S. T., Stilwell, D. N. (1984). Integrating school psychological education programs: A comprehensive checklist. *School Counselor, 31,* 249-255.

Stilwell, W. E., DeMers, S. T., & Niquette, G. F. (1985). Mental health programs in schools: Primary, secondary, and tertiary interventions. In S. I. Pfeiffer (Ed.) *Clinical child psychology* (pp. 365-397). Orlando: Grune & Stratton.

Zuk, D. A., & Stilwell, W. E. (1984). Taming the beast: A comprehensive model for the implementation of microcomputers in education. *Education, 104,* 377-384.

Figure 1

[illegible] Model for [illegible] Internet [illegible]

[illegible]

Minority Recruitment and Retention in Teacher Education: A Southwestern Perspective [1, 2, 3]

Marigold Linton
Director, Educational Services
Arizona State University

"My uncle left the reservation and I heard he had gone to college. A few years later I heard he had gotten a good job. That seemed pretty good to me, so I decided to go to college -- whatever that was -- and so I did."

An Indian graduate

When I talked to that Indian graduate, although he was two decades younger and our reservations a continent apart, I was irresistibly drawn to ask some questions about the isolation of his reservation. How far was his reservation from the closest town? How large was the town? "There was only one road to our reservation in those days," he said, "and we were 10 miles from the closest town, a hamlet with about 3,000 people." My own reservation 35 years ago had two roads, and was 3 miles from a town of 10,000. So close and yet to both of us "college" -- whatever that was -- seemed unutterably remote from our world.

The concrete teepees that marked the boundary of my reservation created in my mind an unbridgeable chasm between Indian's and White Man's world. Shortly before my 18th birthday, passing symbolically between those stone teepees, I went away to college. I was filled with terror and with questions which, even when I could articulate them, no one answered adequately. I have always felt this wrenching experience was trivialized by calling it "culture shock." A shock connotes to me a brief, or transitory phenomenon. It might better be called "cultural tectonics" to convey the idea of land masses coming together and resting uneasily upon each other. Even when their coexistence is quiet, there is the promise of additional adjustment, contortion, and change. The impact I experienced was devastating at first, and it remained a powerful and pervasive force in my life for more than two decades.

I know now what I did not even suspect at 18, that I was asking, not "What is college?" but "What does college mean in White Man's world?" "What does college mean to an Indian?" "Who am I going to be after I have 'gone to college'?" "Who am I and what am I doing?" Those were not easy questions to answer in the '50s, and are not easy questions to answer now, even if the listener can understand the plea for help behind the quiet question.

These experiences directly inform the recruitment and retention program my office has developed for minority students at Arizona State University's College of Education. In the 1990's, at universities as large as this 42,000-student institution, minority recruitment and retention operations are enormously complex. We appreciate the contributions of many individuals and programs althoughwe are unable to describe specific linkages or acknowledge them in this paper .

A caveat: although this information seems not to be widely understood, I trust that individuals involved in minority recruitment and retention recognize that by this time in our history there is no standard Native American (just as there is no standard Hispanic or African American or person of other ethnic background). Native Americans come from different tribes with different traditions (in Arizona there are 14 different tribal groups and 20 reservations in addition to urban Indians whose tribal roots span the country), they may or may not be attached to a reservation (relocation efforts have been going on almost intermittently from our country's beginning so that Indian attachment to reservation comes in every degree), and they have a full range of skills, experiences, and aspirations. Not every Indian wishes to return to the reservation just as not every Indian aspires to the "better life" off the reservation. And, students change over time in their understanding of themselves as Indians and of their relationship to their reservation/people.

In response to strong community pressures to increase the number of minorities in Arizona State University's teacher preparation program, the College of Education, some years ago created an Office of Educational Services whose responsibilities included the recruitment and retention of minorities. Among minority students, although education is perhaps less attractive than engineering or business, there has been considerable interest in teaching. Many students who wish to become teachers, however, encounter serious difficulties in reaching this goal. Thus the Office of Educational Services's primary task has been to nurture and assure the success of those individuals who have already indicated a strong interest in the teaching profession.

In this paper I focus on the major challenges students face before they even begin the teacher preparation course work The Office of Educational Services provides one cornerstone "service" to minority students. In response to the demand for better teachers, the Arizona State Legislature some years ago imposed a requirement that students must pass a basic skills test, the Pre-Professional Skills Test (PPST), before being admitted to a teacher preparation program. As will become clear later, this test is a curious mixture of a barrier and a unique opportunity. Our office helps minority students to pass this test -- and uses this period of contact to create stable and lasting relationships with students.

In the following section I discuss only how the test and the services are made understandable to the students. ("I've just learned I have to pass the PPST -- whatever that is.") The importance of making programs understandable cannot be overstated. In a later section I describe tutoring and its relationship to recruitment.

MAJOR CHALLENGE #1: "NO ONE EVER TOLD ME."

One poignant comment we often hear from minority (but especially from Native American) students is "No one ever told me that." The comment has been applied to virtually every element of the College's requirements, criteria, deadlines, etc. Because the College and University provide numerous orientations, and since all of the deadlines, criteria, and the like are published in bulletins, handouts, and posted on walls, staff hearing yet another "No one ever told me that" are understandably irritated and impatient.

More than other students, ASU's minority students fail to attend orientations, fail to respond to announcements about deadlines, fail to petition when their program is derailed, and so on. It is obvious that if students are to succeed they must absorb this material. Are our students merely careless or thoughtless? Do they expect to be catered to? Are they doing things on "Indian time?" In finding my own answer I think of the student who said, "So I decided to go to college -- whatever that was." I think of the years of puzzlement I experienced when I first left the reservation -- about social and academic cues that I missed. Humans are very similar on this score. We can only focus on and absorb a limited number of novel stimuli at one time. When we are inundated with the novelty of a different world our ability to cope becomes diminished.

Can it be as easy for the minority student to absorb endless new and alien information as it is for you or me? Sometimes the scale of change required is enormous. Students have questions about everything. "What is college or university all about?" "How do I pay for my college education?" "How will my education affect my relationships with my spouse, my family, my people?" "What will I do with my degree?" The problem for university staff is to provide information so it is less alien, so it can be absorbed into the education or life schema the students presently possess. How do you present information so it can be processed and understood and so that students can make decisions that will meet their needs?

We discover, as parents do in trying to provide their children much needed information about the worlds of work, of sex, or of education, that students/children only hear messages when they are ready, when they are motivated, when the message becomes salient. The problem thus becomes, not only how to present the information, but how to be available when the students are ready for the message.

Pushing "Readiness before the Crisis." A number of critical issues were encountered in developing the College's recruitment/ tutoring program. Of primary importance, minority students must be alerted to the basic skills requirement and begin work on it as early as two years before they wish to enter the teacher preparation program.

Because the PPST is the most time consuming barrier to the students' progress, we focus a major portion of our energies around it. We identify students as early as possible, help them understand how crucial it is to begin planning for the PPST immediately, and then persuade them the preparation should start TODAY.

Although staff, faculty, and the students themselves lose track of the need for such a long preparation period, the need is made clear by the following statistics: 1) In the state of Arizona 38% of Hispanics pass the test on the first occasion, 26% of the Blacks, and only 10% of the Native Americans. In contrast, 64% of the nonminorities pass the test on the first occasion. 2) The last qualifying test (that is, the final test students can complete and still have their scores posted in time to permit admission) occurs 6 to 9 months before the beginning of the target semester. 3) Many minority students require from 25 to 200 hours of special classes, tutoring or other forms of psychological and academic support to prepare them adequately for the test. These facts leave little question about the urgency of notifying minority students of the basic skills requirements and seeking them out for early tutoring and support.

Minority students who seek services a prudent six months before they plan to enter the teacher preparation program, often wonder why "no one ever told them" about this requirement. Some, it is true, have simply never heard of the test. Most, however, lack experience with the degree of planning necessary to negotiate a complex set of time locked demands like these. And the dismal truth is that the Native Americans, with their low PPST pass rates and their lack of experience in negotiating their way through the university's complex pathways, are presented with a problem many times more difficult than the one facing their minority and nonminority colleagues.

A typical persuasive session asks the students "When do you plan to enter the program?" "When do you suppose is the last test that will permit you to enter our program?" Most students are very much surprised by the answer. Sadly, despite our outreach, about one third of the students have already missed the qualifying test for their projected admission date when we talk to them the first time. (We assure they get advice on classes to take during the "time out" semesters.) When we have identified the (next) appropriate qualifying test, we begin to talk about their plans to prepare for the test. Our goal at this point is to induce them to take our "NEW IMPROVED FREE DIAGNOSTIC BASIC SKILLS TEST." The diagnostic test, we promise, is the first important step toward teacher certification. The test, we emphasize, tells them where they stand right now. On the basis of the test results, we will advise them specifically about the amount of work they need to prepare for the

PPST and provide them, at no cost, the tutoring they need.

Packaging, and thinking from the students' point of view, is crucial throughout this process. When we originally developed our basic skills support program this preliminary test was conceptualized as a "pretest" whose primary value was to tell us about program effectiveness. This thought is so alien now it is hard to imagine the frame of mind from which it seemed natural. We were struggling with the kinds of classes or tutoring we should provide. We were struggling to justify our funding. Our first priority seemed to be, "Would the program work?" (The question was important because one early 15-week math class we offered lowered students scores an average of one point.)

Although students were happy to receive tutoring or to take classes, wild horses could not get them to take the "pretest". Reconceptualizing the test as one that tells students, rather than us, where they stand, and the inspiration to relabel the test as a "diagnostic test" has transformed this early test into a best seller. In 1990 alone we gave about 200 diagnostic tests to minority students with the number increasing each year.

We try never to let students out of our clutches without obtaining names and telephone numbers, and without making a specific appointment for them to take the diagnostic test or to begin tutoring. All of our students have busy lives around which we must schedule our activities. We give them the test, at their convenience, at any time during the 40-hour work week. (We would love to offer night or weekend tests, but we simply cannot staff the office at those times.) They either make an appointment, or we set a time when, after checking their schedules, they will call us. They are told that if they fail to call us, we will call them. We remind them that getting started right now is important, that we do not want them to put it off.

In most cases we make our sale and the students take the diagnostic test. We must then bridge the gap between this excellent behavior, and the next set of crucial behaviors -- planning some specific and timely preparation for the anticipated PPST. About one in 25 of the minority students we serve are ready to take the test immediately. After a round of cheers, we direct them to the University Testing Service which conducts the test, but ask that they report back to us if they have any difficulties.

The remaining students must be provided clear and useful feedback regarding their own basic skills performance. This feedback which may be disastrous to the individuals' self-esteem must be provided sensitively but in a form that spurs them to further action.

We begin our discussions about the students' basic skills armed with information from either their diagnostic test or their latest PPST. In one case we have PPST scores, in the other PPST-like scores. The PPST's curious scoring system in which 150 means no items correct while 190 indicates perfect performance, often misleads students (both minority and nonminority) about their chances of succeeding the next time they take the test. For example, students see a score of 165 in reading, place themselves implicitly on the number line from 0 to the passing score of 173 and understandably conclude they are indeed very close to passing. They conclude wrongly but reasonably that no one so close to passing, should require tutoring.

In the early phases of our program it seemed obvious to us that students needed to understand the scale, and we explained the scale carefully. We tried to convince students that they still had a long way to go and that considerable work was necessary. We were surprised that these efforts to focus students' energies on preparing for the test were not improved by explanations about the scale. How then were we to prevail? As a first step in solving the problem, we shifted to descriptions of student performance in terms of grade levels. For example, a person with reading scores of 163 has difficulty with 6th and 7th grade comprehension questions. Thus we might say, "You are reading at about the 6th grade level. You must read and comprehend at the 10th or 11th grade level in order to pass the test. You have a lot of work to do before the next test -- can we schedule you for a tutoring appointment?" Our candor did not, as many feared, scare students off. We found, however, that this feedback had only slightly more impact on student attendance at tutoring sessions than did feedback about the scale. Students still did not do "a lot of work" in preparing for the test.

Again we asked, "Why not?" and decided that the students did not share our sense of what "a lot of work" meant. We were presenting an alien concept, an alien test and suggesting some alien strategies to deal with them. How could we make the information more user friendly? Our second relabelling inspiration was to translate scores into number of hours of work required. Our best guess was that five hours of tutoring on the average produced about one point change on the test. Although our scheme for determining the number of hours of assistance students need is somewhat more complex, we basically take the number of points a given student needs to improve, multiply by five, and sum across tests. But we do not stop there. We learn what test students want to pass, a target that may be 2 weeks, 2 months, or 6 months away. We divide the number of hours of tutoring required by weeks remaining and tell students how many hours of preparation they require each week.

The outcomes were a revelation to everyone. We had been thinking in general terms of 20 to 40 hours of preparation (although we knew from experience that this was not enough for some). Students were thinking of 5 to 10 hours (although students requiring so little work are quite rare). Based on our "1 point/5 hours" rule, our new estimates indicate that most students require 50 to 100 hours of individualized remedial preparation!

Providing this highly specific feedback has been remarkably successful with students. They understand the requirement of "7-hours work each week for the next two months." When students are not diligent, we adjust the number of hours per week. Sometimes these increasing number of hours per week remind students cogently of the task facing them. Where choice is possible we plan tutoring for "light semesters," for summers, or over Christmas vacation. We may work on reading for two months, have them pass in this area and then move on to math. We are flexible and work to maintain the students' comfort at the same time we increase their skills.

We have just completed two pilot semesters using this improved feedback. Although our statistics are not complete, we have doubled the number of students in our tutoring program, and have doubled their number of tutoring hours. Moreover, students who follow our recommendations are likely to pass, while those who do not regularly fail. We were gratified (and somewhat surprised) that our estimate of an average of 5 hours of remedial work for each deficient test point has almost always been confirmed. (Our ongoing efforts at further refinements in both prediction and tutoring are another story.)

We have succeeded in our first objective, that is, students see our tutoring help as a useful resource and we have generally succeeded in bringing them into regular and continuing contact with our office. In these contacts we interject trouble-shooting sessions to permit us to continue identifying current and future problem areas and to plan appropriate solutions. In addition, we work to integrate students into the larger College and University system, assure that they understand the complex process of admission to the teacher preparation program, and assist them in understanding -- and in meeting -- the deadlines. We promise students that we stand ready to go to bat for them if they encounter bureaucratic difficulties, but we try to be very clear about what we can and cannot do for them.

A major activity of our office is to help students plan,

prioritize, and organize their lives so they will succeed. Whenever we capture their attention we remind them of remaining opportunities, deadlines, and challenges, and we help them take the first steps to position themselves on these dimensions.

MAJOR CHALLENGE #2. "BASIC SKILLS: IT IS MORE THAN JUST READING WORDS"

"When they say that minorities can't read," he said, "they don't mean 'they can't read,' they mean, 'they can't understand.' Isn't that right?" In one way or another many of our poor readers express misunderstanding and anxiety about comprehension. "Why do they ask us about things that they don't actually say?" "I like reading fine, but I have trouble with this thinking thing." "I like practical things, but I don't care for this AB-STRACK thought." And anxiety about mathematics seems to breed mysteriously in the dark corners. "I can do calculations and even algebra, but what do all those words have to do with math?" "When I start working on math, my hands sweat and my stomach hurts."

The PPST is frightening to our students precisely because it demands abstract thought, understanding the meaning of words, and well-developed problem solving skills. For some students these are the ultimate alien demands of an alien culture.

We have brought our students to the table. Once again we try to expand their worlds, to help them see not only this but all other educational experiences in a more holistic way. And, we do provide them the basic skills that they require. Let me begin by describing the framework from which we work, and then in a later section I shall briefly outline some of our tutoring methods. We view all of these methods as crucial to our recruitment and retention efforts.

We follow several simple principles. 1) We emphasize the value of basic skills. We avoid suggesting that the basic skills test is simply a hurdle placed there to cause minorities difficulty. Most students present themselves as being "done in" by test anxiety. While acknowledging this, we emphasize the virtue of improving basic skills themselves. We view the PPST as an attention- capturing device. During the brief period we have their full attention we want to provide them as many gifts/skills as we can. We emphasize the value and the joy of having high skill levels. 2) We emphasize the importance of life-long learning. We model curiosity. We play simple intellectual games (ones that we enjoy, but that they can understand). 3) We emphasize that all of us are in the learning process together. We don't, for example, have smart staff and dumb students. We model staff trying to solve problems and sometimes solving them and sometimes not. The activity is always done with good humor and gusto, and with the promise of returning to try again if the problem can not be solved today. 4) We talk a lot about the values they themselves have, both the good and the bad, that they will pass on to their students. We remind them how important it is that their fear and avoidance of math not be passed on. We remind students that all of us have areas in which learning is difficult. The issue is not to avoid the anxiety, not to move off to other things, but to work through it and emerge victorious at the end.

<u>How do we gauge the success of these interventions?</u> When I read

descriptions such as the preceding, I always wonder what authors mean and how these grand notions should be translated. But it is obviously important for us to assess how well we do and how well our students succeed. We judge the success of our interventions in some of the following ways: Students may report that they have taken a hard class that they had previously avoided. They may stop selecting classes on the basis their being the easiest ones available. They may stop saying "I hate biology" and move to "Biology is not bad" to "I'm starting to get an idea of what biology is all about" to "That classification stuff we talk about is the same thing they're doing in my biology class, isn't it?" And words start to have unique and complex meaning. Students often say, "I don't think I ever really understood some of this stuff I was reading."

We see students rigid, frightened, and controlled approach to problems become more relaxed and cheerful. Our office always has a student or two working on both the PPST and their present college algebra class. Most impressive to passersby are the shrieks of joy as students exclaim, "I can do it, hah! that's not so hard." One student, after going up several grade levels, reported she passed the math section of the PPST without doing any calculations. "All you have to do is think, compare, and eliminate." A major breakthrough!!

Tutoring itself. Students like the ones we deal with are remarkably interesting intellectually. Many of them are very bright. Many are very hard working. Most are extremely anxious.

Many have sets of skills that would never be predicted from their performance on a standardized test. Unpredictable and often surprising pieces of knowledge or skills may be missing while areas of sophisticated knowledge may be present. Crucial yet unexpected errors are sometimes made (e.g., a student who is passing a statistics class may believe that the products of 0 x 5 and 1 x 5 are both 5). Likewise it is not uncommon for functional classification schemes to be missing from students' schemas. For example, students may miss many PPST questions because they do not confidently know that "oranges" and "apples" are both "fruits", and that "vegetable," not "potato" is at the same level of abstraction as "fruit". Whenever we encounter such lacunae in student knowledge, we stop working on PPST-like problems and try to fill in the gaps.

Within the tutoring program itself we focus on the following things: 1) Tutors, if they do not already know how, are trained to elicit problem solving and thinking behaviors in students. We find this training a persistent and difficult task, and in particular, student tutors require considerable practice before they become effective in giving the students a chance to think, and letting the student do the work. (My rough rule is: if you, the tutor, are talking, and if you have the pencil in your hand, you are doing it wrong.) This "letting the student think it out and do the work" is particularly difficult because both tutors and students have been socialized to consider this the wrong role for tutors. Students love it when someone explains things to them. They hate it when they have to figure something out. It is always so clear when someone else solves the problem. "Now I know how to do it," they say. Of course, most often they do not.

2) We have a simple and effective "tutoring tracking" system in which student activities, assignments, scores, and other data are summarized. The tracking system makes it possible to see at a glance where the student is. In addition, the students have their own copy of materials and scores (because busy offices always lose things). 3) We perform "placement diagnostics" which tell us quite specifically where students are having difficulty. (The PPST tests tell us only how much trouble they are having.) 4) Once we have defined the problem arena, we have numerous materials to deal with a wide range of problems. For example, we have endless pamphlets, books, and exercise sets for fractions and percentages, an enduring scourge among students. 5) We have "PPST-like" tests with which we regularly test students. Regular testing is important for three reasons: First, it familiarizes students with the types of items students are likely to encounter and helps to reduce anxiety. Second, regular feedback is necessary because students often have difficulty assessing their own skills and understanding. Third, students make steady progress and seeing scores improve, is wonderfully motivating.

6) Students work alone on worksheets and other instructional materials, grade their own work and then come to the tutor to discuss problems. It is particularly important that students be able to work independently, both because encouraging independence is

essential, and because our tutors are busy and at any time each may be working with four or five students. 7) Tutors are responsible for identifying commonalities among the kinds of errors students make, and for helping to focus on possible general solutions to these problems. The struggle then becomes, how to devise strategies to help the student make the next leap in understanding. 8) We have perhaps our greatest success in improving writing. About tutoring of writing I would like to say a little more.

Our greatest difficulties are with students whose use of prepositions reflects usage from another language. We have no tricks for teaching why you get into a car, and on a bus. (I know there is someone who can make prepositional usage crystal clear, but it is not I.) We merely start with the most frequent problems, and work our way through grammar usage.

PPST essays are designed to request responses from well within the range of a typical student's experience. We have found, however, that the test or questions may be alien in a wide variety of ways. We have some remarkable and unusual essays that result from students bringing a totally different world view to bear on questions. We respond by giving a crash course on "white man's perspective." Who is going to read this question, and how are they going to understand the answer? What, for example, are the odds of a Navajo teacher reading the essay?

When we begin our training, we frequently get back empty pages reflecting 30-minutes of work. Students report that they have never had the experience they were requested to share, sometimes they say they are not supposed to talk (or write) about those things, or that they couldn't think of anything to say. Here we can greatly help students. Brainstorming can be taught. Students can be assured that it is OK to write something that is not literally true. "You need not lie," we say. "You can do something safely within your own traditions, by telling a story." One student reporting a pass (she got 11/12 points on the essay) described the heart-rending story she had told, and gleefully added, "And it was ALL made up."

We tell students that it is all right, nay, desirable, for essays to be interesting, that they should be creative, and that they should select their own unique perspective in attacking their essays. Coherence is essential. Humor is fine. Descriptions are great (and relatively easy to write). We add that their only goal is to persuade two readers that they can write. Everything is fair within that context. Many students feel they have been liberated. They love to write. No more "formula, three paragraph essays." "Go for it," we say, and they do.

Evaluation. We are dealing with a large amorphous pool. We define students into it by our contacts with them. We have a pool of minority students that numbers in the hundreds. Only a dozen of these students pass the PPST on any particular date. The others are confronting barriers (sometimes we know about them, often we have no knowledge of them). Some individuals find life's challenges too great and give up. They may be faced with hostile spouses, unsympathetic employers, too much work and too many mouths to feed, terminably unreliable transportation, exhaustion, too many classes, the intractable University bureaucracy, too great a distance from the University -- the list is endless.

We attempt to maintain contact with students (although efforts are inhibited by lack of telephones, too frequent moves, etc.). A surprising number of students reappear after long periods of time when their circumstances change or when the success of their friends inspire them.

We provide services for more than half the students in the teacher preparation program. On average we increase the test performance of students one point for every five hours they spend with us. Students spend more and more time improving their basic skills, and consider these skills to be important. They tell their friends about our services, and they come back repeatedly over time for assistance with other significant matters. ASU's students pass the PPST at a higher rate than their counterparts at the other Arizona institutions. Although the interpretation of this result can be argued, we like to think that at least part of this difference results from the services we provide our minority students.

MAJOR CHALLENGE #3. CREATING SYSTEMS ON REMOTE SITES.

In the course of the past year, the College of Education at Arizona State University has worked to develop preliminary feeder programs for several proposed off-campus teacher preparation programs. Arranging these programs, identifying staff, locating funds, and identifying and encouraging students has been enormously complex and time consuming. Each program involves minority teacher aides. One program is based in downtown Phoenix (20 minutes away), the second is located on a reservation a four-hour drive away. In each case, basic skills preparation, which I argue is central to the mission, was initially treated as a secondary issue -- something to be dealt with after staff have been found, after funds have been located, after the students have become committed, after they have completed their liberal arts courses, etc.

Statistics, such as, "on the average students will require 120 hours of tutoring or small-class work" were sobering to administrators. However, they were apprehensive that nontraditional students would be scared off by these statistics.

In one case, as a compromise, we were permitted to offer the "diagnostic test" optionally when we described our program one evening in a traditional presentation to the Indian community. Not to embarrass myself I took only 10 tests with me. On that short notice, a few hours later nine teacher aides took the test. No one passed. Scores indicated that everyone needed to do a lot of work. We wrote a clear, friendly letter of explanation, and provided an adaptation of our "Feedback Sheet." We had warned that our response might take more than a week. Because it is important in attracting students that you maintain close contact, provide clearly understandable information and show enthusiasm, we mailed our letters out in under 48 hours.

Although the full planning team did not make it back to the Reservation immediately, the testing team received a special invitation and was told that 40 people at two sites 60 miles apart wished to be tested. (Students appear to be more robust than the administrators.) Forty-one students showed up for the second test. Again we provided the feedback quickly. Although we have now exceeded the total number of Indian aides that we had anticipated in the program, we continue to receive calls indicating that additional groups of students wish to take the test.

Individual test scores were provided to the students, and group or collective scores to the administrators. At this point basic skills training moved from a peripheral to a central role in the program. It is not yet clear how we shall provide appropriate basic skills training on the Reservation but we are working to create an on-site program that captures the attention of the students. We have already become aware that the Indian students in the community are very reluctant to take "precollege" courses.

We recognize that one of our challenges will be to repackage these courses so that this stigma is lessened. The other challenges will be to encourage teaching of courses that, like ours, give students the skills they need to achieve at a high level at the university. Finally, we must find external funding to fully implement these classes.

<u>Conclusion</u>: This paper talks about preparing minority students to enter the teacher preparation program. Before the College of Education can achieve its mission of increasing the number of minority students <u>completing</u> the teacher preparation program a number of related activities must be successfully completed. Each of these processes recognizes the pervasive differences among our

student clients. We have found that providing students repeated opportunities to see the larger picture combined with frequently repeated painstakingly detailed information about how to approach their next educational steps makes it possible for students to move successfully toward at their goals.

Large numbers of students seek out our program and appreciate its immediate consequences of helping them pass the state mandated basic skills test. We hope that for some students it also produces long term changes in their approach to the educational world.

Coda

At the beginning of this paper I suggested the phrase "cultural tectonics" to label the powerful and pervasive conflicting forces that dominated my life for more than two decades. I am concerned that this implies that at middle age these powerful forces have utterly disappeared. The following vignette suggests how permanently our vastly different experiences shape our world view.

"It was so terrible, they came and took Grandma away, put her in the hospital, hooked her up to all those tubes. It was sad to see her that way."

Grieving Indian woman, B.A., M.A.

(About the same woman.) "It was so terrible, the old woman pulled out the IVs, somehow got out of the hospital, and crawled out behind a bush. We couldn't find her and she died there in the dirt. We couldn't have saved her but we could have made her comfortable during those last hours. I feel so terrible that we failed her."

A White M.D.

(About the same woman.) "At least Grandma escaped that place. She was able to die at peace and with dignity."

Grieving Indian woman, B.A., M.A.

Footnote 1. This chapter is organized in a nonlinear way. Those who find this style difficult to read should either skip the chapter or go directly to the section: "Major Challenge #1: No One Ever Told Me" where a more systematic description begins.

Footnote 2. In this paper I move back and forth between describing a program for Native Americans and for minorities. Indeed most of our students are non-Indian, although we have an impressive number of Native Americans in the pipeline. Our procedures are highly flexible, we fine tune them to meet the needs of each student who enters our office. As a result we have experienced success with a wide range of students.

Footnote 3. I wish to acknowledge my tutor/collaborators on this project who have shared the vision, have been responsible for insights, and who have implemented programmatic changes with remarkable speed. Without this group of flexible and caring individuals such a program cannot succeed. In 1990-1991, Karen Brighton, Prasad Vajjhala, and Roza Ferdosmakan comprised this remarkable team. For the anecdotes and quotes, I am indebted to a number of people. Karen Brighton and Phyllis Gagnier have been especially rich sources of the ideas these stories reflect. Phyllis Gagnier has been a collaborator from the beginning of our support services and continues to lend wise counsel. Gina Mascolo-Saleh, a teacher in preparation, also made a major contribution to our office during the years she worked here.

National Forum on Personnel Needs for Districts with Changing Demographics

Staffing the Multilingually Impacted Schools of the 1990s

May 1990

This Forum Report was prepared with partial funding from the United States Department of Education, Office of Bilingual Education and Minority Languages Affairs (OBEMLA). The opinions expressed in this report do not necessarily reflect the positions or policies of OBEMLA or the United States Department of Education.

ACKNOWLEDGEMENTS

On January 11-12, 1990, with the support of the Secretary of Education, Dr. Lauro F. Cavazos, the Office of Bilingual Education and Minority Languages Affairs (OBEMLA) convened a National Forum of educators to assess the personnel needs of districts with changing demographics. This is the first time that OBEMLA has invited school superintendents and other educators to Washington, D.C. for the express purpose of soliciting their advice. The objective of the Forum was to solicit input for planning and establishing OBEMLA's training program priorities for the coming decade. Forum participants identified several areas of concern and made recommendations to address staff training needs, in light of the rapid increases now taking place in the numbers of limited English proficient (LEP) students. OBEMLA will take their suggestions into consideration in planning and establishing future training priorities.

The Forum could not have been possible without the support of Secretary Cavazos. I would like to take this opportunity to thank him for his leadership.

I would also like to thank the following members of my staff for their contribution to the development of this report:

Dr. John Ovard
Ms. Harpreet Sandhu
Mr. William Wooten
Ms. Catalina Wilkison

In addition, I would like to recognize Ms. Robin Billington and Ms. Velma Robinson for providing logistical support for the Forum.

My special thanks to Dr. James Alatis and Dr. Rudy Chavez for their invaluable comments during the preparation of this report, and to Mr. Douglas Katz of Wasserman-Katz, who played a vital role in facilitating the Forum sessions.

Finally, I would like to express my appreciation to the Forum participants for their valuable contributions and for taking time out of their busy schedules to attend this Forum.

Rita Esquivel

CONTENTS

FORUM PARTICIPANTS

Dr. James Alatis
Dean, School of Languages and Linguistics
Georgetown University

Dr. Charles Almo
Interim General Superintendent of Schools
Chicago Public Schools

Dr. Jack Ammons
Superintendent
Brownsville Independent School District

Dr. Robert Bailey
Superintendent
Busby School District

Dr. Leonard Britton
Superintendent
Los Angeles City Public Schools

Dr. Rudy Chavez
Director, MRC
Arizona State University

Dr. John R. Correiro
Superintendent
Fall River Public Schools

Dr. Rudolph F. Crew
Superintendent
Sacramento City U.S.D.

Mr. Peter A. Eissele
Assistant Superintendent for Human Resources
Albuquerque Public Schools

Dr. Donna B. Evans
Dean, College of Education
Wayne State University

Dr. Herman S. Garcia
Associate Professor of
Bilingual Education
Texas A&M University

Dr. Terrence Garner
Director of Personnel
Dade County Public Schools

Dr. Tom Giugni
Superintendent
Long Beach U.S.D.

Dr. Ira Goldenberg
Dean, College of Education
Florida International University

Mr. Angel N. Gonzalez
Deputy Superintendent
Houston I.S.D.

Mr. Benjamin Gutierrez
Director of Personnel
Edgewood I.S.D.

Dr. Mark Karadenes
Assistant Superintendent
Santa Monica-Malibu U.S.D.

Ms. Carolyn Kelly
Personnel Director
Tucson Unified S.D.

Dr. Margie K. Kitano
Associate Dean for Faculty Development and Research
San Diego State Univ.

Ms. Michele Kostem
Assistant Superintendent
Bethlehem Area S.D.

Mr. Hank Oyama
Associate Vice President
Multi-disciplinary Education and Services
Pima Community College

Dr. Ronald S. Lemos
Assistant Vice Chancellor
The California State University System

FORUM PARTICIPANTS CONTINUED

Mr. Andrew Raicevich
Executive Director
Division of Human Resources
Denver Public Schools

Dr. Alba Rosenmann
Associate Professor
of Secondary Education
Director, Bilingual Education
Ball State University

Ms. Nilda Soto Ruiz
Deputy Executive Director
Office of Recruitment
and Counseling
New York City Board of Education

Dr. John Steffens
Assistant Vice Provost
Public Responsibility
and Current Affairs
University of Oklahoma

Dr. Maria Torres
Director, Program in
Bilingual/Bicultural
Education
Columbia University
Teachers College

Dr. James R. Wood
Superintendent
United Independent S.D.

U.S. Department of Education

Dr. Ted Sanders
Under Secretary
U.S. Department of Education

Dr. Daniel Bonner (A)
Deputy Assistant Secretary
Office of Elementary
and Secondary Education

Ms. Rita Esquivel
Director
Office of Bilingual Education
and Minority Languages Affairs

Dr. Leonard L. Haynes, III
Assistant Secretary
Office of Postsecondary
Education

Ms. Nancy Kennedy
Assistant Secretary
Office of Legislation
and Congressional Affairs

Mr. Charles E. M. Kolb
Deputy Under Secretary
Office of Planning,
Budget and Evaluation

Dr. John T. MacDonald
Assistant Secretary
Office of Elementary
and Secondary Education

Dr. Gilbert D. Roman
Deputy Assistant Secretary
for Operations
Office of Civil Rights

Dr. William L. Smith (A)
Assistant Secretary
Office of Civil Rights

OBEMLA Senior Staff

Ms. Robin Billington
Mr. Rudolph J. Munis
Dr. John S. Ovard
Dr. Carmen Simich-Dudgeon
Ms. Catalina Wilkison
Mr. William A. Wooten

EXECUTIVE SUMMARY

On January 11-12, 1990, the U.S. Department of Education, Office of Bilingual Education and Minority Languages Affairs (OBEMLA) sponsored a Forum on "Staffing the Multilingually Impacted Schools of the 1990s."

KEY FORUM FINDINGS

Forum participants reported a rapid and significant increase in the number of limited English proficient (LEP) students throughout the country. In this regard, they made the following observations:

- Local education agencies (LEAs) are experiencing significant increases, both in the total number of LEP students and in the number of languages represented.
- Increases in the number of LEP students are occurring even in school districts with declining enrollments.
- Many students of all ages are entering school with limited or no previous schooling in addition to the inability to speak English.

The rapid increases in the number of LEP students is compounding the existing problem of bilingual/ESL (English as a Second Language) staff shortages. Participants voiced the following concerns with regard to their ability to staff LEP student classrooms:

- It is difficult to locate trained and certified teachers to work with LEP students.
- It is difficult to retain bilingual/ESL staff due to a variety of factors, such as competition among districts striving to attract bilingual/ESL staff through salary incentives.
- There is a need for re-training of monolingual teachers in school districts where the decline in overall enrollment does not permit the hiring of trained bilingual/ESL staff.

At the conclusion of the two-day Forum, participants made the following recommendations:

- Certification requirements for bilingual/ESL personnel should be streamlined.

- The corporate (private sector) community should be encouraged to take a more active role in promoting the educational success of LEP students.
- Dialogue and collaboration among institutions of higher education (IHEs), local education agencies (LEAs), and the U.S. Department of Education should be increased.
- A greater effort should be made to disseminate information about effective and promising practices in the field of bilingual/ESL education.
- LEAs should encourage school principals to fully integrate bilingual/ESL education staff into the school program.

Additional recommendations recorded in the conference proceedings, call for:

- The establishment of career ladders to provide formal training for aides, para-professionals, and other support staff.
- The involvement of more community colleges in the training of bilingual/ESL staff.
- The use of discretionary points to favor grant applications of first time applicants, i.e. schools not previously funded.

FORUM REPORT

On January 11-12, 1990, the U.S. Department of Education, Office of Bilingual Education and Minority Languages Affairs (OBEMLA) sponsored a Forum on "Staffing the Multilingually Impacted Schools of the 1990s." School superintendents, personnel directors, and university representatives from key institutions across the nation, along with Department of Education personnel, met to discuss the staffing needs for bilingual education in the coming decade. This report presents the findings and recommendations of the Forum participants.

I. FINDINGS

The Demographic Setting

National school enrollment information for 1988 indicates that of the 40 million children in public schools, almost 2 million, or 5 percent fit the definition of limited English proficient. The information provided by the Forum participants confirms these national figures. Additionally, they identified four growth patterns affecting staffing needs. The first is the continued rapid growth of LEP enrollment in districts with previously large concentrations of LEP students. The second is the proliferation of a variety of native languages in school districts. The third is the increase in the number of districts enrolling LEP students. Last, but perhaps most significant, is that these trends exist even in those districts that are reporting overall decreases in total school enrollment.

Los Angeles typifies school districts which are experiencing continued growth in their already significant LEP populations. Their LEP student population has grown from 15 percent of the total population in 1980, to 31 percent in 1989. For the state of California as a whole the number of LEP students increased by 16 percent in 1988, after averaging an 8 percent increase for the previous four years. For example, Long Beach Unified School District, had a LEP enrollment of 18,000 in 1989 (an increase of 20 percent from 1988) representing 44 languages. In two Texas school districts, Brownsville and Laredo, the LEP population is one third of the total enrollment (51 percent of the K-6 enrollment in Brownsville is LEP). More importantly, the future trend is for an increasing LEP population.

Urban centers such as Chicago and New York provide examples of the nationwide proliferation of various native languages. Each has student bodies which include speakers of over 100 languages. Although Spanish is the most frequently encountered language in federal bilingual/ESL programs, over 30 percent also serve students speaking such diverse languages as Apache, Arabic, Cherokee, Chinese, Greek, Korean, Russian, Tagalog, and Urdu. The LEP population seems to be scattering throughout the country as various ethnic groups seeking jobs, move from their original ports of entry and resettle elsewhere. For example, Fall River, Massachusetts, an area with a traditionally low LEP enrollment, experienced an increase of 67 percent from 1985-1990, and now has joined Brownsville and Laredo, Texas in having a one-third LEP enrollment. Similarly, Lowell, Massachusetts, has experienced an increase due to secondary migration. According to Superintendent Leonard Britton of Los Angeles (previously Superintendent of Dade County, Florida), "The situation will have an impact on the entire country during the coming decade." To address this need OBEMLA conducted a special grant award competition in 1989 to assist recently (within the previous two years) impacted school districts. Fifty-five school districts applied for funds to serve recent enrollees. In recognition of this need Secretary Cavazos has proposed to conduct a similar competition in 1991.

Finally, all these gains and redistributions in LEP enrollments are occurring at a time when overall student enrollments are declining. Districts as geographically separated as Chicago, San Antonio, Busby (Montana), and Santa Monica (California) reported significant increase in LEP students despite a decline in their overall enrollment.

Staffing the Schools of the 1990s

The Forum participants, consisting of superintendents, assistant superintendents for personnel, and representatives from various colleges and universities, described four demographic trends that have major implications for staffing patterns in school districts. The most widely shared findings on this issue were: qualified new staff are hard to find and equally difficult to retain; existing staff are not adequately prepared to provide services to LEP students and the problem is aggravated by the increasing number of LEP students; and staffing needs extend beyond the classroom and include a wide array of support staff such as counselors, psychologists, nurses, and therapists.

In the field of bilingual/ESL education, as well as in others, teacher education, in the broader sense of the word, is still the heart of the matter. As people with a first language other than English choose to live in a wider variety of communities, it becomes crucial that teachers and schools are prepared to serve children who are either LEP, or come from a home where a language other than English is spoken. Whether or not bilingual/ESL staff are available, the monolingual teacher must be trained to meet the special needs and concerns of these children.

Although Los Angeles considers itself successful in its recruiting and hiring efforts for bilingual/ESL education staff, their success has been tempered by an ever increasing number of LEP enrollees. The system faces a shortage of almost 2,500 trained bilingual elementary teachers and 400 trained bilingual secondary school teachers. The California State Department of Education's latest report of the Superintendents' Task Force on LEP Student Issues, published in May 1990, estimates the present shortage of bilingual teachers and language development specialists (ESL) at 20,000. Additionally, they are struggling with the problem of having over half of their present bilingual staff teaching under waivers. In many other districts these shortages are a present day reality as eligible LEP students can not receive bilingual or ESL instruction for want of trained instructional staff.

Finding trained and certified staff is difficult in bilingual/ESL education. One reason is the number of additional courses and the language proficiency required for certification. Another is the variability of certification requirements over time and from state to state. Finally, in some districts, a vacancy must occur before a bilingual/ESL teacher can be hired. According to one Forum participant, Dade County, Florida could use 1,500 qualified bilingual/ESL teachers, but has no vacancies to hire them. Once staff are recruited they face the "last-hired first fired" practice common to most school districts.

II. IMPLICATIONS

The changing demographics of the American classroom and the demand for qualified, talented, well-trained teachers has already affected the entire education system. The special instructional needs of LEP children are highly significant within the context of these changes. The way we respond to their needs will influence the nature of the American work force in the next century, and perhaps the very nature of the American society. Will we be able to continue as a nation which offers opportunity to succeed to all students, or will we foster a two-tier society? The participants at the Forum believed that we must take action now to ensure that this opportunity is available to all American school children.

Forum participants concluded that IHEs, LEAs, and state education agencies (SEAs) must set aside questions of "turf" and "precedence" and be prepared to assist one another to meet the current challenges. They called for the federal government to do a better job of providing leadership and facilitating improvements in staff training. Forum participants recognized that funding increases, although desirable, are not likely. However, better targeting of available funds and dissemination of the results of successful projects can help fill funding gaps. Finally, they stressed the importance of developing an awareness within the private sector (corporations and community service organizations) of the significance of educating LEP children. Support from the private sector will help provide children with the tools to fully participate in our society, while ensuring that the American workforce remains competitive in the international arena.

III. RECOMMENDATIONS

New Modes of Cooperation

Institutions of higher education, local and state education agencies, the federal government, and the private sector must cooperate more effectively. The following are areas specifically targeted by Forum participants.

Certification Requirements

A comprehensive catalogue of state certification requirements should be compiled to determine which competencies and qualifications are shared. Greater reciprocity among states should be explored. IHEs should facilitate transfer of credits in bilingual/ESL education from one institution to another and should be more mindful of certification requirements. Alternative certification should be pursued particularly for persons speaking "non-traditional" languages, such as Cambodian and Hmong. Research is needed on the impact of various state certification policies on bilingual/ESL education program achievement and the potential role of paraprofessionals (non-certified) or alternatively certified teachers in the classroom.

Private Sector Involvement

As the demographics of the workforce change the private sector should become more interested in improving the English language proficiency and education level of future workers. Also, the educational community should take on a more active role in soliciting support for bilingual/ESL education programs from the private sector.

Federal Leadership

The U.S. Department of Education can assist in these activities by:

1. Encouraging more dialogue and collaboration among IHEs, LEAs, and the Department of Education;

2. Facilitating business roundtables to discuss the importance of these programs for the workplace;

3. Encouraging better coordination and flexibility of federal resources at the local level (Migrant Education, Head Start, Bilingual Education, etc.);

4. Providing leadership in the review of certification requirements and increased reciprocity between states; and

5. Improving dissemination of information about effective and promising practices.

New Modes of Personnel Development

Forum participants believed that preparation of personnel for the bilingual and ESL classrooms and school settings could be improved in the following areas:

Recruiting and Encouraging Bilingual/ESL Education Staff

LEAs need to emphasize the recruitment of staff prepared to serve LEP students. LEAs should establish career ladders to prepare bilingual aides for teaching positions. Once recruited, staff should be supported and fully integrated into the school program. LEAs should encourage principals to ensure that the bilingual/ESL education program is not thought of as an adjunct program.

Enhancing Training

Inservice training should include: the most up-to-date assessments of student needs and effective teaching techniques, strategies for teaching previously unschooled students, and methodologies that are effective in teaching subject matter areas such as mathematics and science. Specific training in bilingual/ESL education should be required, not only for teaching positions, but for a variety of support and administrative staff positions. At a minimum, training should develop awareness of difficulties facing LEP children. A bilingual/ESL education component should be incorporated into existing staff development programs and focus especially on monolingual teachers who have LEP students in their classrooms.

Schools of Education

Participants agreed that institutions of higher education need to reassess the type of services they deliver, and the mode of delivery. They should consider inservice, on-site training as a legitimate component of their certification programs. They should consciously design programs for training the monolingual teacher who may never acquire bilingual/ESL certification, but has an important role in the education of LEP children. Finally, they should be conscious of the needs of non-teachers (administrators and other support staff) in the school setting for training in the dynamics of bilingual/ESL education.

Federal Leadership

The U.S. Department of Education can assist in these activities by:

1. Identifying and disseminating information about additional funding sources for staff development efforts as a supplement to Title VII funding;

2. Identifying and disseminating information to IHEs and LEAs on effective training techniques such as faculty institutes, demonstration areas, and conferences, etc;

3. Encouraging the funding of first time IHE applicants through priority points; and

4. Providing funding for programs to train non-bilingual/ESL staff, both teachers and administrators.

Conference Proceedings

National Forum on Personnel Needs for Districts with Changing Demographics

Theme: Staffing the Multilingually Impacted Schools of the 1990s

January 11-12, 1990

Introduction

On January 11-12, 1990, a representative group of school superintendents, assistant superintendents/personnel directors, and deans from institutes of higher education (IHEs) from around the country attended a Forum sponsored by the Office of Bilingual Education and Minority Languages Affairs (OBEMLA). The Forum was designed to elicit from people in the field their impressions concerning the need for bilingual education in the 1990s and to allow them to make recommendations for a plan of action to address those needs.

The Forum was divided into smaller work sessions where participants were asked to respond to the following topics:

Topic I: The District Need. What is your sense of the demographic trends of limited English proficient (LEP) students in primary and secondary schools?

Topic II: The Personnel Need. As local education agencies (LEAs), can you obtain the staff you need?

Topic III: How to Address Personnel Needs. What modifications in bilingual/English as a second language (ESL) staff development programs do you think will help in the coming decade?

Topic IV: Next Steps. What future steps should be taken by LEAs, IHEs, and the Department of Education to better meet the needs of LEP students?

Topic I. The District Need

A number of Forum participants introduced recent studies on the numbers of LEP children needing bilingual/ESL services. Some studies have identified between 3.5 and 5 million LEP children. The school districts represented, made the following points regarding LEP students:

1. There is an increase in the number of limited English proficient students, even in school districts with declining populations.

2. There is an increase in the number of languages represented, especially Southeast Asian and some middle-Eastern languages.

3. Many students are arriving--at all grade levels--with limited prior schooling. (Many have no schooling at all).

4. The enrollment problems, which are likely to continue, affect school districts of all sizes.

5. Many districts across the nation are not yet in full compliance with their state's regulations governing minimum services required for LEP students. In some states 50 percent of the districts are not currently in compliance.

Topic II. The Personnel Need

According to a recent projection (Reynaldo F. Macias, Bilingual Teacher Supply and Demand in the United States, 1989), there is a current demand for 175,000 bilingual teachers, assuming a 20:1 student-teacher ratio. Forum participants made the following points about personnel needs:

1. There is a definite need for qualified bilingual/ESL teachers.

2. Qualified staff are hard to find and hard to retain.

3. Certification and other bureaucratic roadblocks impede the hiring of bilingual/ESL teachers. Alternative approaches (i.e., waiver of traditional requirements) are being used in some states and look promising.

4. Attracted by salary incentives (many districts offer dollar supplements as high as $5,000 for bilingual teachers), some bilingual teachers have transferred to the bilingual program but have not fully espoused bilingual teaching philosophies.

5. Burnout is high among bilingual/ESL teachers. This is often due to such factors as:

   a) A lack of administrative support for bilingual/ESL education at the local level (exacerbated by racial and gender tones of the LEA hierarchy);

   b) Lack of collegiality with their monolingual colleagues (bilingual teachers commonly enjoy the help of aides, have smaller class sizes, and are better paid);

c) Demanding school-community activities (many bilingual/ESL teachers have to make regular home visits);

d) Advocacy responsibilities that transcend the school day into many late-evening community meetings;

e) A belief among many staff outside of the bilingual/ESL program that LEP children have less ability than other children;

f) An accountability system that ignores important student characteristics (e.g., students do not excel in tests that are in a language they have not yet mastered);

g) The strain of responding to the special needs of many LEP students who arrive in the United States with no prior schooling;

h) Inadequate number and quality of appropriate instructional materials; and

i) The general lack of a local support system for bilingual/ESL teachers.

6. Bilingual/ESL teachers tend to migrate to other districts in search of higher pay and better working conditions. Some bilingual/ESL teachers who remain in the district transfer to non-bilingual/ESL positions.

7. There is a universal shortage of bilingual/ESL teachers who have specialized in subject-matter areas, especially the sciences, special education, and vocational education. Bilingual staff qualified to serve in ancillary staff positions (e.g., psychologists, physical therapists, early childhood specialists, and administrators) are also in short supply.

8. Some districts with increasing LEP enrollment, stable or declining overall enrollments, and a stable, tenured, monolingual teaching staff cannot determine how to provide bilingual/ESL services.

9. Districts do not have effective college recruiting programs.

10. Only a minority of graduates from IHE bilingual programs are native speakers of the target language. This is because of inadequate financial aid; most students from low-income homes cannot afford to go to college.

Topic III. How to Address Personnel Needs

1. LEAs need to tell IHEs what they need concerning all aspects of the training of bilingual/ESL teachers. Working through college presidents and deans may be an effective way to do this.

2. Bilingual/ESL teachers will need to respond to the diversity that exists within today's LEP student population.

   a) Teachers need training to handle previously unschooled children.

   b) Teachers need more indepth training in teaching methodology.

   c) Subject matter areas (e.g., math) need to be addressed more vigorously.

3. IHEs need to train more bilingual psychologists, physical therapists, teachers for vocational education, special education, and early childhood education, as well as counselors, administrators, and other ancillary professionals.

4. Monolingual staff need to be trained to be more effective with LEP students.

5. SEAs, LEAs, and IHEs together need to develop a way that will streamline certification requirements for bilingual/ESL personnel.

6. School systems need to develop support systems sensitive to the special needs of bilingual/ESL teachers (e.g., peer acceptance, top-down support, community relations, accountability systems).

7. Existing scholarship aid should be increased to attract native bilingual students (full-time or part-time) from low-income backgrounds.

8. Since "good teachers" are good within the context of their particular learners, educational research needs to be more cognizant of learner characteristics.

9. The U.S. Department of Education can strengthen the public support for bilingual/ESL education by spearheading more meetings with national leaders on the district and IHE levels, convening business roundtables to discuss the importance of bilingual/ESL personnel in the workplace, disseminating experiences of other countries with bilingual/ESL education, and by supporting organizations such as the National Association for Bilingual Education (NABE) and Teachers of English to Speakers of Other Languages (TESOL).

10. Bilingual/ESL teachers who are on the front line of curriculum change should realize that not having full public acceptance from all sectors may be "the burden of innovation."

11. There is a need for improved communication among all those involved in bilingual/ESL education programs. IHEs and LEAs need to talk more practically about how to make bilingual/ESL education programs more effective. Deans and university presidents need to become more involved. Teacher trainers need to be more in tune with current practices and needs. Areas to be discussed should include recruitment, course development, and training.

12. Many LEAs need to incorporate a bilingual/ESL component into existing staff development/inservice training programs. The U.S. Department of Education may want to support research in identifying particularly successful inservice strategies.

13. IHEs and LEAs need to establish closer relationships with the private sector.

14. Since learning conditions differ from district to district, continued experimentation with diverse bilingual/ESL methodologies is encouraged.

Topic IV. Next Steps

OBEMLA

1. Include requirements in regulations for coordination and collaboration between IHEs and LEAs, not just in proposal preparation, but also in research design and in the processes of program and staff development.

2. Focus on the <u>quality</u> of staff development rather than on the <u>numbers</u> of people who are involved in staff development. For example, project plans that include training 1000 teachers in two workshops a year should

receive less support than plans that provide long-term development for 30 teachers.

3. Consider the following incentives for IHEs:

   a) Research component with any training that is provided;

   b) Administrative support (release time) for project directors who are trying to get tenure. Working towards tenure requires extensive research and writing, tasks that compete with everything directors have to do administratively; and

   c) Special consideration to IHEs and LEAs that are closely involved with the problem.

4. Provide LEA funding for staff training and development and for "procurement" of IHEs, and alternative delivery systems.

5. Encourage more involvement of community colleges in the training of bilingual/ESL staff. In request for proposals, OBEMLA could promote more collaborative efforts between two and four-year colleges. OBEMLA should not penalize community colleges and small LEAs for having a small proposal writing staff. OBEMLA could also set aside funds specifically for community colleges, especially those in urban areas, for use in training bilingual/ESL teachers.

6. Study the effects of standardized testing procedures on bilingual/ESL program accountability. For instance, some non-English students are tested in English and some English-only students are tested in another language.

7. Test both the bilingual and the ESL education components.

8. Initiate faculty institutes, to include demonstration and research centers and to train IHE faculty to work with LEAs. A center focusing on language might also be initiated.

9. Continue the drive to solve basic problems concerning certification and appropriate models of bilingual/ESL education.

10. Compile lists of required competencies for bilingual/ESL teachers according to different types of certifications.

11. Conduct a comprehensive study to identify and compare certification requirements throughout the country to determine what competencies/qualifications are shared and which ones are most likely to bring about the desired results. The whole issue of reciprocity should be examined carefully.

12. Promote the development of mechanism among IHEs to facilitate the transfer of student credits in bilingual/ESL education from one institution to another.

13. Contract a study to identify state certification requirements for bilingual/ESL teachers and to propose ways to streamline these requirements.

14. Share with certifying agencies the mechanisms for certifying teachers in languages that are not taught in colleges.

15. Establish a career ladder for aides and paraprofessionals and provide a formal training program for aides and other support/ancillary positions.

16. Broaden the number of languages that are underwritten to include more "nontraditional" languages.

17. Research is needed in the following areas:

    a) The effect of teacher expectations on student achievement;

    b) The uses of technology in improving bilingual/ESL programs and reducing the cost of providing services;

    c) Effects of the early and late exit processes;

    d) The role that parents and communities play in bilingual/ESL programs;

    e) The role of paraprofessionals in the classroom;

    f) The impact of various state certification policies on bilingual/ESL program achievement and drop-out rates;

    g) Issues affecting drop-out rates and student and teacher retention;

h) Ways to improve teacher retention to include characteristics that positively affect teacher retention in bilingual/ESL education;

i) Strategies for teaching students who are not literate in their native language;

j) Teacher orientation; and

k) Promising practices (This research could be compiled and disseminated, possibly during a series of conferences. There is no need to continually re-invent the wheel.)

18. There is a need to identify additional funding sources appropriate to bilingual/ESL programs as a supplement to Title VII funding. Possible sources might include Special Education, Teacher Corps, Migrant Education, Bilingual Education, and Head Start. OBEMLA should pull agencies together to see what can be done collaboratively. State sources might also be included.

19. Before approaching outside programs and agencies, review the effectiveness of the existing program structure. As a radical move, one participant suggested that OBEMLA consider abolishing all departments of bilingual education bureaucracies at the LEA and IHE levels and replacing them with joint appointments. The local hierarchy of IHEs and LEAs would be abolished. Others recommended that OBEMLA continue to support the bilingual/ESL education program hierarchy, as currently established, and the developmental bilingual education programs, grades K-12. These should produce a larger pool of students who can return to LEAs and provide better teachers.

20. Facilitate the involvement of the corporate world. Such involvement would make a case for corporate benefits. Perhaps a forum with the corporate community would be helpful.

21. Continue funding existing teacher preparation programs. (Two Forum attendees were former OBEMLA fellows.)

22. Fund regional demonstration areas staffed by IHEs, LEAs, and the Department of Education. These areas might be responsible for providing demonstrations, information dissemination, and training.

23. Provide additional funds for classes for non-bilingual teachers. OBEMLA should be more flexible in funding and give preference to districts with the demographics

that document the need for more funding of bilingual/ESL programs.

24. Provide more funds for quality staff development. More statutory change is needed to allow LEAs to apply for additional staff development dollars.

25. As a follow-up to this Forum, sponsor a Policy Resolution Conference. This conference could be scheduled separately or held in conjunction with an already scheduled conference.

26. Set targets for student achievement and community involvement, and give rewards and penalties when these targets are or are not met. OBEMLA might also set target incentives for IHEs to cooperate with LEAs or for LEAs to meet accountability standards.

27. Relax proposal writing requirements. Project staff spend too much effort writing proposals. OBEMLA could specify page limits for proposals.

28. Consider the use of discretionary points or other mechanisms to favor funding applications from first time applicants, i.e., schools not previously funded. For these first time applicants, perhaps no proposal would be required.

29. Incorporate desired outcomes into any Requests for Proposal (RFPs) that are released.

LEAs

1. Push for more on-site training by IHEs.

2. Support programs to teach second languages to populations that are English speaking.

3. Support language retention in those students who are fluent in a native language. Those who have the language should be encouraged to maintain it and become literate in it.

4. Organize a forum with IHEs to discuss national issues concerning certification.

5. Stay committed to the cause of bilingual/ESL education and the children who are being served. Field staff have first hand knowledge and understanding of the students' needs and should speak and act in the students' behalf.

IHEs

1. Reach out to teachers on-site to do collaborative research.

2. Increase contact with and involvement of community colleges.

3. Continue to generate innovative training models for inservice teachers.

4. Be more involved in LEA on-site inservice teacher training.

5. Review requirements for pre-service training and the language requirements for all undergraduate students.

Other

Dr. Leonard Britton of the Los Angeles City Public Schools recommended that during the development of bilingual education programs, special emphasis be placed on the following areas:

a) Proper identification of students whose primary language is other than English (linguistic minority students);

b) Proper placement of linguistic minority students in classes by using valid instruments, appropriate bilingual personnel to administer the tests, and appropriate student support services such as guidance and counseling, psychological evaluation, and special education/learning disability or exceptional child education;

c) Proper placement of qualified bilingual staff in the public school system;

d) Proper location of bilingual classes;

e) Utilization of relevant instructional materials;

f) Development of adequate training in bilingual education for school personnel through bilingual education/ESL and foreign languages;

g) Propose competency-based model for teacher training in multilingual/multicultural education;

h) Participation of parents in school activities; and

i) Expansion of services provided by the U.S. Department of Education.

Dr. Donna Evans of Wayne State University in Detroit, Michigan presented for consideration the following recommendations that appeared in the January 10, 1990 issue of the Chronicle of Higher Education:

1. Insure that language minority students start school prepared to learn.

2. Insure that academic achievement of language minority youth is at a level that will enable them, upon graduation from high school, to enter the workforce or college fully prepared to be successful and not in need of remediation.

3. Significantly increase the participation of language minority students in higher education, with a special emphasis on the study of mathematics, science, and engineering.

4. Strengthen and increase the number of teachers of language minority students.

5. Strengthen the school-to-work transition so that language minority students who do not choose college leave high school prepared with the skills necessary to participate productively in the world of work and with the foundation required to upgrade their skills and advance their careers.

6. Provide quality out-of-school educational experiences and opportunities to supplement the schooling of language minority youth and adults.

Early Identification and Recruitment of Hispanic Teacher Candidates

Minorities

Jesse T. Zapata

While America's minority student population is increasing, the teacher pool is becoming increasingly white. For Hispanics, the country's fastest growing minority, the situation is critical. Zapata reviews the issues regarding Hispanic involvement in teaching and presents *Project: I Teach* as a viable model for recruiting Hispanic high school students into teaching.

Zapata is Associate Professor, Division of Education, University of Texas at San Antonio.

At a time when America's classrooms are beginning to reflect the significant increases in minority populations already apparent in the general population, the teacher candidate pool is becoming increasingly white. The National Retired Teachers Association ("Minorities Need," 1987) reports that by the year 2000 minorities will account for only 5% of public school teachers compared to 12% today. At the same time, the minority student population will expand from 29% to 33%. Concurrently, there is wide agreement that a situation where the vast majority of teachers is white and where most students are minority is not ideal for the psychological development of minority students.

Traditionally, teaching has been the first stepping stone to a professional life for first generation college graduates. It continues to offer opportunities for upward mobility. Teaching is also a decidedly conservative enterprise: teachers enculturate by curricular design and personal example. To the degree that they accomplish that, minority teachers become role models for minority students and examples of competence for students who are already in the mainstream.

The literature on educational reforms repeatedly addresses the family's influence on attitudes toward and success in school. Teachers from backgrounds like those of their students can serve as liaisons between home and school, making linkages that are trusted and credible in minority communities.

Jackson (1986) discusses shared identity in teaching and learning. He argues that teachers base their instructional decisions on their own ways of learning more often than on how their students learn. In effect, they pattern their teaching on the ways of learning that have worked for them. In most cases, especially those where teachers and students are from decidedly different socio-cultural backgrounds, the assumption of shared identity as learners is tenuous at best. If learning style is influenced by one's sociocultural environment, it follows that teachers and students from similar backgrounds may have greater likelihood of similarity in ways of learning. Accordingly, teachers from minority backgrounds may be better prepared to meet the learning needs of an increasing proportion of the school population than teachers from other backgrounds.

There is, then, a need to attract more minority students to careers in teaching. This need is especially critical for Hispanics because that population is the fastest growing minority population in the country (Hispanic Policy Development Project, 1984). This paper provides a view of the problem relative to Hispanics pursuing careers in teaching. In addition, it presents a model, *Project: I Teach,* for attracting, encouraging, and supporting Hispanic high school students interested in teaching careers. While the model presented focuses on Hispanics, it is applicable to other minority groups and communities.

Hispanics in Teaching

In 1980, Hispanics constituted 2.6% of all elementary school teachers and 1.7% of all secondary school teachers (Orum, 1986). More recent data from the two states with the greatest concentration of Hispanics underscore the problem. In Los Angeles, California, where Spanish-background students make up 53% of the school population, about 10% of teachers are Hispanic (Crawford, 1987). In Texas, the school-aged population is growing at an annual rate of 2%, and the ethnic composition of the school population is rapidly changing. In the period between 1972 and 1983, the white student membership dropped about 3%, the Black student population increased 1.5%, and the Hispanic population increased 32.9% (State Board of Education, 1983). In 1984, Hispanic students comprised 30.4% of Texas's student population (Hodgkinson, 1986).

Yet, while Texas's Hispanic school age population is growing, the corresponding number of employed Hispanic teachers has remained relatively constant at about 12% from 1982 through 1986 (Texas Education Agency, 1987a). In Bexar County, which includes San Antonio, the percentage of Hispanic teachers has remained about 25% from 1983 through 1986. But Hispanics represent about 58% of the student population there (Texas Education Agency, 1987b).

Projections for the future are generally bleak. While the national college enrollment increased 7% during the first four years of this decade, the percentage of Hispanic high school graduates going to college dropped from 35.8% in 1976 to 31% in 1983 (Orum, 1986). In addition, because fewer Hispanic students than Anglo students finish high school, only about 4% of undergraduate students are Hispanic (Santos, 1986).

Those Hispanic students who do attend college often experience more stress than do their Anglo counterparts (Munoz, 1986). This difference in stress relates first to concerns about finances and secondly to academic concerns. Concerns about finances actually may begin before Hispanic students enter college as they and their parents attempt to deal with complex financial-aid applications and often miss deadlines for all nonreimbursable programs and thus have to rely more on loans than do Anglo students (Olivas, 1986). The college academic experience is also more stressful for Hispanics than for Anglos in areas ranging from "uncertainty of being accepted by a university" to "seeking help with academic problems." These differences in stress might account for the higher attrition rate for Mexican-American students (Munoz, 1986).

Finally, data collected in 1987 suggest that the number of students preparing to be teachers may be on the rise (Rodman, 1987). However, those same data suggest that the number of Hispanic students choosing teaching as a career is relatively small. Specifically, the data reflect that 90% of these students intending to become teachers are Anglo, 4.6% are Black, 2.8% are Hispanic and 1.4% Asian or Pacific Islander.

The problem with the potential pool of applicants may be worsened by the current reform in education movement which places a heavy emphasis on standardized tests as a vehicle for demonstrating educational excellence and as a way of determining who is entitled to move up the educational ladder. In California, only 46% of Hispanics finishing teacher training in 1984-1985 were able to pass the California Basic Education Skills Test. In addition, barely 15% of Hispanic high school graduates were even eligible for admission to California's two university systems in 1984-1985, suggesting that the potential pool in California is becoming progressively smaller.

In Texas, students wanting to become teachers must first have passed a variety of tests required for graduation from high school (Texas Educational Measurement of Students, TEAMS), for admission into teacher education programs (Pre-Professional Skills Test, PPST), and for the granting of teacher certificates (Examination for the Certification of Educators in Texas, ExCET). Hispanic students pass these tests at far lower rates than Anglos do. Through 1986, only 43% of the Hispanics who took the PPST passed it and through 1987 only 64% had passed the ExCET. Of white students taking those tests during those same periods, 79% had passed the PPST and 91% had passed the ExCET (Texas Education Agency, 1987c). This, of course, is resulting in fewer and fewer Hispanic students qualifying for teacher certification.

Project: I Teach

The overall goal of *Project: I Teach* is to increase the number of Hispanic students pursuing teaching careers. Given the research reported here, it was clear that what was needed was a project that focused on the early identification of Hispanic students interested in teaching careers. It was also clear that the goal could best be accomplished through a collaborative effort that was multidimensional in focus. This collaborative orientation is consistent with the current emphasis on collaborative activity. Such collaborative activity has been pioneered in several instances. The California State University System (1984) instituted "bridge" programs to improve minority students' preparation for college. The Carnegie Foundation for the Advancement of Teaching's special report (Maeroff, 1983) on school-college partnerships illustrates existing programs of considerable diversity, all designed to improve minority students' opportunities for both attempting and succeeding in post secondary studies. But few reported programs focus on the recruitment and retention of minority teachers. In areas where minority populations are large, university-school partnerships must give high priority to the search for minority students with talent for teaching and offer them programs to nurture that talent. Accordingly, *Project: I Teach* was created.

Project Goals

Given the complexity of the issues regarding Hispanics and higher education, any effort to recruit and retain Hispanic teacher candidates must be well-planned and aimed at addressing all of the problems defined here. Specifically, any such program would have to address the academic and financial needs of the students as well as encourage and reinforce the desire to attend college and pursue careers in teaching. Those issues guided the development of project goals which included:

1. To provide academic support to Hispanics wanting to pursue teaching as a career but who lack the academic skills to do so.
2. To provide test-taking and study skill development to Hispanics wanting to pursue teaching as a career.
3. To provide emotional and psychological support to Hispanics with an interest in pursuing a career in teaching.
4. To provide knowledge about, if not actual, financial support to Hispanics expressing an interest in pursuing teaching.
5. To facilitate the transition from

high school to college for Hispanics expressing an interest in teaching as a career.

6. To provide Hispanic role models for students interested in teaching as a career.

The Collaborating Institutions

The institutions involved in *Project: I Teach* include a university (The University of Texas at San Antonio), a test development company (the Educational Testing Service), and local school districts (the San Antonio and Edgewood Independent School Districts). Each of these agencies recognized the need for and advantages of a collaborative effort aimed at increasing the number of Hispanic teacher candidates and committed themselves to this activity. The commitments took different forms and resulted in varied costs.

The University of Texas at San Antonio (UTSA) provided a project director whose responsibility would be to develop, coordinate, monitor, and evaluate project activities. UTSA also provided office and classroom space and secretarial support.

The Educational Testing Service provided two staff members who assisted in planning, developing, coordinating, implementing, and evaluating the project. These staff members also assisted in assessing students' academic needs and in designing and developing materials and seminars on test-taking and study skills.

The two local school districts each identified one high school with high concentrations of Hispanic students (95% and 98%) and provided a school counselor who acted as campus coordinator. This coordinator assisted in developing project goals, planning project activities beginning with student recruitment and selection, and acted as a liaison between the project director at UTSA and project participants. In addition, the school districts agreed to employ project participants as teacher-aides during the districts' summer school programs. This last commitment would give the students early practical exposure to teaching as well as much needed summer employment.

The First Year

During the fall of the project's first year, overall goals were agreed upon by the participating institutions. It was also agreed that the project's goals for the first year should be modest in terms of the number of students involved, with the long-range plan being to use this "pilot" year as the basis for seeking financial and institutional support for maintaining and expanding the project's activities. For that reason, it was agreed that the focus should be on two high schools (one from each participating school district) with the expectation that 30 students would be recruited to participate. In addition, there was a strong conviction that the project should focus on students far enough along in their high school careers to have a general idea as to their career goals but not so far along that efforts to remediate or redirect them would have diminished chances of succeeding. For that reason, students in their junior year of high school were targeted.

Recruitment of students was begun early in the spring semester. Since one of the project's goals is to provide Hispanic models for the students, a major recruiting device was the use of UTSA Hispanic teacher candidates. The teacher candidates were recommended by members of the education faculty who had those students in their classes and who perceived them as enthusiastic and competent. The project director met with these four students and gave them an overview of the project's goals and proposed activities and then guided them in developing an outline of a brief presentation that they could make when visiting the high schools. These presentations were made in all junior level English sections in the two high schools and focused on (a) the teacher candidates' reasons for choosing teaching as a career, (b) reasons why high school students should consider teaching as a career, and (c) what *Project: I Teach* could offer high school students interested in teaching as a career.

As an additional strategy, teachers and counselors in both schools were encouraged to recommend students who they thought might have potential as teachers. Teachers were sent letters describing the project and an attached nomination form. Counselors, of course, already knew and understood the intent of the project. The selection criteria (outlined later in this article) were described, but teachers and counselors were encouraged not to exclude students who might not be strong academically but who did demonstrate a strong desire to learn and/or to become teachers.

Finally, at one of the schools, it was also possible to identify students with an interest in teaching by reviewing the results on an interest inventory, the California Occupational Preference System Interest Inventory (COPS). These students were mailed personalized letters asking them to consider participating in *Project: I Teach*.

Criteria for admission into the project included (a) completion of an application, (b) two letters of recommendation, (c) a written statement including the student's interest in becoming a teacher and in participating in *Project: I Teach,* and (d) at least a C average. Twenty-three students applied for admission into the program. Of these, 20 nominated themselves, and two were nominated by a counselor or teacher. Twenty-one students were accepted into the project. The two who were not accepted had extremely low achievement test scores, below a C academic average, and weak letters of recommendation. Applicants were accepted with C averages and low achievement scores if they expressed a strong desire to become teachers and if they were strongly supported by a counselor or teacher.

The program's focus during the spring semester was on reinforcing in those students selected the desire to pursue careers in teaching. Toward that end, major project activities included meetings on the local school campuses every two weeks, a field trip to UTSA, and a reception at UTSA held in honor of the students and their parents. The meetings varied somewhat from campus to campus but generally adhered to the following sequence:

1. Orientation to program goals and objectives,
2. Self-assessment in terms of qualities needed to become a teacher,
3. Speakers addressing the need for teachers in Texas.

The Summer Program

The high school students in *Project: I Teach* had little or no exposure to a college campus; some indicated that they had no idea where UTSA was located. Because a major goal of the project was early exposure to college life, financial assistance was sought and obtained for a summer camp that would allow the students to experience college life to the fullest. The Summer Camp provided the students with the opportunity to spend a week at UTSA and to stay in university housing. In addition, the Summer Camp provided a setting in which intensive effort could be directed to helping students develop needed knowledge and skills.

Summer Camp activities focused on the development of (a) writing and reading skills, (b) test-taking and study skills and (c) problem solving strategies. In addition, the students were exposed to varying perspectives on teaching through lectures by education faculty, to possible career options through presentations by teacher certification personnel and student members of Kappa Delta Pi, and to alternative ways of financing a college education through a presentation by the University's financial aid director.

Finally, special evening activities were planned to expose students to issues important to them because of their ethnicity and/or socioeconomic status. Activities included (a) reviewing and discussing the recently released, *La Bamba,* a movie focusing on Mexican-American rock and roll star, Ritchie Valens, (b) a dialogue with the Executive Director of the Mexican-American Legal Defense and Education Fund, and (c) a visit to a local bookstore where the students were each given a small stipend to be used to buy books.

An evaluation of the Summer Camp was conducted in two ways. The students responded to a questionnaire that asked them to indicate the degree to which camp objectives were reached and pre and post measures were taken regarding the objectives focusing on skill development. Pre and post data are being tabulated and analyzed and are not currently available.

Results from the student questionnaire are available. Students were asked to rate on a 5-point scale (with one being low and five being high) the degree to which they thought Summer Camp objectives were met. Items were clustered into five categories (see Figure 1 for sample items): writing/reading; problem-solving strategies; test-taking/study skills; guest speakers; special events. Generally, item means suggest that the students thought that the Summer Camp had successfully accomplished its goals. From the students' perspective, the Camp was most successful at helping them learn problem-solving strategies, with means for those objectives ranging from 4.55 to 4.91. Overall, means ranged from a low of 3.73 for two writing/reading objectives ("applying starter and organizing strategies to personal and expository writing" and "applying prereading strategies to reading") to a high of 4.91 for one problem-solving objective ("making logical inferences for answering a question or solving a problem").

Figure 1
Sample Questionnaire Items

I. **Writing/Reading**

1. Apply a variety of starter and organizing strategies to personal and expository writing.
2. Understand the reading/writing connections.

II. **Problem-Solving Strategies**

1. Look for clues in the details of an object or problem to find solutions.
2. Make logical inferences for answering a question or solving a problem.

III. **Test-Taking/Study Skills**

1. Develop study and test-taking techniques.
2. Become acquainted with the PSAT and the SAT.

IV. **Guest Speakers**

1. Acquire information about financial aid available to attend UTSA.
2. Acquire information about possible teaching fields.

V. **Special Events**

1. Become aware of special issues concerning Mexican-Americans and education.
2. Understand problems in how American-Americans are portrayed in films.

The Second Year

The second year of *Project: I Teach* will focus on reinforcing experiences from the project's first year, most notably the Summer Camp. In addition, there will be a greater focus on preparing students for the transition to college life.

Writing and reading activities were emphasized during the Summer Camp and will continue to be emphasized throughout the second year. Four workshops are planned for the students in the fall semester. These workshops will focus on topics identified through assessing the students writing and reading skills during the Summer Camp and/or topics in which the students expressed an interest.

Study and test-taking skills also will continue to be emphasized. The Educational Testing Service suggests:

1. Quarterly meetings with the students to enhance their test-taking and study skills. The meetings will be held before SAT administrations so that students can be better prepared for the tests.
2. Assessing the SAT and PSAT scores of the students and providing an evaluation of the results for the students.

Counselors at the respective high schools will continue to meet with the students every two weeks. The focus of these meetings will be on helping students maintain their career direction through activities and discussions that help clarify their interests and skills relative to teaching. Examples of these activities include discussing their experiences as summer teacher aides (only one of the school districts was able to provide this experience for the students), conducting interviews about the teaching profession with teachers, and on helping the students make the transition from high school to college by providing guest speakers from the University and assistance in completing applications for admission and financial assistance. In addition, each participating student will be assigned a "mentor" from the University who will maintain contact with the student beginning in the fall of the students' senior year. These mentors will be students enrolled at UTSA who are active members of Kappa Delta Pi, and their responsibility will be to ease the students' transition to UTSA.

Future Plans and Evaluation

The ultimate goal of *Project: I Teach* is to increase the number of Hispanic students choosing to pursue teaching careers. *Project: I Teach* has started by focusing on a limited number of high schools and students to be used as the basis for, at the least, maintaining the project at its current level. The real hope is to expand the pilot project by using its demonstrated effectiveness and its collaborative nature as the basis from which to seek additional financial and institutional support. The collaborating institutions are already committed to maintaining the project at least at its current level by supporting the selected students through their senior year in high school and their first two years in college. The Educational Testing Service and UTSA are committed to helping these students succeed and will be developing plans to ensure that success.

Plans for the students' entry into UTSA are already being made. Given the problems encountered by Hispanic students attending college, emphasis will be placed on providing students with psychological, academic, and financial support. The students will be assigned "mentors" recruited from Kappa Delta Pi and education classes. A "special problems" course will be developed for the students that will emphasize a variety of activities including providing mutual support, involving education faculty in special projects, and recruiting (and then tutoring) other prospective Hispanic students. The Educational Testing Service will continue to provide assistance in developing testing and study skills, and the University will provide tutorial assistance. In addition, the University's financial aid office will be involved to ensure that the students are aware of and apply for all possible financial assistance.

Several measures will assess the project's effectiveness. Students' performance on standardized tests, especially the SAT, the PPST and ExCET will provide one set of evaluative data. Measures of test-taking and study skills will also contribute information on the program's value for improving student growth in feelings of control in testing situations. Measures of growth in critical thinking skills and in writing and reading strategies will also be made.

The students' satisfaction with the experiences offered by the program will be examined through interview schedules administered at the end of each school year. The final test of the program's success, of course, will be the degree to which project participants succeed in completing teacher training programs. Of the 21 students that were originally accepted into *Project: I Teach*, 19 are still actively involved in the project. The two students no longer involved withdrew for nonacademic reasons. One student decided against a career in teaching, and the other moved to another school. Of the 19 students still involved in the project, 16 are still committed to a career in teaching; the other three are still interested but are actively exploring other career interests.

Finally, the current crisis regarding the recruitment of minority students into teaching has resulted in money being made available for the recruitment effort. In the summer of 1987, for example, the Texas Education Agency announced the availability of grants totalling $320,000 and ranging from $40,000 to $80,000, each of which will support projects whose goal is the early identification of minority students interested in pursuing careers in teaching.

Conclusion

Project: I Teach is a pilot project attempting to identify strategies for recruiting high school Hispanic students into teaching careers. It also is an effort to identify strategies that will be helpful in increasing the likelihood that those students will complete successfully teacher training programs. To meet the critical shortage of minority teachers facing this nation, efforts similar to but broader and more extensive than *Project: I Teach* need to be implemented.

References

Brown, P. (Ed.). (1983). *Cooperative activities between high schools and colleges.* Washington, DC: Association of American Colleges.

California State University. (1984). *Academic challenges: University and high school partnerships.* Long Beach: Office of the Chancellor.

Crawford, J. (1987, April 1). Bilingual education: Language, learning, and politics. *Education Week*, pp. 19-50.

Hispanic Policy Development Project. (1984). *The hispanic almanac.* Washington, DC: Author.

Hodgkinson, H. L. (1986). *Texas: The state and its educational system.* Washington, DC: Institute for Educational Leadership.

Jackson, P. (1986). *The practice of teaching.* New York: Teachers College Press.

Maeroff, G. I. (1983). *School and college: Partnerships in education special report.* Princeton, NJ: Carnegie Foundation for the Advancement of Teaching.

Minorities need apply: Schools consider new recruitment programs as the number of minority teachers dwindles. (1987, July-August). *National Retired Teachers Association*, p. 8.

Munoz, D. G. (1986). Identifying areas of stress for chicano undergraduates. In M. A. Olivas (Ed.), *Latino college student* (pp. 131-156). New York: Teachers College Press.

Olivas, M. A. (1986). Financial aid for hispanics: Access, ideology, and packaging policies. In M. A. Olivas (Ed.), *Latino College Student* (pp. 281-295). New York: Teachers College Press.

Orum, L. S. (1986). *The education of hispanics: Status and implications.* Washington, DC: National Council of La Raza.

Rodman, B. (1987, February 25). Numbers preparing to be teachers may be rising. *Education Week*, p. 1, 19.

Santos, R. (1986). Hispanic high school graduates: making choices. In M. A. Olivas (Ed.), *Latino college student* (pp. 104-130). New York: Teachers College Press.

State Board of Education. (1983). *A policy statement: A state in motion in the midst of a nation at risk.* Austin, TX: Author.

Texas Education Agency. (1987a). *Personnel rosters: 1983-1986.* Unpublished raw data.

Texas Education Agency. (1987b). *Ethnicity for students in Bexar County.* Unpublished raw data.

Texas Education Agency. (1987c). *Teacher testing fact sheet.* Unpublished raw data.

From *Action in Teacher Education*, vol. 11, no. 2, Summer 1989, pp. 47-50. Reprinted by permission of the publisher and the author.

Preparing Minority Teachers for the 21st Century: A University/Community College Model

Leo W. Anglin

In *A Profile of Teachers in the United States*, Feistritzer (1986), states that public school enrollment is projected to be one-third minority by the year 2000. Only six percent of public school teachers, according to Feistritzer, are Black while two percent are Hispanic. In Ohio, a shortage of qualified minority teachers has reached epidemic proportions, especially in urban areas, largely due to early retirement programs for teachers. It was the local need for minority teachers as well as a national call for the recruitment of minority teachers that led Kent State University to open dialogue with Cuyahoga Community College regarding the development of a teacher education articulation program between the two institutions.

The objective of this article is to describe a plan to recruit minority students from a large urban community college into a university-based teacher preparation and certification program. This proposed program has generated hope that positive steps can be taken to recruit, prepare and support the development of capable minority teachers from the ranks of the community college population. The need for teachers from underrepresented groups is so great that, although this proposed plan focuses upon recruitment from the community college, other entry levels (e.g., traditional students, midcareer professionals, and non-traditional students) are also addressed in the plan.

Leo W. Anglin is Associate Dean of the College and Graduate School of Education at Kent State University, Ohio.

The Dilemma

Why are we experiencing such renewed interest in recruiting, preparing, and retaining minority teachers? The data illustrating the dilemma is not new.

As stated earlier, public school enrollment is projected to be one-third minority by the year 2000. Other data that illustrate this situation have been widely reported. For example:

> Today, Black teachers constitute about 8 percent of the elementary/secondary teacher pool and projections indicate that-they may compose as little as 5 percent of the teaching force by 1990 (Hodgkinson, 1985).
>
> Of our largest 25 cities, 23 currently report that the majority of students are from minority populations (Graham, 1987).
>
> Urban universities certify less than 10% of the nation's newly certified beginning teachers (Haberman, 1987).
>
> A smaller percentage of members of minority groups are selecting education careers (Haberman, 1987).
>
> It is projected that in the year 2020, the minority birthrate is expected to exceed the birthrate for this country's white, Anglo-Saxon majority (Hodgkinson, 1985).
>
> Despite aggressive and costly recruitment strategies by many school districts in Ohio, there are only 39 more Black teachers in October 1987 than in October 1986 (Loehr, 1988).

This is only a sample of the compelling data that illustrate the magnitude of the situation. These data, coupled with the fact that the graduating class of the year 2000 is currently enrolled in our first grade classrooms, make it clear that action steps must be taken immediately. In other words, we must increase the pool of minority applicants in teacher education programs and provide support systems that enable them to graduate and become successful career teachers.

Recruiting Teacher Education Students from the Community College

There are many interesting plans and programs being proposed and in some cases implemented that are designed to build the minority teacher resource pool (Haberman, 1987). Fifth-year programs or alternative certification programs are short-term efforts. Other strategies, such as the revitalization of future teacher organizations in schools with a high concentration of youth from underrepresented groups, are long-term efforts that will take five to ten years to have impact. Recruiting teacher education students from the community college environment is an alternative that can complement both short- and long-term efforts.

Community colleges enroll 43% of the United States' undergraduate students and represent a microcosm of American society. According to the Center for Education Statistics (1988), 55% of Hispanic, 57% of Native American, 43% of Black, and 42% of Asian undergraduates attend community colleges. The population of community college students represents a wide range of academic abilities, ages, and career interests. It is from this rich environment that Kent State University has developed plans to recruit prospective teachers capable of providing leadership in the urban schools.

Kent State University/Cuyahoga Community College Partnership

Kent State University, a member of the Holmes Group, supports large comprehensive undergraduate and graduate programs. Over the past three years, plans have been implemented to downsize the undergraduate teacher education program and increase enrollment in graduate programs. The downsizing is occurring as a result of more stringent admission standards. The positive result of this policy change has been an observed increase in the capabilities of the entering students. However, the institution has also experienced a decrease in the number of minority students who major in education. A strong institutional commitment to develop capable minority teachers coupled with internal policy and program changes have created an atmosphere that supports several innovative programs. Our Cuyahoga Community College teacher recruitment program is among these efforts.

Cuyahoga Community College, the largest comprehensive community college in Ohio, serves over 25,000 full- and part-time students from the Greater Cleveland area. Kent State and Cuyahoga first joined forces in 1983 with a "High Schools for the Future" project. Through these collaborative efforts, a level of trust and admiration developed among personnel at both institutions. In 1984, initial plans were developed for a jointly sponsored faculty development program to be based at one of Cuyahoga's campuses. As a result of initial collaborative projects, a formal memoranda of agreement between the two schools was developed and signed by the respective presidents in 1988. The memoranda described six collaborative projects that will be jointly sponsored by the two institutions, including the teacher recruitment component.

Teacher Education Student Recruitment Plan

The agreement allows Kent State University College of Education personnel to recruit outstanding students enrolled in Cuyahoga associate of arts and science degree programs. Criteria used to guide the recruitment process include high achievement, high motivation, maturity, and residence in urban centers. Target students for this program tend to be nontraditional, adult students who historically have not chosen teaching as a career.

The memoranda of agreement provided the groundwork for three important actions which were critical to the planning phase. First, a joint advisory committee, composed of faculty and administrators from both institutions, was established. Communication, cooperative planning, and formative evaluation are the primary responsibilities of this group. Second, the agreement provided an opportunity for KSU College of Educational faculty to develop and implement an articulation and dual enrollment agreement in partnership with the Cuyahoga personnel. Finally, the agreement provided the foundation necessary to design and staff a community college/university liaison position. This jointly funded position provides on-going facilitation for the venture.

One additional factor is important to note regarding the project's support system. In 1987, the position of Assistant Dean for Recruitment and Student Life was established at KSU. The person holding this position is responsible for providing a social and academic support system for College of Education students. It is through this office that ongoing support will be provided by KSU for students articulating from Cuyahoga.

Proposed Project

The primary goal of the proposed project is to prepare 30 minority teachers at KSU each year. Kent State personnel, in cooperation with personnel from Cuyahoga, will select candidates for the program and provide academic and personnel support through cohort groups at Cuyahoga. Most students selected for the program will complete an associate's degree and then transfer to KSU academic programs.

These individuals will be certified to teach once they satisfactorily complete a bachelor's degree at Kent State and pass the National Teacher Exam (NTE). Agreements will be developed with participating Ohio school districts that will facilitate the hiring of the students; ongoing staff development support will be provided cooperatively by the participating school districts and Kent State University. Three years after initial certification, each minority teacher will have completed three years of successful teaching experience in Ohio, a master's degree, and will meet or exceed National Board Certification requirements for teachers.

In addition to substantially increasing the number of minority teachers prepared by Kent State, this project will also provide leadership in the following areas:

1. Focusing the mission of the University and State of Ohio education programs toward encouraging members of underrepresented groups to become teachers.
2. Developing high quality, model teacher education programs for minority students. Quality is indicated by successful academic and teaching performance, above average National Teacher Exam scores, and completion of National Board Certification requirements.

3. Encouraging minority teachers to complete their careers in Ohio.

The majority of student participants for this program will come from Cuyahoga Community College. Options will be provided that will allow other qualified minority students, e.g., transfer students, traditional university students and non-traditional students to enter the program. Although Cuyahoga is the primary source for minority teacher education candidates, the overriding goal of this project is to demonstrate that qualified minorities from a variety a backgrounds are interested in actively pursuing teaching careers.

The community college environment can expand the pool of potential teacher education students. The large number of minority students, a strong developmental curriculum, and an atmosphere that is supportive of collaborative programs with universities provide the necessary ingredients for success. Community college students who have the potential for teaching typically do not identify themselves. Early participation of a teacher education institution's faculty in partnership with the community college's counselors and faculty is critical. Through this partnership students can be identified and advised about teaching careers and appropriate coursework. Once identified students transfer to the university, it is imperative that support systems be continued to offset social and academic problems. Finally, actual teaching experience under the supervision of professors and master mentor teachers in an urban school environment should provide the capstone academic experience for these students.

References

Center for Educational Statistics (1988). Unpublished data.

Feistritzer, C.E. (1986). *Profile of teachers in the United States.* Washington, DC: National Center for Education Information.

Graham, P.A. (1987). Black teachers: A drastically scarce resource. *Phi Delta Kappan, 68*(3), 598-605.

Haberman, M. (1987). *Recruiting and selecting teachers for urban schools.* Reston, VA: Association of Teacher Educators.

Hodgkinson, H.L. (1985). *All one system: Demographics of education—Kindergarten through graduate school.* Washington, DC: Institute for Educational Leadership.

Loehr, P. (1988, October 5). The urgent need for minority teachers. *Education Week*, p. 32.

From *Action in Teacher Education*, vol. 11, no. 2, Summer 1989, pp. 51-58. Reprinted by permission of the publisher and the author.

NEW DIRECTIONS IN PRESERVICE TEACHER EDUCATION PROGRAMS IN HISTORICALLY BLACK COLLEGES AND UNIVERSITIES: THE CHALLENGE OF THE 1990'S

Ora Sterling Anderson

Ora Sterling Anderson is Dean of the Division of Education at Coppin State College, Baltimore, Maryland.

The Problem

An *Education Week* report (1985) indicated that in 1963 Florida A&M University, the state of Florida's largest producer of Black teachers, graduated more than 300 teachers each year, but in 1985 it graduated fewer than 100 and 66 percent of those graduating failed the state's teacher certification test. The Florida A&M example is far from unique. It is what educators warn is a growing national problem—the erosion of the minority teaching force. Ironically, as the minority teacher slowly vanishes, minority school enrollment is the fastest growing segment of the nation's youth population. It is estimated that by the year 2000, the minority student enrollment in urban schools will approach three-fourths of the enrollment population (Baratz, 1986).

On the contrary, the statistics on minority enrollment in colleges and universities indicate a serious decline in enrollment of minority youth. According to statistics from the U.S. Department of Education, Office for Civil Rights, Blacks have constituted a very small percent of the nation's total college enrollment since the mid 1970's.

Secondly, the number of minority college students choosing education as their field of study is decreasing. The number of bachelor's degrees in education awarded to Blacks declined by 52 percent— from 14,209 in 1975-76 to 6,792 in 1982-83 (Cooper, 1986). The proportion of undergraduate degrees awarded to Blacks in that same period dropped from 9.2 percent to 6.9 percent. A recent survey of teacher education statistics (Cooper, 1986) in ten Southern states found that the number of Black teachers had decreased by 6.4 percent between 1980-81 and 1983-84 while the total number of teachers in those states rose by one percent.

G. Pritchy Smith, Chairman of the Division of Curriculum and Instruction at the University of North Florida and considered by many to be one of the nation's leading authorities on the effect of teacher testing on minorities, concluded that based on the available data and if present trends continue, the minority representation in the nation's teaching force could fall to five percent by the year 2000. This fact indicates that the ability of predominantly Black institutions to attract Black students to the teaching profession is decreasing (*Education Week*, 1985). Black students need Black role models to encourage them to achieve and consider teaching as a career possibility.

According to Reginald Wilson, Director of the Office of Minority Concerns for the American Council on Education, through the late 1970's the majority of Blacks and Hispanics chose education as a major (Cooper, 1986). Presently, however, the choices of majors for these groups closely mirror those of White students. Those studying the phenomenon of the vanishing minority teacher agree almost unanimously on this point. The broadening practice of competency testing for teachers, prospective teachers, and graduates seeking certification has been likened by a Florida A&M professor as "an academic electric chair." If historically Black institutions of higher education are not willing to change the status quo, the Black teacher will become an "endangered species" within the next few years. There is a need for the historically Black institution to reconceptualize recruitment and retention strategies to increase the pool of Black teachers as the year 2000 approaches.

The next section describes programs designed to improve preservice education and teacher education student retention strategies utilized by one predominantly Black institution of higher education. These programs are making a difference in developing effective preservice teacher competencies.

Programs Making a Difference

Teaching Effectiveness Network (T.E.N.)

In an effort to promote teacher education program change and improvement, the Maryland State Department of Education (MSDE) designed a collaborative preservice program improvement project, The Teaching Effectiveness Network (T.E.N.), consists of MSDE teacher certification personnel, five institutions of higher education (IHDs), and local education agencies (LEAs). Coppin State College is the only predominantly Black IHE involved in the project.

The basic purpose of T.E.N. is to ensure the development of effective teacher preservice competencies through a focused core of content across the program continuum beginning with the early experiences of educational psychology and field experiences, methods courses, lab and clinical experiences, student teaching, and supervisory conferences. The project also provides a support system in the first year of teaching (MSDE, 1984).

The training provided faculty and teachers in LEAs that train minority teachers is vital to aiding an historically Black institution train competent minority teacher candidates. There is dearth of Black teachers at a time when the 1987 U.S. Department of Education statistics report indicates an escalating national high school dropout rate among Black students. The literature indicates that a growing number of competent Black teachers are needed nationally.

T.E.N. objectives include:

1. Promote teacher education program change through the use of Madeline Hunter Mastery Teaching principles integrated throughout a program sequence.
2. Support supervisory reinforcement of Mastery Teaching principles during clinical and practicum experiences.
3. Facilitate the connection between preservice programs and school observation sites.
4. Support the development of supervision and coaching skills by col-

lege/university supervisors and LEA supervising teachers.

5. Support the ongoing training for a cadre of IHE teacher educators and LEA supervisors, who will become trainers for additional persons in the project.
6. Coordinate the collection of data for evaluating the T.E.N. program improvement and training process and the teacher education graduates' competence, using an external evaluator.
7. Promote possibilities for individual and/or collaborative research studies using or related to the overall T.E.N. project (MSDE, 1984).

To achieve the objectives, one-week training institutes are scheduled each summer in Mastery Teaching Principles and on-going training for all participants is provided throughout each year. The project is presently concluding the fourth year of activities.

The teacher decision-making model (Hunter, 1982) focuses on the teacher as the key to effective instruction. The theory was developed on the premise that teaching is a decision-making process. The model is researched-based and is built on effective use of motivation, reinforcement, and practice theory, and uses effective lesson design as a basic delivery strategy. Effective training in Mastery Teaching principles is essential to successful implementation of the model.

Transfer of learning occurs through appropriate application of skills learned through a combination of training elements. Each of these elements contributes to the effectiveness of the training. After analyzing more than 200 studies in which researchers investigated the effectiveness of various types of training methods, Joyce and Showers (1980) concluded that a specific set of training components contribute to the impact of training. The major components are:

Presentation of Theory for skill or strategy.

Modeling or demonstration of skills or models of teaching.

Practice in simulated and classroom settings.

Structure and open ended *feedback*.

Coaching for application (hands on, inclassroom assistance with the transfer of skills and strategies to the classroom). (p.380).

Southern Regional Education Board (SREB) Project

Coppin State College was one of three historically Black institutions involved in the Southern Regional Education Board Project "Improving the 'Pass Rate' of Minority Students on the National Teachers' Examination and other Standardized Tests" funded by the Fund for Improvement of Postsecondary Education (FIPSE). The project was designed to be implemented over a three-year period, 1984-1987, to achieve the following objectives:

1. Train a cadre of faculty in three historically Black colleges and universities to act as resource persons to other institutions in a) test construction, b) item analysis, and c) assessing curriculum and instructional methodology and materials.
2. Establish a model to improve the performance of students on standardized tests.
3. Increase the pool of minority public school teachers locally, regionally and nationally.

The four model components were 1) faculty development, 2) curriculum development, 3) student development, and 4) student assessment. The faculty development component focused on developing and/or improving the skills of faculty in test construction, test-taking strategies, test familiarization, and writing test items. Faculty members were assisted in reviewing and analyzing standardized and teacher-made tests in relationship to curriculum objectives and their relationship to test specifications. The faculty development and curriculum development training was conducted by a team of consultants from Educational Testing Service.

The general focus of the curriculum development component was assessment of course syllabi to determine the degree to which course objectives are stated behaviorally, course content is designed to meet the objectives, and effective measurement strategies are utilized to determine achievement of the objectives. Faculty were assisted in translating findings into curriculum change geared to strengthen programs and student achievement. The student development component emphasized strengthening the reading, writing, and test-taking skills of students. The program became mandatory for students in need of reading skills enhancement beginning with the Fall 1986 semester (Cooper, 1986).

Student assessment was designed to provide feedback on the effectiveness of instruction as well as program placement. Program planners and curriculum developers utilized the assessment data to make appropriate program adaptations and changes.

Significant progress has been made during the past decade in producing knowledge that describes effective testing (Joyce & Showers, 1980; Arends, 1985). However, there is an insufficient knowledge base to support one type of teacher preparation program over another (Arends, 1985). The writer was interested in determining what historically Black institutions are doing to meet the national demand for minority teachers. As a result, a survey of historically Black colleges and universities which have teacher education programs was conducted using a questionnaire response format to determine the recruitment and retention practices in existence. The questionnaire was mailed to the 89 historically Black colleges and universities which have preservice education programs. Replies were received from 62% of the institutions surveyed. A summary of selected findings follows.

Selected Program Characteristics

The number of teacher education students enrolled in seventy percent of the historically Black institutions is between 100 and 300 (Table 1). The

Table 1

Student Enrollment in Preservice Education Programs at Historically Black Institutions	
Number of Students	*% of Institutions*
100 to 200	43%
200 to 300	27%
300 to 500	13%
500 to	7%

students enrolled represent 10 to 20 percent of the total enrollment in the majority of institutions (Table 2).

Table 2

Percentage of Total Undergraduate Enroll	
% of Student Body	*% of Institutions*
10 to 20%	79%
20 to 30%	7%
More than 30%	2%

The largest number of historically Black institutions training teachers have been in existence more than fifty years. The next largest number of institutions have been training teachers between 30 and 50 years. (Table 3).

Table 3

Length of Time Institutions Have Preservice Teachers	
Number of years training Preservice Teachers	*% of Institutions*
More than 50 years	46%
30 to 50 years	29%
20 to 30 years	7%
less than 20 years	9%

Generally, each institution requires a combination of basic skills for admission to teacher education and utilizes a variety of screening procedures. (Table 4).

Identified Recruitment Strategies

Although the majority of institutions use a combination of at least three of the recruitment strategies indicated, the strategy utilized most often by the majority of institutions is professionally designed brochures. The percentage of institutions engaging in collaborative internships with the public schools appears extremely high. In view of the responses to similar items, it is likely that many respondents interpreted this item as being the same as field experiences such as internships or student teaching. (Table 5)

A variety of personnel are involved in recruiting preservice education students at most institutions surveyed. The group used most often by the majority of institutions is teacher education fac-

Table 4

Basic Skills Required for Admission to Teacher Education	
Basic Skills Required for Admission to Teacher Education	*% of Institutions*
Acceptable written communication	80%
Acceptable oral communication	70%
Acceptable level of reading skills	57%
Speech screening	30%
* Other (Math screening, reading test, etc.) (5)	

* 5 = actual number

Table 5

Recruitment Strategies	
Strategies	*% of Institutions Using Strategies*
Professionally designed brochures	73%
Letters to prospective candidates	63%
Collaborative internships with public schools	46%
Communicating to students the need to become a part of a solution to a national crisis in education	43%
Press releases to news media	39%
Telephone prospective candidates	39%
College prep courses for high school	16%
Internship arrangements with industry	7%

Table 6

Personnel Involved in Recruitment	
Personnel	*% of Institutions*
Teacher Education Faclty	75%
College/University Recruiters	66%
Organized alumni activities	55%
Admissions personnel only	38%
Other groups	
* Retirees (1)	
* Junior Division Students (2)	
* Graduate Students (1)	
* Parents (1)	

* Numbers indicate the number of institutions

ulty. However, 38% of institutions still depend on college admissions personnel only for recruitment. (Table 6)

Retention Strategies

As a result of the national concern about the quality of teacher education programs, forty-four states presently have in place competency assessment measures for admission to teacher education; the remaining states are preparing for some type of assessment (Imig, 1985). Students in historically Black institutions are held accountable for achievement in a variety of ways. (Table 7)

While the largest percent of institutions indicated that achievement is monitored in direct classroom experiences, most of them used a combination of two to four strategies for monitoring achievement. Only three institutions indicated the use of only one monitoring strategy. When the use of only one strategy was indicated, it was usually

Table 7

Strategies for Monitoring Achievement	
Monitoring Activity	*% of Institutions*
Direct expereinces in the classroom	63%
Competency - based instruction	57%
Achievement Tests	48%
Use of Mastery Teaching principles	45%
Use of Mastery Learning programs	39%
Use of competency checklists	36%

Table 8

Test-Taking Skills Instruction	
Activities Designed to Develop Test-Taking Skills	*% of Institutions*
Test-taking strategies workshops	66%
Instruction in test-taking strategies	54%
Assistance to faculty in designing effective tests	43%
Students recommended or required to take the National Teachers Exam (NTE)	43%
Tests designed in NTE format	41%
Course designed to teach test-taking skills	16%

achievement testing or direct classroom experiences.

Achievement on standardized tests is a critical factor in completing certification requirements in the majority of states. Black teachers have demonstrated a very low pass rate nationally. Therefore, it is essential that preservice education programs provide assistance to Black teacher candidates in improving test-taking skills and abilities. The findings relative to training or some type of preparation in test-taking skills are presented in Table 8.

This summary of strategies for recruitment and retention of preservice education in historically Black institutions indicates the diverse approaches used by different institutions. There appears to be limited activities of a collaborative nature with public schools and industry. A lack of indicated use of research for developing a knowledge base upon which to build practice is an area of serious concern. Although the problems related to the training of Black teachers who can compete for teaching positions which must be acquired by passing competency tests are serious, we appear to be going about business as usual.

The nation faces a national emergency for meeting the needs for role models for minority children in the classrooms as well as for the preparation of minority teachers in preservice education programs in Black schools. Despite the barriers, continuous efforts must be made to ensure that the teaching profession reflects the racial diversity which has made America great. David Imig (1985) warns:

> Let us not forget the oldest lesson from previous change strategies, i.e., change can come only from within—it cannot be dictated — it must emerge through self determined change in the behavior and commitment of those responsible (p. 15).

It is imperative that Black teacher educators develop an agenda to deal with the pending crisis. I believe that there are three areas of focus to facilitate change from within institutions. We must focus on:

1. attracting qualified and talented Black preservice teachers,
2. improving the capacity of teachers educators and the capability of teacher education programs to prepare effective beginning teachers, and
3. utilizing creative collaborative strategies to train and retain qualified Black teachers.

The available data for historically Black institutions indicate that the effective change agents are within the institution. I recommend a ten-point agenda for excellence:

- Use a variety of strategies to attract talented Black preservice education students, i.e., collaborative efforts with business, industry, high schools, other school system personnel, alumni, and community colleges;
- Develop and maintain rigorous standards for admission to teacher education programs;
- Demonstrate and model for preservice teachers how research on teaching effectiveness and effective schools can guide educational practice;
- Establish a coherent program identifying competencies to be mastered and inform preservice teachers of the competencies to be demonstrated;
- Develop and use an effective repertoire of instructional strategies which include: using technology in learning and practice; modeling Master Teaching principles; coaching as a teaching and instructional management strategy;
- Analyze teaching in the college classroom and in practice via video taping and microteaching;
- Develop a strong relationship with school system personnel who can provide practice opportunities and models for preservice students;
- Increase the attention to conducting and applying research on teaching and teacher training in teacher education (Mills, 1984).
- Operate the preservice program on an "excellence philosophy" (McPhail, 1982). Excellence breeds excellence and mediocrity spawns mediocrity (Imig,1985);
- Develop solid realistic exit criteria using competency examinations to measure pedagogical achievement.

The ten-step agenda is only the beginning step in the important task of developing quality programs and producing quality products. Once the institution has identified the necessary reform measures, the task of program delivery becomes a very difficult challenge. The trend in education in the past five years has been reform to improve undergraduate preservice education. A variety of alternative training programs have been developed to prepare teachers. There has been much discussion about how to improve the professional knowledge base and translate the recommendations from research into practical experiences for the development of competent teachers.

Teacher education programs face a tremendous challenge to build strong programs to satisfy public demands for teachers who can demonstrate excellence in preparation. Meeting this challenge demands strong leadership and commitment to reshape teacher education programs, sorting out relevant recommendations and making appropriate program decisions.

References

Arends, R.I. (1985). Teacher education: A decade of neglect. In H.E. Behling (Ed.), *The quality of teachers, teaching, and teacher development*. (pp. 17-20). Baltimore: Maryland State Department of Education.

Baratz, J.C. (1986). *Black participation in the teacher pool*. Paper presented to ETS for the Carnegie Forum's Task Force. Princeton, NJ: Educational Testing Service.

Cooper, C.C. (1986). Strategies to assure certification and retention of black teachers. *Journal of Negro Education*, *55*, 46-55.

Education Week, (1985, September 4).

Hunter, M. (1982). *Mastery teaching*. El Segundo, CA: TIP Publications.

Imig, D.G. (1985). What should be the national agenda in teacher education? In H.D. Behling, Jr. (Ed). *The quality of teachers and teacher development*. Baltimore: Maryland State Department of Education.

Joyce, B., & Showers, B. (1980). Improving in-service training: The messages of research. *Educational Leadership*, *37*, 374-385.

Joyce, B., & Showers, B. (1982). The coaching of teaching. *Educational Leadership, 39*, 117-122.

McPhail, I.P. (1981) *Agenda for urban education: Implications for teacher education from the study of successful low-income minority schools*. Keynote address at the Second Annual Conference on Urban Education, Dallas.

Maryland State Department of Education (1984). *Teaching effectiveness network*. Baltimore: MSDE.

Mills, J.R. (1984). Improving teacher education through the use of research information. *Journal of Teacher Education, 35*, 9-23.

THE REVITALIZATION OF TEACHER EDUCATION PROGRAMS AT HISTORICALLY BLACK COLLEGES: FOUR CASE STUDIES

Antoine M. Garibaldi, Ph.D.
Xavier University of Louisiana

August 1989

SOUTHERN EDUCATION FOUNDATION

TABLE OF CONTENTS

INTRODUCTION

"A Rising Tide of Mediocrity" and First Wave Reforms

In the early 1980's this country witnessed the beginning of a major education reform movement. The chief catalyst for this movement was the 1983 final report of an 18-month, 18-member commission established by Education Secretary T. H. Bell. The now famous report of the National Commission on Excellence in Education, *A Nation at Risk: The Imperative for Educational Reform*, analyzed the condition of America's educational system and focused special attention on the content and quality of elementary and secondary education in the nation's school districts. A critical assertion in the document which gave impetus to immediate action stated that "...the educational foundations of our society are presently being eroded by a rising tide of mediocrity that threatens our future as a Nation and as a people."

Because of this landmark report, school systems, educators and citizens gave heightened emphasis to the importance of a learned society, effective schooling processes and well-prepared teachers. The results of the first wave of elementary and secondary reforms, which occurred less than two years after the report's publication, were characterized by significant increases and changes in the number and types of academic credits required for high school graduation in more than 45 states. Subsequent to the addition of academic units in science, mathematics, and English in many schools across the country, attention then shifted around 1986 to discussions on a second wave of reforms focused on teachers and teaching practices. The rationale for these proposed changes was based on the belief that only effective instructional processes by current classroom teachers, as well as a higher quality of beginning teachers, could raise the academic achievement of all elementary and secondary school students.

Second Wave Reforms: Teacher Education

The second wave of reforms emanating from *A Nation at Risk* primarily focused on the improved preparation of teachers. However, because of the fact that close to 1300 institutions prepare teachers in this country, it was much more difficult to achieve consensus among this group on the types of curricular and structural changes that were necessary to produce the most prepared teachers for the nation's schools. While states and school districts hastily increased elementary and secondary curricular requirements, major reforms in teacher education programs were slower to occur as teacher unions, national associations representing teacher education, state organizations of education deans, and others deliberated and disagreed on the merits and manner of revised preparation programs for teachers.

Due in large measure to the lack of unanimity on these issues, the agenda for the discussion of "second wave" reforms relating to the teaching profession were chiefly set by two groups: the Holmes Group, representing more than two dozen graduate schools of education at major research universities, and the Carnegie Task Force on Teaching as a Profession, a diverse commission of business leaders, legislators and educational organization representatives. In 1986 both groups released two notable reports, Holmes' *Tomorrow's Teachers* and Carnegie's *A Nation Prepared: Teachers for the 21st Century*, which called for, among other things, higher salaries for teachers; career ladder programs; differentiated licensure and certification tests; dissolution of four-year undergraduate programs for teacher education majors, the development of five-year programs and master's degrees for entry level teachers; higher academic standards and more stringent admissions and exit requirements for education majors; more clinical experiences for education majors and closer linkages between local schools and colleges and universities; as well as the establishment of a national board for professional standards. These recommendations prompted discussion, as well as debate, among a wide cross-section of individuals, schools, colleges and universities, and also state lawmakers about what the curriculum content of teacher education programs should be as well as who should be allowed to enter and exit from schools, colleges and departments of education.

While all of the above recommendations did not receive immediate implementation, many states acted swiftly to raise teacher salaries and initiated some changes to improve the quality of teacher education programs. Many of the initiatives have been charted in the annual fifty state survey of legislative and administrative actions in teacher education by the American Association for Colleges of Teacher Education. Several of these reforms were described in a state-by-state summary conducted by the *Chronicle of Higher Education* in the Spring of 1988 (Leatherman, 1988). Among its results, the *Chronicle* found that between 1986 and 1988:

- admissions standards had been increased in 26 states;
- certification tests had been approved for entry level teachers in 26 states;
- curricula for teacher education students had been changed in 32 states, with some eliminating the four-year teacher education degree and requiring that students major in an academic field; and,
- some states initiated financial incentives to attract more students into the profession (e.g., scholarships and forgivable loans) while 11 developed special alternate certification procedures for individuals with bachelor's degrees in other fields but who wanted to teach.

Those changes, coupled with other mandates, many of which were legislated, prompted further discussion among, and some criticism from, teacher educators. As a result of this, most of the approximately 1300 schools and academic units responsible for teacher education in this country internally evaluated the quality, strengths and weaknesses of their programs. These self-studies were important to each institution's programs of teacher preparation and epitomized their ways of constructively responding to the sweeping changes and recommendations that were being proposed nationally and within states.

The Decline of Minority Teachers

While discussions ensued on proposed revisions to the structure and content of teacher preparation programs, less attention was being devoted to an equally inportant and related issue, namely, the decline in the number of teacher education majors and graduates in the early 1980's. Of even greater concern to large urban public school districts where the majority of students are non-white has been the dwindling pool of minority teacher education students and the shrinking percentage of non-white teachers. A 1987 survey by the National Education Association, for example, estimated that less than ten percent of the teaching force in 1985-86 was non-white, with Black-Americans representing 6.9 percent, Hispanic-Americans 1.9 percent, Asian-Americans and Pacific Islanders 0.9 percent and Native-Americans 0.6 percent (National Education Association, 1987). These and other data have prompted many researchers to predict that the minority share of the nation's teaching force will be less than five percent by the year 2000 if current enrollment trends continue and if the natural attrition of veteran teachers, especially those who are non-white, occurs as expected. This severe decline in the supply of non-white teachers is as critical as the issue of restructured teacher education programs since there is an urgent need to assure some minimal representation of teachers from different cultural and racial backgrounds as the nation's schools become more racially homogeneous.

The Role of Historically Black Colleges in Teacher Education

One group of colleges and universities have traditionally produced the majority of non-white teachers in this country, namely, the approximately 100 historically black colleges. Despite the fact that they represent less than eight percent of the nation's teacher education programs, they have been responsible for producing between two-thirds and three-fourths of all black teachers. As recently as 1981 these same institutions, located primarily in the South, graduated 48 percent of all black teacher education students in this country (Trent, 1984). These institutions clearly still play a pivotal role in the production of black teacher education students even though their enrollment in this field declined in the late 1970's and 1980's. These declines have occurred partially because of greater opportunities for blacks and other minorities in other career fields as well as a result of some of the reforms mentioned previously, especially those related to higher entrance and exit standards.

The tremendous decline of black teacher education graduates in Louisiana was emphasized in this author's 1986 Southern Education Foundation study which analyzed graduation trends in education between 1976 and 1983. In that study it was discovered that while the five historically black colleges in Louisiana graduated 745 education students in 1976, only 242 education degrees were awarded by them in 1983. (A total of 3386 degrees were awarded by the 21 schools and colleges of education in the state in 1976, but only 1864 were awarded statewide in 1983.) Nevertheless, the data showed that the five historically black colleges still accounted for 63 percent of all black education graduates in Louisiana in 1983 (Garibaldi, 1986).

Despite the fact that their enrollment and graduation rates, like other teacher education programs, are smaller than those figures of the early and mid 1970's, there have been many significant and proactive academic changes in the teacher preparation programs at historically black colleges and universities. Since many southern states initiated teacher education reforms in the late 1970's and early 1980's, historically black colleges and universities were among the first to reform, transform and revitalize their teacher education programs. Many of these initiatives were implemented prior to the "second wave" of national education reforms, and even before the 1983 release of *A Nation at Risk*, and occurred when enrollments were declining and when admissions standards were being raised.

The Revitalization of Teacher Education Programs at Historically Black Colleges

Because these institutions continue to provide the major share of non-white teachers to the nation's elementary and secondary schools, this monograph has been prepared to illuminate some of the proactive initiatives which have taken place in four historically black colleges' teacher education programs: Bethune-Cookman College in Florida; Norfolk State University in Virginia; Tuskegee University in Alabama; and Xavier University in Louisiana. Specific attention is devoted to those critical institutional changes which have occurred over the last five years as each has worked to improve the quality of their education graduates and their pre-service teacher preparation programs while successfully coping with enrollment declines, higher admissions standards and major proposals calling for restructured teacher education programs.

This qualitative study was designed to obtain information on the following key variables:

1. Enrollment and Graduation Patterns in Teacher Education since 1985-86

(What have been the enrollment and graduation trends in education since 1985-86? If there has been growth in the program, to what specific recruitment strategies and/or special incentives are these incentives attributable?)

2. **Academic Standards and Curricula**
(What kinds of changes have been made over the last three years or earlier related to teacher education standards, curricula, or admissions criteria that have improved the quality of the teacher education program?)
3. **Performance on Competency and/or Certification Examinations**
(What recent data are available to document the performance of students and graduates on competency and certification tests?)
4. **Other Departments/Institutional Initiatives**
(What are some of the other starategies that have been developed to increase the quality and numbers of students who will become teachers, e.g., education minor programs, future teachers clubs in local schools; programs geared to community college transfers, military personnel, teacher aides, etc.?)
5. **Placement Rates of Graduates**
(What are the placement rates of graduates in schools, where do they go to teach and/or do they go to graduate school?)
6. **Other Items of Importance Related to the Success of the Program and the Potential Impact of State Policies on Their Future Success**

Each institution was visited in the summer of 1988 to collect the above information and to discuss various aspects of the academic programs with faculty and staff.

Even though these are four private and public institution in different states and of varied size, the reader will discover many similarities. For example, all have high academic standards in their programs; all have a strong liberal arts core curriculum; all have been experiencing rising enrollments and the passing rates on certification exams by students have improved. But of greatest importance is the fact that teacher education reforms were initiated, first and foremost, at the institutional level. Each of the institutions also, for example, offers special scholarships to academically talented students who are interested in becoming teachers. Each also has evaluated its entire curricula, in conjunction with Arts and Sciences faculty, to improve the liberal arts components of their respective programs. And all of the institutions' graduates are in great demand by school districts and graduate schools throughout this country.

The following four case studies demonstrate that many positive academic initiatives have been occurring for the last few years at historically black institutions which have teacher education programs. Though two of the institutions, Bethune-Cookman and Norfolk State, have obtained state funds for special initiatives in their education programs, the real financial costs of the transformation and revitalization of these four education programs have been very small. Change has essentially been achieved through institutional commitment, collaboration and the determination of faculty to design programs that will produce the best teachers for elementary and secondary schools. Even though successful performance by students on certification tests is still perceived by many as a key indicator of a teacher education program's success, the institutions highlighted here are much more proud of the comprehensive transformation of their academic programs. The training of teachers is still a premier mission of historically black colleges and as more positive attention is devoted to the need for more black teachers, education enrollments at these institutions will undoubtedly swell to a level comparable to that of the 1970's

REFERENCES

Carnegie Task Force on Teaching as a Profession. (1986). *A Nation Prepared: Teachers for the 21st century.* Hyattsville, MD: Carnegie Forum on Education and the Economy.

Garibaldi, Antoine M. (1986). *The Decline of Teacher Production in Louisiana and Attitudes Toward the Profession.* Atlanta: Southern Education Foundation.

Holmes Group. (1986). *Tomorrow's Teachers.* East Lansing, MI.

Leatherman, Courtney (April 20, 1988). "Reforms in education of school teachers face tough new challenges." *Chronicle of Higher Education.*

National Education Association. (July, 1987). *Status of the American Public School Teacher, 1985-86.* Washington, DC: National Education Association.

Trent, William T. (May, 1984). "Equity considerations in higher education: Race and sex differences in degree attainment and major field from 1976 through 1981." *American Journal of Education.*

BETHUNE-COOKMAN COLLEGE

Institutional Profile

Bethune-Cookman College is a private, church-related (United Methodist) institution of higher education located in Daytona Beach, Florida. Upon the merger in 1923 of Cookman Institute for Men, founded in 1872 by the Reverend D.S.B. Darnell, and Daytona Normal and Industrial Institute for Women, founded in 1904 by Mary McLeod Bethune, the institution became the Daytona Cookman Collegiate Institute and was taken over by the Board of Education of the Methodist Church. The name was later changed to Bethune-Cookman College.

The college awards only undergraduate degrees through its five divisions: Business, Education, Humanities, Science and Mathematics and Social Sciences. In 1987, Bethune's undergraduate enrollment was slightly less than 1900 students. Between 1982-83 and 1986-87, the Division of Business had awarded the largest number of degrees (561), followed by Social Sciences (226), Education (221), Science and Mathematics (129), and Humanities (121) for that five-year period *(Bethune-Cookman College Factbook, 1987-88)*. In the Fall of 1987 the Division of Education, which includes Psychology and Health and Physical Education, had the third highest number of majors (324), preceded by Business (759) and Science and Mathematics (365), which includes Nursing majors. Social Sciences had 263 majors and Humanities had 177 in Fall 1987.

THE EDUCATION DIVISION

Bethune-Cookman College offers 14 teacher education programs which are accredited by the National Council for the Accreditation of Teacher Education (NCATE) and the Southern Association of Colleges and Schools (SACS). Despite experiencing a decline in the number of graduates in education since 1982-83 when 72 degrees were awarded, compared to an average of 37 degrees for the subsequent four year period, the number of education majors at Bethune has been increasing. In the 1985, 1986 and 1987 academic years, for example, there were 208, 216 and 244 majors, respectively, in the fields of Elementary, Special (Exceptional Child) and Physical Education *(Bethune-Cookman College Fact Book, 1987-88)*. These increases in majors were primarily the result of targeted academic efforts at the institution and the establishment of a Teacher Education Institute (TEI) funded by the Florida Department of Education. The Institute and its various components, as well as other support programs, are discussed later in this chapter.

The education program is governed by the Teacher Education Council whose responsibility it is to:

1. provide leadership and direction in the development and implementation of the teacher education program;
2. manage and evaluate all components of the teacher education program;
3. promote research designed to improve the teacher education program and teacher effectiveness at the local, state, and national levels;
4. coordinate the school's teacher education program with the State Department of Education;
5. screen applicants seeking admission to the teacher education program and to review applicants seeking approval for student teaching;
6. aid in recruitment for teacher education;
7. assist with the general advising of students in the teacher education program; and,
8. supervise all field-based experiences of the teacher education program *(Bethune-Cookman College Catalog)*.

The Teacher Education Council is comprised of all faculty members in the Division of Education as well as those faculty from the other four divisions who work with secondary education majors.

Education Admissions Requirements

As required by the state, students admitted to teacher education must have a score of at least 17 on the ACT or 835 on the SAT to be eligible later for a Florida Teaching Certificate. Students who are admitted to the college and who wish to become education majors must first successfully complete all general education requirements (56 credit hours) in their first two years. They must also: have a cumulative GPA of at least 2.5; attain scores at the 80 percent level of proficiency on entrance examinations in the areas of reading, writing, mathematics and speech, which are administered by the Division of Education; and be formally admitted into the Teacher Education Program. All students must also achieve the prescribed qualifying scores on the Florida Teacher Certification Examination (FTCE) which was instituted in 1983 by the state. The FTCE is a test of minimal entry skills for all prospective teachers in the state of Florida. The test is administered four times a year and includes four subtests. The four sections are: Writing; Reading; Mathematics; and Professional Education.

Another state test required of all college students who receive Florida financial aid from a variety of statutory programs is the College Level Academic Skills Test (CLAST). The CLAST, which now satisfies the first part of the FTCE for current education majors, includes four components: an essay section; a section on reading comprehension; objective writing; and computation. According to the law, students who have received an associate of arts degree since August 1, 1985 or who have completed sixty semester hours of credit, or the equivalent, in academic work applicable to an associate of arts or bachelor's degree at a Florida public or independent institution, are required to meet the state's minimum qualifying scores on the CLAST. Students who attend private institutions have been required to take the test but have not been mandated to pass it as of this writing.

Nevertheless, all sophomore level students at Bethune were required to "pass" the test in Fall 1988 as a prerequisite to taking junior level course work at the college. This requirement for students in all academic divisions at Bethune will obviously serve as another assessment measure of students' basic academic proficiencies as they matriculate to upper division status. Additionally, it should greatly assist education majors who must ultimately take the Florida Teacher Certification Examination, since the content of the CLAST is very similar in scope.

The Teacher Education Institute

The key to much of Bethune-Cookman's recent success in teacher education is its Teacher Education Institute (TEI), an innovative recruitment and retention program. An unsolicited proposal was submitted by Bethune for the institute and it has been funded since 1986-87 by the Florida Legislature at an annual level of $250,000. The institute was principally designed to enhance recruitment, admissions, preparation and retention, and the certification of students interested in obtaining degrees in teacher education.

Furthermore, the institute was developed to advance research and training, to improve those specific criteria required for state and national accreditation in teacher education, to enhance professional development and to promote leadership skills. The program objectives of the institute, as identified by the Division of Education, include the following:

1. to increase the number of teacher education graduates and to provide the necessary financial assistance to attract more highly able students into the Division;
2. to improve the retention rates of teacher education students through counseling, academic assistance, and professional preparation;
3. to examine alternative models, structures, and designs for professional teacher preparation; and,
4. to examine the knowlege base of teacher education and teacher competency.

The institute's academic and retention components are based on a team approach, providing an elaborate network of support for future teachers through mentoring activities and professional seminars whereby students learn leadership skills and effective strategies for personal and social adjustment. Specially selected staff members from around the university, e.g., in career placement and counseling, admissions, and testing offices, are integrated into the activities of the program and play major roles in the institute's success. It is important to note that these activities supplement, rather than replace, the traditional responsibilities of the university's advising program.

The institute's program at the university is augmented by a Competency Based/Computer Assisted Teacher Education Program, funded by a federal Title III Institutional Aid grant, to improve students' performance on and preparation for the Florida Teacher Certification Examination. The computer laboratory which has been developed also allows faculty to become more proficient in computer literacy skills, provides a mechanism for faculty to revise courses in teaching methods and educational foundations, as well as improves their ability to design competency-based instructional packages.

Specific activities have been developed under each of the aforementioned objectives of the Teacher Education Institute. To increase enrollment and recruitment, a Teacher Education Institute brochure has been developed to make students, high school teachers and counselors, and parents aware of the institute's purposes and offerings. Increased recruiting has been conducted throughout the state, linkages have been developed with school systems and the university's admissions office, and informational workshops have been held to advertise scholarship opportunities under this program as well as those offered by the university.

The primary focus of the TEI program is directed toward the improved academic performance and retention of teacher education students at Bethune-Cookman. The extensive list of activities includes:

1. orientation seminars for education majors where they can obtain accurate information about university and state requirements for graduation and certification, respectively;
2. a structured academic advising system where students are placed into one of eight teams which has a faculty Team Leader, Mentor and Area Specialist/Advisor; (Each team meets as a group monthly and students meet weekly and individually with their mentors.)
3. a personal counseling system to advise students about financial aid, scholarship opportunities, housing and other matters related to student life and college adjustment;

4. a special advising and counseling program to identify students who show early signs of dropping out of the teacher education program;
5. an integrated program of extra curricular activities for students, in-service staff development activities for students and faculty, and annual interviews of each students;
6. a system to review and revise curricula to improve the preparation of students in content-related courses; and,
7. a multi-faceted academic support system of tutorial assistance, study hours, workshops, and conferences, as well as mandatory attendance at the monthly professional seminars.

The retention component's successful "team" activities of advising and mentoring are undergirded by an experimental scholarship assistance program, known as The Challenger Program, whereby teacher education students can obtain as much as $1000 annually, in addition to their other federal and state grants or scholarships, provided that the academic performance requirements of the scholarship program are maintained. (Any students who applies to the college with a high school grade point average of 3.0 and an ACT of 17 may qualify for an academic merit scholarship from the university. Presidential Scholarships are also awarded to students with high school GPA's between 3.5 and 4.0 and an SAT of 1000 or an ACT of 23.) This supplemental financial assistance which is offered through the Challenger Program serves as an excellent incentive for students as well as minimizes the possibility that students will withdraw from the college because of insufficient student aid.

The Teacher Education Institute's professional development component provides faculty with the necessary resources (1) to regularly revise the content of curricular offerings, (2) to improve students' test taking skills and their professional knowledge for successful performance on the state certification test, and (3) to carefully evaluate students' clinical experiences. These examinations of teaching competencies and the knowledge base to teach effectively are supplemented by summer professional development and leadership skills seminars for faculty and students, as well as a minority teacher education training research program.

A final feature of the programmatic activities of the institute which deserves mention is its use of diverse faculty from all divisions of the college. Many of these professors are used as mentors and advisors and thus are able to inform, and possibly entice, students in other Arts and Sciences fields about the need for more teachers and to communicate their own personal satisfaction with teaching as a career. These kinds of informational talks by other Arts and Sciences faculty have been very effective with students who are majoring in other academic fields but who may be interested in learning about their options to teach after graduation. Furthermore, retired teachers who have had productive careers in the profession come to the college to talk about their many satisfying years in the classroom. These individuals, as well as other major speakers, who are invited in for the professional seminars serve a useful retention purpose by sustaining students' interest in the teaching field.

Graduation and Placement

Between 1984-85 and 1986-87, approximately 70 teacher education majors graduated. In 1988, 33 teacher education students received degrees in education. As noted earlier, all students must pass the Florida Teacher Certification Exam to graduate and obtain their regular teacher certification license. (Students must also be evaluated in their first year of teaching through the Florida Beginning Teacher Program. When this has been successfully completed, the new teacher receives a five year academic professional teaching certificate. More than 90 percent of Bethune's graduates have passed the Beginning Teacher Program.) Most of the degrees in education over the last four years have been conferred in elementary, special and physical education. Very few have been awarded in the secondary fields. However, more than 95 percent of the graduates are teaching or are in graduate school. Most graduates remain in Florida to teach but others are also employed in the Midwest and in various southern states.

Summary Analysis

Bethune-Cookman's success in the recruitment, retention and graduation of teacher education students has been due in large measure to its initiative and success in obtaining state funds for the establishment of the Teacher Education Institute. This institute has received a quarter million dollars annually since 1986 for the enhancement of the teacher preparation program's professional curricula and its academic advising process, the development of tutoring and mentoring activities to help students meet performance standards for state and national certification, and provided financial support for faculty research and training as well as professional seminars for faculty and students. Similarly, Bethune-Cookman's Title III-funded Competency Based/Computer Assisted Teacher Education Program has provided a computer laboratory to help students prepare for the state's teacher certification examination and where faculty can design competency-based instructional packages and revise their courses.

The aggressiveness by Bethune-Cookman in seeking these funds is testimony to the fact that the institution views the production of teacher education graduates as an important part of its mission and recognizes that academic support services are essential to the maintenance of high retention rates in these programs. Bethune's state-funded Challenger Program, which has given scholarships to education students, has also served as an innovative strategy for the recruitment and retention of majors. The success of the students on the Florida Teacher Certification Examination and also in the Florida Beginning Teacher Program is not only commendable but also imperative since the state requires that 80 percent of an institution's graduates must pass the FTCE and 90 percent must pass the Florida Beginning Teacher Program. Bethune-Cookman's experimental models for recruitment and retention, as well as the high priority which the institution has placed on basic skills proficiency by requiring that all students take and pass the CLAST, are proactive steps toward educational excellence. However, like many other small private colleges, Bethune-Cookman will have to continue to be aggressive and innovative in securing external funds to maintain the successful recruitment and retention programs it has developed.

NORFOLK STATE UNIVERSITY

Institutional Profile

Norfolk State University, an urban institution enrolling more than 8000 students, has gone through several transformations since its founding in 1935. Originally the institution was named the Norfolk Unit of Virginia Union University but in 1942 the College became the independent Norfolk Polytechnic College. In 1944 it became a part of Virginia State College be an Act of the Virginia Legislature, offering essentially a two-year junior college program. In 1956, the institution was able to offer its first bachelor's degree as its mission was expanded. In 1967 the college was separated from Virginia State College and became fully independent. In 1979, the institution obtained university status and is today one of the largest predominantly black universities in the nation.

The School of Education's origin dates back to 1944 when the institution became a part of Virginia State College. At that time a two-year teacher education curriculum was developed and patterned after the program at Virginia State College. When the institution's mission was expanded in the mid 1950's, teacher education programs were included and the college granted its first Bachelor of Science degrees in 1958. By 1969, when the College became an independent four-year degree granting institution, the Division of Teacher Education was offering 16 teacher education programs. In 1970 the teacher education programs were awarded accreditation status by the National Council for Accreditation of Teacher Education (NCATE) and received approved program status by the Virginia Department of Education. In 1979 the Division of Teacher Education became the School of Education when Norfolk's status was elevated from a college to a university.

THE SCHOOL OF EDUCATION

The School of Education has six departments (Early Childhood/Elementary Education/Library Media; Health, Physical Education and Recreation; Reading; Secondary Education and School Management; and Special Education) and five centers (Professional Laboratory Experiences; Multicultural Education; Instructional Resources; Reading and Study Skills Centers; and the Teacher Education Assessment Center). Six undergraduate and five graduate degree programs are offered in the School of Education. Each leads to a Virginia Collegiate Professional Teacher Certificate or to a specific non-teaching education career. The School of Education also coordinates and provides professional education courses for 44 teacher certification programs offered through other schools at the university.

It is worth noting that Norfolk State University's teacher education programs, like others in the state, will be restructured as mandated by the Virginia Department of Education. By 1990, all undergraduate degrees in education will be eliminated. Each teacher education student will earn an undergraduate degree in an arts and sciences field and will be allowed to take no more than 18 semester hours in education, plus student teaching. The School of Education will initiate a new Master of Arts in Teaching degree program and a graduate level non-degree certification program as a part of this restructuring process.

While Norfolk State University's School of Education has experienced declines in enrollment similar to other institutions since the mid 1970's, enrollment is on the upswing due to increased recruiting efforts, scholarship incentives, and improved curricula. Since 1985, the School of Education has graduated an average of 80 undergraduates, compared to their average of 200 graduates in the late 1970's. Passing rates in the National Teachers Examination fluctuated in the early 1980's but since 1986 the passing rate has been 80 percent or better, with more than 20 students taking the test at each administration.

Recruitment Initiatives

As a result of extensive investigations by the faculty and the university's Council on Teacher Education, significant improvements have been made by the School of Education in several areas. Recruitment and the attraction of more students hve been top priorities in the School of Education and special attention has been devoted to increasing the number of highly able students. These efforts have been greatly enhanced by the availability of special scholarships targeted at education majors. In 1983, for example, the president of the university approved the establishment of full tuition scholarships for teacher education students. Through this program, the Harrison B. Wilson Honors in Teaching Program, named after the president, twenty education majors became Teaching Fellows. This program has been renewed each year.

In addition to the institutional scholarships, an average of 34 students for the last two years have received $1500 annual Pacesetter Scholarships. Funds for the Pacesetter Scholarships come from a special two-year grant of $500,000 which was awarded by the state in 1986 to improve the performance of students on the NTE. (Specific academic components of this project are discussed in the next section.) The Pacesetter students receive these awards based upon their academic averages (a GPA of 3.0 for sophomores and 3.2 for juniors and seniors) and leadership ability. The students participate in monthly seminars on such topics as leadership, stress management, self-esteem, motivation, and others.

Norfolk State University has also been very successful in obtaining private and state support for its students. In 1987-88, for example, five students received scholarships of $1500 from the Metropolitan Life Foundation. (Norfolk received the highest number of scholarships in the Metropolitan Life Foundation's invitational competition.) Fifteen students also received awards in the Virginia Teaching Scholarship Loan Program. Norfolk State University's School of Education is also developing a special program for the recruitment of former military personnel into teaching. Given the university's location to military installations in the Norfolk-Virginia Beach area, this opportunity has great potential for the training and retraining of individuals in mid-careers. The small planning grant for this activity comes from the Hazen Foundation.

Finally, a special collaborative recruitment project is also underway with eighth, ninth and tenth grade students in the Norfolk Public Schools. By way of example, Norfolk State University's School of Education adopted Ruffner Middle School in 1985. Through this program the teacher education students provide tutorial assistance and enrichment activities for pupils in the school. Teachers and parents also receive rewards and incentives as well as special assistance from the School of Education faculty. This program is co-sponsored by the Virginia Department of Education.

Academic Standards and Activities

A student wishing to pursue a teacher education degree is formally admitted to the Professional Education program in one of the prescribed programs after he/she has completed all of the first and second-year curriculum and has met the prescribed standards of the department. For example, the student must have obtained a score of 700 or higher on the SAT; a cumulative average of at least 2.3; passed the first two sections of the National Teachers Examination; and met other specific academic requirements. The student must maintain the above academic standards to remain in the program and must have a cumulative GPA of at least 2.5 to be eligible for student teaching. Academic standards and the quality preparation of prospective teachers are carefully monitored, and revised as necessary, by the earlier cited Council on Teacher Education (CTE)—a university-wide advisory and policy making board which discusses and evaluates curricula and requirements for education majors.

The academic program of the School of Education and the performance of teacher education students have been significantly improved by the state-funded NTE project at Norfolk State. All components of the project have been very successful and the monies have been used primarily for staff development activities, curriculum revisions and resource materials, in addition to the student scholarships. Specific activities under this program include: tutorials, workships, seminars and a special test preparation class to improve NTE passing rates. A supplemental grant for two years, $90,000 annually, has been approved by the state for the continuation of these enrichment efforts and scholarships.

The special class referred to above, Seminar in Assessment and Evaluation, is a course which has been redesigned to specifically address the necessary test-taking skills which students must have to improve their performance on the NTE. This course incorporates test-taking skills and strategies, uses a professional laboratory where students can practice on content-based learning modules, and uses professional test preparation consultants in seminars for students and faculty. Students meet for two hours a week, attend a regular three hour Saturday workshop, and they must obtain a minimum grade of "B." Students also do not officially receive a grade for this course until they have passed the first two sections of the NTE.

All teacher education students also have access to the services and materials offered through the state-supported Assessment Center. In the center are:

1. self-paced, computer-assisted tests in early childhood education, reading, special education, physical education and health education;
2. a comprehensive basic skills computer instructional program;
3. specially developed test batteries in communication skills (listening, reading, English, essay development); general knowledge (mathematics, biology, physical sciences, social studies, fine arts and literature); professional knowledge; and in the education specialty areas of Music, Business, Home Economics, Physical and Early Childhood Education;
4. video-taped assessments of students' teaching performance through observations of interviews, tutorials and micro-teaching; as well as opportunities to view films and film strips and video-taped lessons for "study-test-study" sessions; and,
5. test-taking study guides, faculty-developed instructional modules and books on developing analytical thinking skills and general testing skills.

The student teaching program has been revised to support the new program thrusts. Special efforts, for example, are being made to prepare students for the Virginia Beginning Teacher Assistance Program (BTAP). The BTAP assesses the performance of beginning teachers in specified competency areas and provides them with the support to be effective teachers during their first two years. After the individuals have successfully demonstrated mastery of specific teaching competencies, they are awarded the regular five-year revewable Collegiate Professional Certificate.

Placement

Graduates of Norfolk State's teacher education programs are recruited actively by nearby urban school systems as well as out-of-state school districts. While the Dean and the faculty are thoroughly aware of the great demand for their gradutes across the nation, special collaborations have been initiated between a few local systems and the School of Education. One of these school system programs is called the Early Contracts Program, whereby the districts allow students to do student teaching in their schools and offer them contracts before the experience.

The School of Education also developed an innovative program in 1984-85 with a local system whereby teacher aides in that district are prepared to obtain a teacher education degree and full certification. These individuals attend classes in the evening and by special arrangements. Each school system arranges the student teaching experience to facilitate the individual's needs. The first two individuals from this program were graduated in 1988 and others are reaching the end of their academic programs. Participants in this program, however, must have completed at least two years of college level work to enter the program. This is a program with great promise and can be replicated across the country, especially where teacher aides are used and where junior colleges exist.

Summary Analysis

Like Bethune-Cookman, Norfolk State University has been very successful in obtaining external support to improve the recruitment, preparation and retention of education majors. Coupled with the institution's commitment to promote teacher education with the president's allocation of full tuition scholarships for education students since 1983, the School of Education was awarded more than a million dollars by the state to improve the performance of its students on the National Teacher Examination, to revise its curricula and to develop retention strategies and incentives. Furthermore, Norfolk State has also secured private funding to attract non-traditional students (e.g., military personnel, mid career professionals and teacher aides) into teaching.

Collaborations with school districts have also been established (e.g., Early Contracts Program, Future Teaching Clubs, etc.) and these types of consortial arrangements must be promoted since these kinds of cooperative projects may be most instrumental in luring more non-white students into teaching. Since 1980, Norfolk State University's teacher education program has also given significant leadership in addressing the shortage of minority teachers. Long before the issue received national prominence, Norfolk State initiated and has continued to convene annual conferences related to the supply and quality of black teachers for the nation's public schools. Those forums have provided the opportunity for participants to not only discuss this important natter but also to share successful education recruitment and retention strategies.

The future of Norfolk State's teacher education programs and their ability to produce more black teachers will depend largely on the success of their newly restructured teacher education program called for by the state board of education. The state's Ad Hoc Committee on Teacher Education and its Teacher Education Advisory Board will need to closely evaluate whether these restructured programs in teacher preparation are not only producing higher quality education graduates but also whether five- or six-year preparation programs are discouraging minority students from entering the profession. Regardless of the incentives available to students and the standards required to become a teacher, non-white students will certainly weigh the financial costs of an extra year of schooling with their potential earning power as a teacher before they choose teacher education as a major. The impact of those policies can only be assessed after the programs have had a chance to be implemented.

TUSKEGEE UNIVERSITY

Institutional Profile

Tuskegee University, one of the nation's most well known institutions of higher education, has been producing teachers since its founding in 1881 by Booker T. Washington. At that time the Alabama State Legislature enacted a bill, with an annual appropriation of $2000, to establish a school for blacks in Macon County. First known as Tuskegee Normal School for the training of black teachers, the co-educational university is today privately controlled but also state-related. The university has grown tremendously in its one hundred plus years of existence and offers 45 undergraduate and 22 masters degrees, a Master of Architecture, and a Doctor of Veterinary Medicine. The academic organization of Tuskegee includes a College of Arts and Sciences, Schools of Engineering and Architecture, Nursing and Allied Health, and Veterinary Medicine.

The university in the Fall of 1987 had a total student body enrollment of 3235 students, with 2851 in undergraduate programs. The remainder were in graduate programs and the first professional degree program in veterinary medicine. Over the last three years, enrollment in the School of Education has averaged approximately 250 students. Almost one-fourth of the total student body comes from Alabama, 68 percent from 41 other states, and the remaining seven percent from United States possessions and foreign countries. And, 61 percent of the 238 faculty hold the doctorate or professional degrees (*Tuskegee University 1987-88 Fact Book*).

THE SCHOOL OF EDUCATION

The establishment of the School of Education took place in 1927, when baccalaureate degree programs in teacher education were instituted. In 1944 graduate degrees in education were authorized. All programs are approved for state certification by the Alabama Department of Education and accredited by the Southern Association of Colleges and Schools. The School of Education offers 11 undergraduate degrees in education, as well as psychology, and 12 masters degrees in a variety of education fields.

ADMISSIONS AND ACADEMIC STANDARDS

All students who enroll as teacher education majors at Tuskegee must first complete two years of preprofessional studies before they are formally considered for admission into the professional teacher education program. The preprofessional studies program primarily consists of: general education courses required by the university, subject-matter content related to the student's chosen specialization area, and other elective courses. When the education student who plans to obtain teacher certification is at the sophomore level, he or she must formally apply for entrance into the School of Education, provided that the requisite academic standards have been met. Chief among these are: a minimum score of 16 on the ACT or 750 on the SAT (mandated by the state in 1985); completion of at least 60 semester hours of general education coursework; a cumulative GPA of at least 2.2 on all coursework attempted; minimum grades of "C" in courses in English, Speech, and first year seminar courses in teaching; a grade of at least "B" in the introductory professional education course; as well as successful performance on both the state and university English proficiency tests, and satisfactory completion of the institutional reading requirements. Students submit their applications for admission, and two letters of recommendation from faculty members, to the Committee on Admission to Professional Teacher Education who determines their eligibility for advanced professional studies in teacher education. Students who are not eligible, or who are denied admission, are not permitted to take professional education courses.

In order to remain as an advanced student in good standing in the School of Education and to be eligible for student teaching, the education major must have a minimum cumulative GPA of 2.2, and a GPA of 2.4 in the major area of specialization. To graduate, the education major must also obtain a minimum grade of "B" in student teaching and perform satisfactorily on the Core Battery and specialized tests of the National Teachers Examination. To obtain a teacher certification license, the graduate must also pass the Alabama Initial Teacher Certification Test (AITCT), the state-approved comprehensive examination, with a score of 70 or higher. (Currently, the AITCT covers the teaching content area only as a result of a racial discrimination case initiated in 1981 by three plaintiffs against the state board of education. Recent rulings on the case, which is now a class action suit, called for the elimination of the professional knowledge section of the AITCT.)

The Transformation of Tuskegee's School of Education

The School of Education at Tuskegee began the transformation of its teacher education programs in 1983. A "Blue Ribbon" committee, chaired by a vice president emeritus of the College Board, was established at the request of the president to assess the School of Education. The report of the committee was favorably received by the president and the Board of Trustees who went on record as saying that "there will be a School of Education on this campus and it will get support if it produces." This expression of commitment and support to the School of Education from the university leadership was important to the faculty and set the tone for the kinds of changes that have been taking place since that time.

One of the first overt changes was the immediate move to a renovated facility on the campus. This physical change was significant because it was designed to create an atmosphere conducive for teaching and learning, with laboratories and also offices where the education faculty could consult with each other in a central location, rather than in their previously disparate sites. The School of Education faculty thus began to discuss and implement the recommendations suggested by the Assessment Committee as well as the results of a 1984 state accreditation review. The "value-added approach" which the faculty developed focused primarily on the improved quality of both existing programs and current and future majors, especially where the potential of success was greatest. The faculty essentially agreed that the most attention should be placed on areas where ample resources were already available. Thus, producing quality graduates, as had been suggested by the Assessment Committee, served as the cornerstone for the transformation of the School of Education.

As critical first steps, the Dean and the faculty began (1) to stringently enforce the academic requirements of the various teacher education programs and (2) eliminated programs where there had been few majors in recent years and where there were insufficient resources to maintain quality programs. Approximately 15 certification programs and all programs **beyond** the master's degree were discontinued. Similarly, courses which had not been offered regularly were eliminated. Each department, therefore, had to justify whether and when a course needed to be offered. Thus, the School of Education accepted the fact that their scope needed to be reduced in direct relation to the enrollment and size of their small departments.

As the process began for improving those programs which were retained, all academic courses were reviewed, 25 were thoroughly revised, and many were strengthened by the incorporation of state objectives into the specific curricula. Furthermore, the faculty used graduates' performance on the state certification test as another guide for revising courses and also developed item banks of test questions related to each of those courses. The latter innovation provided students with the opportunity to take "practice tests" on what they had learned and where they could obtain immediate feedback on their progress.

As mentioned above, the Dean also promoted an atmosphere of and exercised the "enforcement" of the academic standards in the catalogue related to teacher education programs. For example, the formal interview process for entrance into the teacher education program was given increased importance; the "60 hour" rule, which requires students to complete the entire freshman and sophomore general education curriculum before applying to enter the professional phase of the teacher education program, was stringently enforced; and transfer students' academic records were thoroughly scrutinized before being admitted into the program. These and other measures primarily allowed the School to retain those students who were meeting all of the academic requirements. However, the "value added" approach also included giving those students whose performance did not meet the prescribed standards more than one opportunity to succeed before they were screened out of the program. Students not admitted to the program were therefore required to strengthen their academic skills through re-tooling efforts offered by the School of Education.

The academic monitoring of students' progress has been enhanced by a data management program which includes comprehensive information on each student. These profiles include: students' ACT/SAT scores, high school GPA's, performance on university and state-required competency tests, cumulative GPA's in college, scores on the NTE and other critical academic information. These profiles, which are updated constantly, give the School current information on every student in the program. To assist students with their performance on the proficiency tests in English and Reading, tutorial sessions were established. And to improve the performance of those students who wish to be teacher education majors but have not achieved the state required ACT (16) or SAT (750) scores, a peer tutorial program was developed with the support of federal Title III funds. Students and the School of Education have also benefited from a University-Wide Academic Advising program, supported with funds from the Bush Foundation, which emphasizes the role that proper and continuous academic advisement plays in enhancing student performance and matriculation toward graduation. It is important to note that all of the above efforts to enhance students' academic performance have been done in concert with and with the support of faculty in Arts and Sciences.

While the National Teachers Examination is a university requirement, graduates must pass the Alabama Initial Teacher Certification Test (AITCT), currently a test of the specific content areas, to obtain their teaching licenses. Passing rates of Tuskegee graduates on the AITCT increased to 70 percent for each of the academic years since 1985. The 70 percent pass rate of graduates on the AITCT is an important benchmark since the state requires that at least 70 percent of every teacher education program's students, over periods of five years, must achieve the requisite qualifying scores on this test to maintain their state accreditation. Schools or departments that do not meet this criterion will be reviewed by the state department of education.

Before proceeding to the next section, it is important to note that Tuskegee receives credit for the incorporation of an amendment to the previously mentioned policy. That amendment stated that students who took the test could only be counted once during the three administrations of any given academic cycle. The amendment had been proposed because of the fact that an institution's "percentage passing" rate could be adversely affected when a small number of students constantly repeated and failed the test. As a result of the amendment, students who do not successfully achieve the qualifying score must obtain tutorial assistance before they can be "counted" again.

Recruitment and Placement

To increase enrollment throughout the School of Education, recruitment programs were initiated within each department in 1985. The institution has provided support through its annual awards of $3000 scholarships to outstanding students. Eight scholarships were offered to students who were considering Tuskegee as education majors in 1987-88. Additionally, the School of Education has developed relationships with two-year colleges in and outside of the state as another means of attracting quality majors. In some instances, prospective students from the junior colleges have been brought to the institution as a group for two-day (weekend) activities. Through this process, the junior college students have an opportunity to learn more about the university, the School of Education and also have a chance to observe student life and some of the institution's social and athletic activities. These and other collaborative relationships with local school systems have expanded the quality of students who enter the teacher education programs at Tuskegee.

Tuskegee's education graduates are in high demand. While there have been an average of 30 graduates for each of the last three years, many of the students are actively recruited by school districts across the nation. Though most decide to teach in their home areas, several have accepted contracts in other metropolitan areas such as Atlanta, Denver, Boston, Miami, Chicago, Indianapolis, St. Louis, Madison, Wisconsin; Germany and many others. In addition, a number of students are also in master and doctoral programs in major graduate schools around the country.

Summary Analysis

The transformation of Tuskegee University's teacher education program began in 1984 after evaluations by a special committee appointed by the president and a state accreditation review panel. Having received the commitment of the university as well as the designation of one central location for the education faculty, the School of Education embarked on the development of a "value-added teacher preparation plan." But prior to the implementation of this plan, the School of Education streamlined the number of teacher education programs it had, thereby dedicating its resources and focusing its attention on those activities and programs which it believed had the highest probability of success. Thus, it took the bold step of eliminating many certification programs and those beyond the Master's degree.

Tuskegee's "value-added" approach was based primarily on how well students performed. As the Dean at that time indicated: "If something doesn't work or we cannot do it well within our resources, we are committed to changing it or eliminating it." The School of Education's administrative team therefore implemented a system to monitor and evaluate student progress in the teacher education program. But while Tuskegee recognized that their programs have produced students who can meet the minimum qualifications for college admission and professional licensing, they acknowledge that their numbers have not increased dramatically. Even though this enrollment situation is typical of many teacher education programs, and especially those at historically black institutions, Tuskegee has clearly demonstrated that more needs to be done to eliminate the premature screening out of minority students who may have the potential of becoming excellent teachers but who have difficulty passing tests on the first try. Their "value-added" model needs to be replicated by other institutions to prove that minority students can indeed succeed when systematic advising and enrichment activities are provided.

XAVIER UNIVERSITY OF LOUISIANA

Institutional Profile

Xavier University of Louisiana is a private, urban institution located in New Orleans which enrolls more than 2500 students. Xavier was founded in 1915 by Katherine Drexel and the Sisters of the Blessed Sacrament, a Catholic religious community she established to serve minorities in America. Mother M. Katherine Drexel, who was beatified by the Pope in 1988, came to New Orleans at the request of the local Catholic archbishop because of the limited higher educational opportunities for black youth, who had been denied admission to colleges and universities in the area and in the state.

Xavier opened with a college preparatory school in 1915 and added a normal school in 1917 to prepare teachers for the local black community. In 1925 a College of Arts and Sciences was established and, in 1927, a College of Pharmacy was added. In 1933, a Graduate School was established primarily to provide masters level degrees in education, another educational opportunity which many educated blacks had been denied because of the segregation policies of local colleges and universities. The university occupied its present location in 1932 and several buildings have been added over the last 15 years as enrollment has grown significantly in each of the three colleges mentioned above.

More than two-thirds of Xavier's students are day students who commute from the New Orleans area. The others come from over thirty states and a dozen foreign countries. In the Fall of 1988, the university had a total enrollment of 2584 students, a 17 percent increase over 1987's enrollment. Slightly more than 80 percent of the total student body in 1988 was enrolled in the College of Arts and Sciences where the fields of Business (with 348 students), Biology (301), the two-year Pre-Pharmacy program (264) and Chemistry (185) accounted for the largest share of majors. The College of Pharmacy had an enrollment of 275 students and there were 200 students in the Graduate School, both of which had increases of 15 percent and 25 percent, respectively. Almost all fields, however, experienced increases in 1988, e.g., the social sciences (17 percent), the humanities (13 percent), natural sciences (17 percent), business (14 percent) and education (16 percent).

EDUCATION DEPARTMENT

As noted earlier, the preparation of teachers has been a major goal of the university and the mission of the education department is consistent with the mission of the university, namely, to prepare graduates who are "intellectually, morally and spiritually prepared to contribute effectively to the creation of a more just and humane society." The Department of Education's primary responsibility, therefore, is to prepare well-qualified teachers for public and private elementary and secondary schools and who will assume leadership roles in their schools and in the community. Thus, the department's preservice training is focused on preparing future teachers "who possess a deep sense of civic responsibility, who are liberally educated and physically healthy, who possess sound moral character and philosophical principles, and the professional character which is so essential to their vocation and career" *(Department of Education section of the Xavier University 1988-90 Catalog).*

Xavier's 13 teacher education programs are approved by the Louisiana Department of Education and the Southern Association of Colleges and Schools. The Department of Education is also a member of the American Association of Colleges for Teacher Education and the Association of Independent Liberal Arts Colleges of Teacher Education. Xavier's Department of Education is primarily responsible for Bachelors programs in Elementary Education, Early Childhood Education, Special Education and Health and Physical Education. In addition to the above programs, the Education Department is also responsible for the academic monitoring of all state-approved programs in secondary education at Xavier. These programs include: Art, Biology, Chemistry, English, History (Social Science Education), Mathematics, Music (Instrumental and Vocal), and Speech Pathology Education. For those students who are enrolled in secondary teacher preparation programs, advising is jointly coordinated between the education department and the department of the student's major field to assure that students are meeting requirements for graduation and teacher certification.

Admissions and Retention Policies

The education department has a number of prerequisite requirements for students who wish to enter the university's teacher education programs. Though students may enter the university as "education majors," they do not officially become members of the teacher education program until the junior year, after they have completed the first two years of the university's Core Curriculum, and when they have satisfied all of the prescribed requirements. All students must maintain a grade point average of 2.5 and those who transfer into the department from other institutions or from other departments on campus must have a minimum grade point average of 2.2 to be considered for admission into the preprofessional program. Other requirements to enter the teacher education program include:

1. Achievement of at least a "C" grade in every course.
2. Completion of all developmental coursework.
3. Demonstration of proficiency on English, Mathematics, Speech and Reading examinations according to guidelines established by the Competency Examination Committee. (All university students must complete this requirement, usually in their second year, after having amassed a minimum of 42 degree credit hours.)
4. Completion of three clock hours of counseling.
5. Obtain passing scores on the Commuication Skills and General Knowledge section of the National Teachers Examination Core Battery by the end of the second semester of the sophomore year.
6. Membership in a professional organization.
7. Satisfactory rating on an interview with the Teacher Education Admissions Committee.

All except the last requirement above must be satisfied by the student before he/she can submit an application for formal admission into the teacher education program during the second semester of the sophomore year. Subsequent to the submission of the application, students are interviewed individually by the Teacher Education Admissions Committee, which is comprised of faculty from the education department and from Arts and Sciences disciplines which have teacher education programs. This committee determines whether the student should be fully or provisionally admitted into the teacher education program. Before students graduate, they must also take the remaining sections of the NTE, i.e., the Professional Knowledge section and the specialty area test in the student's teaching discipline, e.g., Elementary, Early Childhood, Health and Physical Education or a secondary field. (All of the above requirements apply to every secondary education major.) Students in the department who have not passed or taken all sections of the NTE by the beginning of their final semester are also required to pass the department's senior comprehensive examination.

Education Curricula

The structure of all education degree programs, and their related coursework, is organized into three components: (1) the pre-professional, where core curriculum courses are taken and where the students are actively involved in local classrooms during their first two years; (2) the professional, where students who have been formally admitted into the teacher education program and who have met all preliminary requirements take courses in education foundations and pedagogy; and (3) the student teaching experience, where students who have grade point averages of 2.5 and higher and have met all other requirements practice teach with the assistance of an approved cooperating teacher for a full semester.

Students' academic progress is monitored at each of the above stages. Those students who have not met the grade point average requirement and related academic criteria are counseled to pursue other academic fields, typically at the end of the sophomore year. Furthermore, all majors are required to complete three clock hours of counseling with a university counselor to determine whether students' vocational interests correspond closely to those of teaching and the helping professions. Students are also provided with career placement information on the national demand for teachers during these sessions.

All education degree programs have a heavy concentration of liberal arts coursework (i.e., approximately 80 semester hours). These general education courses are supplemented with courses in professional and specialized academic education in the student's respective teaching discipline. All of these academic components are essential to teaching excellence in a variety of settings and with varied students. The foundations courses, for example, provide a contextual framework for making value judgements in education. The methods courses address individual needs and teaching specialties by exposing students to, and giving them experience in, the application of a wide variety of teaching strategies, learning theories and motivational techniques. To provide additional training, most upper division courses in methodology and pedagogy also require students to complete a minimum of 20 clock hours of field experiences and practice.

Students are also required to participate in field experiences in conjunction with courses in their particular fields of specialization, e.g., reading, methods, special education, and health and physical education. Nationally, preprofessional field experiences have been heavily emphasized in all education programs and these observational exercises give students the opportunity to apply what they are learning in actual school settings. To expand these types of practical learning experiences, the department faculty in 1987-88 devoted the entire year to revising the curriculum for the three Introduction to Teaching courses. The curriculum revision in these courses, which are taken by students as freshmen, sophomores and juniors, now includes 15 programmatic areas that students are required to master in addition to completing a minimum of 105 observation hours in schools prior to their senior year and the student teaching experience. These revisions and the sequencing of courses will be evaluated during 1988-89 and 1989-90.

THE REVITALIZATION OF THE XAVIER EDUCATION DEPARTMENT

Like many other institutions of higher education, and especially small, historically black universities, in the late 1960's and early 1970's, many of Xavier's graduates were education majors. But as career opportunities for blacks expanded and as the need for teachers declined, fewer students majored in education during the late 1970's and early 1980's. This decline of Louisiana education graduates, and especially black graduates, between 1976 and 1983 was verified in a 1986 analytic study by this author, who is also Xavier's education chairman (Garibaldi, 1986). In that study, supported by the Southern Education Foundation, the author showed that in 1976 the state's 21 schools, colleges, and departments of education awarded 3384 education degrees, compared to 1864 degrees in 1983. Among the state's five historically black institutions, 750 education degrees were awarded, compared to only 250 in 1983. Using these data and national trends which verified the steadily declining numbers of black teachers, the department was able to more aggressively recruit education students.

As in the transformation of Tuskegee's education program, the department faculty in 1983-84 devoted its attention to the curricula, the academic progress of students and the low passing rates on the National Teachers Examination. The faculty devoted some of its staff meetings, as well as Saturday conferences, to specifically discussing the content of the entire teacher education program, and its professional education curricula in particular. The activities served dual purposes in that they were opportunities to revise and add to the content of courses, as well as useful for the staff to learn more about what each other was teaching.

The enforcement of all of the previously noted preservice requirements was a major initial step in the department's revitalization. In addition, the faculty agreed that students should obtain grades of "C" or better in **all** courses, as well as take the first two sections of the National Teachers Examination prior to being admitted into the Teacher Education Program. (The latter policy was instituted at Xavier one year before the state mandated the same requirements of all sophomore education majors.) While rigid enforcement of the department's regulations did cause enrollment to decline slightly, the academic quality of education students improved significantly. Through this process, students' academic progress has been sequentially monitored and standards have been communicated often, in writing and verbally, at student-faculty conferences and at students' monthly departmental meetings.

Students' low performance on the National Teachers Examination was a major concern of the faculty in the early 1980's. Though they recognized that academic advisement and a strengthened curriculum would help to improve student performance, they developed an optional four hour test taking skills seminar for those students taking the NTE and required that students take the Communication Skills and General Knowledge sections earlier in their four-year program. The seminar is offered one afternoon each semester and is designed primarily to familiarize students with the various components of the tests, appropriate strategies for responding to test items, and other nuances which help individuals to perform better on all tests.

The seminar, in combination with the other standards, has significantly improved the performance of Xavier's education students on the NTE. In 1984 and 1985, 19 of the 30 graduates, or 63 percent of them, had passed all sections of the NTE before graduation. However, 22 of the 28 graduates, or 79 percent between 1986 and 1988 had passed all sections of the NTE **before their last semester of coursework**. The majority of graduates, nevertheless, usually pass the remaining sections of the test during their last semester or during the summer immediately after receiving their degree. (To encourage students to take the final section early, the department offers students the incentive that if they have passed all sections of the NTE before their last semester, they are exempt from taking the departmental senior comprehensive examination.)

To complete the above programmatic changes, the faculty has also added more writing in education courses, placed greater emphasis on lesson plan development and verbal communication skills, and has varied classroom testing formats to aid students in their preparation for the National Teachers Examination.

Recruitment

The Education Department's targeted recruitment efforts have yielded fruitful results in the last two successive academic years. At the beginning of the 1987 and 1988 terms, approximately 30 new majors were enrolled each year, compared to less than 10 in each of the previous four years. Moreover, many already enrolled Xavier students have transfered into the education department as they have become aware of the need for teachers and the numerous job opportunities available to minority teachers across the country. The department has communicated its message and requirements in its brochure at high school career fairs, through the promotion and establishment of Future Teachers Clubs at local high schools, as well as provided potential majors with information on scholarships and forgivable loan programs for teacher education students. Xavier University's founding order, the Sisters of the Blessed Sacrament, also created an annual $2500 scholarship (for a maximum of four years) in 1984 for outstanding Catholic students. The students must commit to a year of teaching in one of the Sisters of the Blessed Sacrament's schools, or another Catholic school, for each year that they have received the scholarship. The program, which graduated its first two recipients in 1988, is designed to increase the number of Catholic teachers in parochial schools.

The most successful of the recruiting efforts has been a program established with the assistance of the university's admissions office and the nationally recognized Xavier premed program. Using strategies from both of these offices' successes, the names and academic records of students who express an interest in coming to the university and in majoring in education in the subsequent academic year are obtained so that students can be contacted during their senior year about the strengths of the university's teacher education programs. This systematic and personalized process allows the department to contact interested students, in writing and by phone, repeatedly during their last year of high school and also to answer any questions that students may have about the education curricula or even job opportunities after graduation. This strategy has been very successful and accounts for the tripling of the first-year education enrollment over the last two years.

The Education Minor Program and the Master of Arts in Teaching

In addition to targeting high school seniors, the department also provides information directly, and through academic advisors, to undeclared majors about the education program and the many available job opportunities in teaching. As another effort to prepare students who may be interested in teaching but who have majored in another academic area, the department developed an education minor program. The program contains a specified, 18 semester hour sequence of professional courses in education for non-education majors who may decide after graduation to teach in their chosen disciplines. The courses selected are those which are almost universally accepted toward certification in all states. Thus, if a non-education student decides to teach after graduation, the amount of coursework required to obtain a teaching certificate will be significantly reduced by his/her participation in the education minor program. The program has been successful during its short existence and has attracted students from several disciplines. Some too have officially transfered into education as a result of being exposed to the education curricula.

To meet the numerous requests of individuals with bachelors degrees who were interested in teaching in their academic areas or other fields, Xavier's Graduate School of Education developed a Master of Arts in Teaching (MAT). Through this program, the prospective teacher takes courses for certification and for a master's degree. (An individual, however, may elect to take only those courses required for teacher certification in the state.) The program has been very successful and there are more than 125 persons currently pursuing certification in a variety of fields. Because the majority of the candidates have full-time jobs, most are part-time students and take courses through the Graduate School's evening program.

Finally, the department receives positive local publicity through the faculty members' community service with the local school systems, community-based organizations and also city government. The same also holds true for national exposure, where the president of the university, a member of the National Commission on Excellence in Education, and members of the department speak on educational issues, serve on several national boards and commissions, as well as publish in professional journals in the fields of education and psychology. All of these forms of public relations and service have had direct, and indirect, influences on the enrollment of students as well as brought national attention to the education department and the university's degree programs.

Placement

Almost all of Xavier's teacher education graduates teach immediately after graduation. Many also have been recruited by major graduate schools and have chosen to pursue master's and doctoral degrees. While many New Orleans students have chosen to remain to teach in the local area, a number of students have accepted contracts to teach in other states over the last three years, e.g., California, Georgia, Florida, Minnesota, New York, and also the Peace Corps in Africa, to name just a few. This trend is sure to continue as rural, urban and suburban districts across the country aggressively recruit black teachers for their school systems. Because more teacher education graduates will be produced in the next few years and with many Xavier alumni already in leadership positions in major school systems, more of Xavier's teacher education graduates are likely to choose other school districts in and outside of the state.

Summary Analysis

Xavier's efforts to revitalize its teacher education programs began with the selection of a permanent chairperson in 1982, a position which had been held by temporary chairs for almost five years. During the latter period, a number of new state policies and higher criteria for teacher education graduates had been legislated while the department was also experiencing declining enrollments. The institution, therefore, affirmed its commitment to teacher education and expressed its serious intent to raise the academic quality of its students rather than concerning itself with the number of majors in the department.

The process of reform was very systematic and extended beyond the departmental level. The university's president, vice president for academic affairs, dean of arts and sciences and dean of the graduate school of education were involved in the initial meetings and a great deal of time was devoted to the national discussions on extended teacher preparation programs at that time. The early planning for change also included: assessments of the need for more teacher education graduates in the state; retreats and meetings by the faculty to discuss current majors' and recent graduates' academic performance and the more stringent enforcement of academic standards within the department; a thorough review of all teacher education programs and professional education curricula by the faculty; an item analysis workshop by an Education Testing Service staff member who discussed, analyzed and provided examples of students' performance on the National Teacher Examination to faculty members in arts and sciences, as well as in education; the requirement that students take the first two sections of the NTE prior to taking junior level courses; the revision of the senior comprehensive examination in education; as well as the extablishment of free test preparation workshops for education majors. All of the above initiatives, as well as others, were implemented between 1982 and 1984 and changes in education majors' academic performance were observed immediately.

Once the fundamental tasks of strengthening the department, the academic quality of students and the enforcement of standards had been completed, special efforts were focused on recruitment. These efforts have been extremely successful with new students as well as other majors on campus since they are now aware of the success which students have on the NTE and the numerous job offers they receive from around the country. The education minor program is also attracting a number of interested students from other disciplines who have come to realize that teaching may be a viable career alternative for them after graduation.

Finally, it must also be noted that much of this change has occurred with a small amount of additional resources. More students, however, are receiving institutional, state and private scholarship support and the institution's participation in consortial programs to address the shortage of minority teachers has provided more incentives to all education majors. These activities are currently increasing and more efforts in the near future will be targeted at junior and senior high school students so they can plan early to major in teacher education.

SUMMARY PROFILES OF INSTITUTIONAL CHANGES

BETHUNE-COOKMAN COLLEGE

Impetus for Change:

— Declining enrollments;

— Changing state requirements (i.e., ACT/SAT requirements for admission, grade point average increases from 2.0 to 2.5, proficiency on College Level Academic Skills Test, successful performance on Florida Teacher Certification Examination, etc.);

Genesis of Changes:

— Reviews and revisions of teacher education curricula;

— Development of proposal for state-funded Teacher Education Institute which includes comprehensive activities focused on recruitment, advising, personal counseling, tutorial assistance, leadership seminars, retention and graduation of teacher education majors;

— Development of Title III-funded Competency-Based/Computer Assisted Teacher Education Program designed to improve students' performance on state certification examinations and to assist faculty in revising existing curricula and the creation of new competency-based instructional packages;

— Development of state-funded Challenger Program to provide scholarships to and improve retention of current teacher education majors;

Resources

— Teacher Education Institute (funded at $250,000 annually since 1986-87 by the state);

— Challenger Program (funded at $250,000 annually by the state since 1986-87);

— Competency-Based/Computer Assisted Teacher Education Program (Title III Institutional Aid grant funded at $250,000 over four years between 1983-84 and 1986-87. This program is now funded by the institution as a part of the teacher education department budget.)

Outcomes:

— Increased enrollments, higher retention rates, successful performance (90 percent and higher) on state-required basic skills and teacher certification tests;

— Curricular revisions and greater participation by Arts and Sciences and education faculty in the teacher education program;

— mentoring and team activities have improved students' leadership skills and classroom proficiency;

— Successful performance in Florida Beginning Teacher Program (90 percent and higher).

NORFOLK STATE UNIVERSITY

Impetus for Change:
- Unstable enrollments;
- Low passing rates on the National Teachers Examination;
- Changing state standards for entry to and exit from teacher education programs, as well as state initiatives for restructuring teacher preparation programs;

Genesis of Change:
- External evaluations by private consultants;
- Institutional commitment to the School of Education and the establishment of presidential scholarships to outstanding teacher education majors;
- Department participation in the revision of curricular content; increased recruitment activities; and improvement of students' test-taking skills through assessment classes and tutorials funded by a major state grant;
- Procurement of private grants to increase retention and provide financial incentives to current majors;

Resources
- Special state grant to provide scholarships and improve students' performance on the NTE ($500,000 total for 1986-87 and 1987-88 academic years and $90,000 annually for 1988-89, and 1989-90);
- Presidential scholarships awarded since 1983 (an average of 20 per year);
- Student scholarships from the Virginia Teaching Scholarship Program (annual awards of $2000 per student) and the Metropolitan Life Foundation Scholarship Program ($1500 annually to upperclassmen);
- Private grant from the Hazen Foundation ($5000) to recruit retiring military personnel into teaching;

Outcomes:
- Significant increases in enrollment and higher passing rates (80 percent or better) by students on the NTE;
- Staff development activities for faculty, revisions of the teacher education curricula and development of a test-taking laboratory and an assessment course for students;
- Revision of student teaching program to improve students' performance in their first year of teaching and to meet the criteria of the Virginia Beginning Teacher Assistance Program;
- Established special programs to (1) fully certify teacher aides as classroom teachers; (2) facilitate the transfer of community college graduates into the teacher education program; and, (3) entice military retirees into teaching;
- Developed Early Contracts Program with two local school systems to encourage graduates to teach in urban settings and established collaborations with local middle and senior high schools to encourage students to go into teaching.

TUSKEGEE UNIVERSITY

Impetus for Change:

— Unstable enrollments and declining institutional resources;

— Changing state requirements for entry to and exit from teacher education programs;

Genesis of Change:

— External evaluations by a special committee appointed by the president and a state accreditation review panel;

— Institutional commitment to the teacher education program by centralization of all education faculty in one facility and dedication of scholarship to prospective majors;

— Review and revision of all education courses;

— Stringent enforcement of teacher education standards;

Resources

— Presidential scholarships ($3000 per student for five to eight students annually);

— Title III grant to establish peer tutoring programs, to improve students' performance on the SAT/ACT and to improve clinical training ($125,000 estimated);

— Bush Foundation grant to establish a University-Wide Academic Advising Program ($80,000 estimated);

— National Science Foundation grant (Collaborative Alliance for the Development of Resource Educators) to enhance the training of math and science resource teachers in Macon County schools ($400,000+ estimated over four years);

— Education alumni contributions for two computers ($5,000 annual gifts for two years) and institutional contributions of computer and resource reading rooms;

Outcomes:

— Elimination of 15 certification programs and all degree programs beyond the Master's level;

— Establishment of a "Value-Added Approach to Qualitative Improvement in Teacher Preparation;"

— Development of a Data Management/Student Advising System to periodically monitor students' academic progress;

— Development of a test-item bank for professional education courses;

— Improvement of all professional courses through systematic evaluations of course content and outlines;

— Improved passing rates (70 percent and higher) on state certification exams.

XAVIER UNIVERSITY OF LOUISIANA

Impetus for Change:

— Declining enrollments and low passing rates on the National Teachers Examination;

— Changing and higher state requirements for entry to and exit from teacher education programs;

— National discussions of extended teacher preparation programs;

Genesis of Changes:

— Institutional commitment to education by the president;

— Review of all education programs and curricula by the faculty for two years beginning in 1982-83;

— Stringent enforcement of standards, systematic academic advising and requirement that students achieve "C" or better in all courses, instead of only professional education courses;

— Required students to take the first two sections of the NTE at the end of the sophomore year;

— Reinstitution of the Teacher Education Admissions Committee;

— Item analysis workshop conducted by ETS consultant for education and Arts and Sciences faculty to review students' NTE performance;

— Careful evaluation of students requesting to transfer into the department;

Resources:

— Southern Education Foundation grant to study the decline of black teachers Louisiana and to develop recruitment materials ($25,000);

— Catholic School Promotion Scholarships from the Sisters of the Blessed Sacrament (approximately $10,000 annually for four students since 1984);

Outcomes:

— Higher passing rates (80 percent and higher) on the NTE;

— Stabilized enrollment and improved quality of students;

— Revised senior comprehensive examination and all Introduction to Teaching courses;

— Targeted recruitment efforts have yielded 300 percent increases in first year enrollment since 1987-88;

— Strengthened curricula and developed test-taking skills seminar to prepare students for the NTE;

— Publicized program standards and screened out students who did not meet the criteria after first four semesters

— Developed education minors program to attract other Arts and Sciences students and undeclared majors into teaching;

— Increased the amount and quality of academic advising of students;

— Assisted Graduate School of Education in developing a Master of Arts in Teaching program for Arts and Sciences graduates who decide later that they want to teach.

About the Author

ANTOINE MICHAEL GARIBALDI

Antoine M. Garibaldi became Dean of Arts and Sciences in August 1989 at Xavier University of Louisiana where he previously served as Chairman and Associate Professor of Education since 1982. A native of New Orleans, he holds a B.A. in Sociology from Howard University (1973) and a Ph.D. in Educational and Social Psychology from the University of Minnesota (1976). Prior to coming to Xavier, he was a researcher with the U. S. Department of Education's National Institute of Education for five years in Washington, DC, where he also served as a staff member of the National Commission on Excellence in Education, which produced the landmark report, *A Nation at Risk.*

A former elementary teacher and Street Academy Director in St. Paul (MN), Garibaldi is the author of seven books and monographs and more than 40 research articles and chapters in scholarly journals and books. His book, *Black Colleges and Universities: Challenges for the Future*, published by Praeger was recognized as one of the outstanding books of 1984 by the American Educational Studies Association.

Garibaldi is very active in professional associations and in his community. In New Orleans, he is Co-Chair of the Urban League's Education Committee and a member of its Board of Directors, Co-Chair of the Mayor's Foundation for Education, and is currently serving his third term as Vice Chair of the Board of Directors of the New Orleans Public Library, where he has been a member since 1984. He also served as Chairman and Study Director of the New Orleans Public Schools' study on the status of black male students during 1987-88 and was the author of the committee's nationally publicized final report, *Educating Black Male Youth: A Moral and Civic Imperative*. Nationally he serves on the advisory board of the *Journal of Negro Education*, the Committee on Policy Analysis of the National Association of Independent Colleges and Universities, the Committee on Research of the American Association of Colleges for Teacher Education, the advisory board of the National Catholic Education Associations's journal, *Momentum*, and many more. He is also a past associate editor of the *American Educational Research Journal.*

He is a nationally recognized scholar and speaker who has received research grants from the Office of Naval Research and the Southern Education Foundation, and he has also served as a Fellow and Consultant to numerous professional and philanthropic organizations. He has also been an Education Policy Fellow with the Institute for Education Leadership in Washington, DC (1977-78) and an Adjunct Research Fellow with the Southern Education Foundation (1988-89).

Minority Student and Teacher Retention Strategies

OVERVIEW

This chapter describes specific activities to encourage the retention of minorities in higher education and in the teaching profession.

The first article describes a successful retention model implemented at the University of Akron. The model is designed to meet the needs of "high-risk" minority students who were academically dismissed.

In the second article, Daughtry describes strategies to ensure that those minority students who wish to be teachers are not only admitted to teacher education programs, but are also retained, graduated, and certified. The strategies recommend the provision of a variety of services.

From *Educational Considerations*, vol. 18, no. 1, Fall 1990, pp. 33-34. © by Kansas State University. Reprinted by permission.

The High Risk Minority Student Retention Program (HRMS) was developed to enhance Black student retention at a large, urban Ohio university.

High Risk Minority Student Retention Model: A Collaborative Program for Black Students

Thomas E. Midgette
Charles Stephens

Introduction

Institutions of higher learning must greatly expand their efforts to increase significantly the number and proportion of minority graduates. Furthermore, they must create an academic atmosphere that nourishes minority students and encourage them to succeed . . . and a campus culture that values the diversity minorities bring to institutional life.

One-Third of a Nation, 1988

The need for institutions of higher education to be more effective for minorities and the poor is imperative. Changing demographics suggest that the nation can ill-afford to waste valuable resources by ignoring students of color. Educators and economists have suggested that the nation's future will depend on Black students' success, thus influencing the social, economic, and political stature of this country.

Our society in the 1990s depends on our institutions of higher education being able to attract and graduate a sufficient number of minorities. Left unchecked, the declining participation of minorities in higher education will have severe repercussions for future generations of Americans (Wilson, 1989; 1988). In addition, we risk developing an educational and economic underclass and creating a culture that ignores the talents of a significantly large number of individuals.

Since a great majority of Blacks are attending predominantly White institutions, it becomes even more critical for these institutions to adopt policies that are innovative in recruiting, retaining, and graduating a greater number of minorities. More importantly, educational institutions must play a pivotal role in developing more sensitive programs and strategies to improve the quality of life of minority students, thus increasing the probability that they graduate (O'Brien, 1988; Penn, 1988).

Dr. Thomas E. Midgette is on the faculty of the Department of Counseling and Special Education at the University of Akron. Charles Stephens works with minority student retention for the Office of Minority Affairs at the University of Akron.

The High Risk Minority Student Retention Model (HRMS)

The High Risk Minority Student Retention model was developed to address concerns about:

a. The declining pool of minority students who enroll in the urban university described below;
b. The high attrition rates of Black students in this predominantly White university;
c. The low graduation rates of Black students in this predominantly White university.

The HRMS Model was implemented in a large (+30,000) northeastern Ohio university. This model was developed for "high risk" students, which consisted of 100% African-American individuals. This model allows African-American students who have been academically dismissed to return to school the next semester if they agree to participate in a highly structured program. The HRMS Program is a contractual arrangement between the student and staff which facilitates skill acquisition and social development.

The American Council on Education suggests that only one out of every four Black high school graduates will enroll in college, despite the fact that high school graduation rates for Black students are at an all time high (Hodgkinson, 1985; Astin, 1982). By the year 2020, it is predicted that minorities will represent about 35% of the population of the U.S. Given this demographic shift, the highly negative impact of the disproportionate representation of minorities in college takes on alarming significance.

According to Bureau of Census data, college enrollment for Black students dropped from 33.5% of high school graduates in 1976 to 26.1% in 1985. U.S. Department of Education figures indicate that only 5.9% of recipients of bachelor degrees were Black, representing a 9.26% decline from the high reached in 1980–81.

Traditionally Black Institutions (TBI) have produced the majority of Black college graduates. However, according to current estimates about two-thirds to three-fourths of the Black students in college are now in predominantly White educational settings (Fleming, 1984).

Operation of the HRMS Program

The program staff pairs each participant selected for the program with a minority faculty mentor, a peer counselor, and an academic adviser. All faculty and staff are chosen for their sensitivity and concern for the needs of minority students. Program participants must attend a college survival skills class. In the fall, students begin participating in a counseling group to enhance student quality of life and self esteem. This personal growth group is conducted in collaboration with the University Counseling Center and the Department of Counseling and Special Education. Students who participate in the HRMS Program have their academic dismissal rescinded and are allowed to return to the university the semester following their dismissal.

Selection Process

Listed below are the steps to implement the program:

(a) Initial retention decisions are made in the usual fashion (i.e., folders of students whose grade point averages are in the dismissal categories are reviewed by the Dean of the University College, or one of his/her designates, along with students' assigned academic advisors).

(b) At the end of each day's retention meeting, a small group of academic advisers selected by the Director of Minority Retention and the Director of Afro-American Studies, reviews the files of dismissed minority students for the purpose of selecting students who might benefit by continued enrollment in a highly structured program for high risk students. The group examines students' high school background, extracurricular activities in high school and college, and ACT/SAT scores and college grades.

(c) The files for students selected for the program are forwarded to the Dean for his approval. Each file includes a written rationale to support the decision, and the name of the High Risk Minority student's (HRMS) adviser to whom the student is assigned.

(d) Letters are sent to approved students by the Director of Minority Affairs explaining the program and encouraging them to participate.

(e) A student who decides to participate in the program makes an appointment with his/her adviser to establish the written contract.

(f) The following activities are mandatory for all participants:

1. Monthly contact with HRMS adviser;
2. Participation in a special Survival Skills Forum;
3. Monthly contact with HRMS mentor;
4. Weekly meetings with a minority peer counselor;
5. Continuous monitoring of grades by faculty/staff;
6. Attendance at social support groups conducted by the University Counseling Center and Department of Counseling and Special Education;
7. Attend Career Planning Seminar conducted by the Department of Counseling and Special Education and University Counseling Center;
8. Other requirements as established by the HRMS adviser.

The HRMS program is evaluated at the end of each semester. Success is measured by students' questionnaire results, adviser satisfaction, grades received in academic courses and mentor-mentee feedback gathered at various points throughout the semester.

Identified Trends

The program began in Fall 1989 with 23 students of African-American descent. Preliminary findings follow:

(a) Twenty-one of the 23 (91%) students have improved their cumulative grade point average;

(b) Nine out of 23 (39%) have received a 2.0 or better grade point average after one semester in the program;

(c) Six out of 23 (28%) students moved out of the dismissal category;

(d) Two students improved enough (after only one semester) to come off probation;

(e) Two students did not enroll Spring Semester because of low grade point average (.5);

(f) Three students elected not to return Spring Semester;

(g) One student initiated a total withdrawal from the university;

(h) The range of the GPAs received after one semester in the High Risk Minority Student Program was 00.0 to 2.9.

Future Implications: A Final Word

Clearly there is a need for more systematic programs that confront the devastating problem of high attrition rates for African-American students enrolled in predominantly White universities. The High Risk Minority Student Retention Program demonstrates that academically dismissed students placed in a highly structured program of skill acquisition and personal attention can be successful in improving their academic performance over a sixteen week period. Future consideration should be given to conducting the HRMS Program for two terms (32 weeks). Two terms of the HRMS Program should produce greater academic improvement and allow stronger mentoring relations to develop and increase the probability that these students will reach their academic and personal goals.

More systematic and longitudinal examination of student data is needed to implement responsive programs for "high risk" African-American students. The faculty and staff who participate in this program should be compensated with appropriate load or release time for making such an investment of time and energy with "high risk" students. The success of many predominantly White institutions may depend not only on how well they recruit these new students, but in the development of innovative programs to retain students of color experiencing academic, personal, and environmental difficulties.

References

Astin, A. (1982). **Minorities in American higher education**. San Francisco, CA: Jossey-Bass.

Fleming, J. (1984). **Blacks in college**. Washington, D.C.: Jossey-Bass.

Gibbs, J. (1988). **Young, Black, and male in America: An endangered species**. Dover, MA: Auburn House.

Harper, E. and Washington, W. (1989). **An ecological analysis of strategies for minority success at predominantly white institutions: A system approach to retention**. An unpublished paper presented at the Fifth National Conference on Black Student Retention, Miami, FL, Fall.

Hodgkinson, H. (1985). **All one system: Demographics of education, kindergarten through graduate school**. Washington, D.C.: Institute for Educational Leadership.

O'Brien, C. (1988). Institutional responsibility and the minority student. **Black Issues in Higher Education**, 5, 11, August 15, 48.

Penn, P. (1988). **Black student persistence to graduation: Summary and recommendations**. Oberlin, Ohio: Oberlin College.

Smith, J., Simpson-Kirtland, D., Zimmern, J., Goldenstein, E. and Prichard, K. (1988). The five most important problems confronting Black students today. **The Negro Educational Review**, XXXVII, 2, April.

The American Council on Education and Education Commission of the States, **One third of a nation: A report on minority participation in education and American life**.

Wilson, R. (1988). The state of Black higher education: Crisis and promise. **The State of Black America**, 1989. New York: National Urban League, Inc.

Wilson, R. and Justiz, M. (1988). Minorities in higher education: Confronting a time-bomb. **Educational Record**, Fall and Winter, 9-14.

4. RECRUITING AND RETAINING MINORITY TEACHERS: WHAT TEACHER EDUCATORS CAN DO

by Jody Daughtry

The demographics of our public school population are changing. Minorities constitute a higher percentage of total enrollment than ever before in our nation's history. Nationally, between 1976 and 1984, the Asian student population increased by over 85 percent and the number of Hispanic students increased by 28 percent (6, p. 64). In large urban school systems, the changes have been particularly dramatic. Boston, Denver, Portland, San Diego, and Seattle, for example, doubled their percentage of minority students between 1970 and 1982. New York, Los Angeles, Chicago, Philadelphia, Detroit, and Houston are among the many cities in the United States where minority students represent at least 75 percent of total public school enrollment. Of the nation's 20 largest public school districts, 13 are composed predominantly of minority students (6, p. 179).

When populations change, the institutions that serve them must also change. With the percentage of minority students rising, the need for minority teachers is becoming increasingly urgent. If school systems across the country that serve large numbers of minority students are to remain viable, they must increase the number of minority teachers, and they must do it quickly. The current status of minority teachers, obstacles to increasing minority participation in the teaching profession, and possible means for overcoming these obstacles are the focus of this chapter. Special attention is devoted to ways in which teacher educators at colleges and universities can help to ensure that schools will have the minority teachers who are so important to the future of public education.

CURRENT STATUS

Recent data compiled by the National Education Association (9, p. 74) indicate that about 10 percent of all teachers in the public schools are members of minority groups, while minority students represent about 29 percent of our total public school student population (6, p. 64). In areas of the country where minority student enrollment is particularly high, the figures are even more dramatic. In California, for example, about 50 percent of the students are members of minority groups, yet only 18 percent of the teachers are minorities (2).

While the disparity between the number of minority teachers and the number of minority students is great at present, the prognosis for the future is even worse. It has been estimated that by the year 2000, only 8 percent of the nation's teachers will be minorities (5, p. iii). Thus, in the next 15 years as the percentage of minority students rises, the percentage of minority teachers is predicted to decrease.

OBSTACLES TO INCREASING THE MINORITY TEACHING POOL

The low representation of minorities in the teaching ranks has been viewed as a result of both adverse socioeconomic factors and inadequate instruction at all levels of schooling, leading to fewer minority graduates at both the high school and college levels. The predicted decrease in the percentage of minority teachers, however, has been attributed to the increased use of competency tests in the field of teaching (5, p. iii). As of 1987, 45 states had adopted competency testing for initial certification of teachers and 31 states had required students to pass standardized tests for admission to teacher preparation programs (7, p. 70). Several states are also using competency tests for continuing certification. Nationally, the success rate for whites on these tests is approximately 86 percent, while the success rate for minorities is only 26 percent (4, p. 47). In spite of the undeniable differential impact of these tests on minorities versus nonminorities, the courts have upheld their use. In short, the use of competency testing presents a formidable barrier to Blacks, Asian-Americans, American Indians, and Hispanics entering the teaching profession, and no legal relief is likely to be forthcoming.

Other obstacles to equitable representation in the education profession include the high dropout rate of minorities at the high school level and the underrepresentation of minorities in the general college population. Resident minorities represented about 15 percent of enrollment at four-year institutions and about 22 percent at two-year institutions in 1986 (8, p. 170). Still another reason for the decline in the supply of minority educators is that academically talented minority students are increasingly choosing to enter fields other than teaching.

SOLUTIONS TO THE PROBLEM

In spite of the obstacles that have been outlined, there are many avenues to increasing minority participation in the teaching profession.

First, minorities can be vigorously recruited to teacher preparation programs. Potential minority teachers should be sought not only among university students, but among community college, high school, and junior high school students, as well as among adults. These individuals should be made aware of the intrinsic rewards of teaching, the high demand for teachers, recent improvements in teachers' salaries, and opportunities for advancement to supervisory and administrative positions.

Prospective Black, Asian and Pacific Islander, American Indian/Alaska Native, and Hispanic teachers can be recruited from the ranks of university students currently pursuing other majors. Programs that involve these students in tutoring can expose them to the rewards of teaching and, in many cases, cause them to change their career goals.

Posters, booklets, and other materials can be prepared for secondary schools and community colleges with high concentrations of minority students to orient both the students and their parents to the profession of teaching. Professional education faculty can be given support, especially in the form of released time and travel funds, to visit high schools and community colleges to talk directly with students about the teaching profession and to work with counselors and teachers who can play a key role in attracting and advising minority students who might be interested in teaching. Minority students who are presently preparing to be teachers can also be enlisted to help in recruitment efforts. Minority members of educational service clubs or honorary societies are usually very willing to talk with younger students about the profession. Clubs for future teachers at the secondary level can also help to foster and maintain interest in teaching.

Community organizations of various minority groups can provide an excellent forum for presenting the benefits of a career in teaching to adults. Financial incentives such as scholarships and forgivable loans for talented minority individuals who plan to enter teaching are a powerful aid to recruitment efforts. More incentives such as these are needed along with more effective dissemination of information about existing financial aid.

Beyond recruitment of minority students, efforts must also be made to ensure that those students who wish to be teachers are admitted to teacher education programs, retained, graduated, and certified. This will involve the provision of a variety of services.

Steps can be taken to identify students with potential problems in their freshman and sophomore years. When necessary, remedial instruction can be offered in basic academic skills such as reading and writing. Early exposure to and practice in taking tests similar to those needed to enter teacher education programs and to become certified can be provided. For those students who lack test-taking skills, direct instruction in this area can be given. Students can learn skills such as how to interpret test questions, how to complete tests on time, and how to guess intelligently.

Faculty, not only from schools and departments of education but also from every other academic department, need to become involved in assisting minority education students. Workshops can be given to make them aware of the content of the tests the students will be taking, what the common areas of deficiency are, how to incorporate test content into existing course objectives and content, and how to write challenging examinations that will give students the opportunity to test their knowledge.

Financial, academic, and personal counseling

available to minority students can also be improved. To supplement the counseling available to all students, minority peer advisors can be hired to provide assistance to fellow students. In addition, faculty mentors can be assigned to ensure that each minority education student receives personal help and encouragement throughout his or her program.

Finally, education faculty can provide positive minority role models. Schools and departments of education without such role models could give high priority to hiring minority faculty and could use minority adjunct faculty as well.

In addition to ensuring that minority students become certified, measures should be taken to ensure that they are hired, retained, and promoted. Placement procedures can be developed to assure that school districts seeking to hire minority teachers are put in contact with minority applicants. Assistance programs for novice teachers can be developed cooperatively by school districts and universities to reduce the attrition rate of new teachers, especially new minority teachers. Such programs can provide many types of aid. New teachers can be mentored by outstanding veteran teachers. Mentor teachers can be paid for their services and both new and mentor teachers can be periodically released from their classrooms to permit classroom observations and other types of professional development activities. Support groups can be formed for new teachers to alleviate feelings of isolation and to facilitate collective problem solving. University faculty and school district personnel can conduct workshops for new teachers on areas of common concern such as how to manage time effectively and how to cope with paperwork.

These services should increase minority graduates' chances of being hired and retained. To increase minority teachers' chances for promotion, fellowships and loans can be provided for those who wish to pursue advanced degrees.

To carry out activities such as those just described, colleges, universities, and school districts need formal, well-coordinated programs that are adequately funded and staffed by professionals. A number of such programs have been implemented around the country. For example, University of Arkansas at Pine Bluff has established the Advocacy Center for Equity and Excellence in Teacher Education to help alleviate the current and future shortage of Black teachers (1); Virginia Commonwealth University in Richmond, Virginia, has instituted a program for recruiting and mentoring minority education students (10); and fifteen school districts in California have initiated pilot projects for assisting new teachers aimed at increasing retention rates for minority as well as nonminority teachers (3, p. 4). Research should be conducted on the effectiveness of such programs and the findings disseminated so that other institutions can adopt those practices that have proved to be successful.

It is clear that much can be done to increase the number of minority teachers in the nation's public schools and that teacher educators have an important role to play in this effort. Equitable representation of minorities in the teaching profession has always been desirable; now it is a practical necessity. Minority teachers are needed to ensure that all schools are truly multicultural in perspective and that minority students have appropriate role models. Above all, minority teachers are needed if the reality of the public schools is to match the promise of democracy.

REFERENCES

1. Antonelli, G. "The Revitalization of Teacher Education at UAPB." *Action in Teacher Education 7,* no. 3 (1985): 63–64.

2. California State Department of Education. *Fingertip Facts on Education in California.* Sacramento: California State Department of Education, 1988.

3. Commission on Teacher Credentialing and State Department of Education. *Draft Vignettes of Fifteen Pilot Projects: California New Teacher Project.* Sacramento: the Commission, August 1988. (Available from Commission on Teacher Credentialing, Box 944270, Sacramento, CA 94244-2700.)

4. Cooper, C. C. "Strategies to Assure Certification and Retention of Black Teachers." *The Journal of Negro Education* 55, no. 1 (1986): 46-55.

5. Goertz, M. E., and Pitcher, B. *The Impact of NTE Use by States on Teacher Selection.* Princeton, NJ: Educational Testing Service, 1985.

6. National Center for Education Statistics. *The Condition of Education.* Washington, DC: U.S. Government Printing Office, 1987.

7. ______. *The Condition of Education*. Washington, DC: U.S. Government Printing Office, 1988a.

8. ______. *The Digest of Education Statistics*. Washington, DC: U.S. Government Printing Office, 1988b.

9. National Education Association. *Status of the American Public School Teacher: 1985-86.* Washington, DC: the Association, 1987. (Available from NEA Professional Library, P.O. Box 509, West Haven, CT 06516.)

10. Reed, D. F. "Wanted: More Black Teacher Education Students." *Action in Teacher Education* 8, no. 1 (1986): 31-36.

Summary/Conclusion

SUMMARY/CONCLUSION

Although the minority teacher shortage is predicted to increase during the 1990s, a number of programs, models, and strategies have been identified to redress the problems. The recommended strategies, however, must be both systematic and consistent, and they will require cooperation and coordination with many different groups. These groups must include state planning and coordinating agencies for higher education, teacher alumni, colleges of education, two-year colleges, school districts, churches, community-based agencies, business groups, and professional associations.

All of these groups working in concert have the ability to reverse the projected negative trends.